The
Nature

The Lessons of
Nature in Mythology

RACHEL S. MCCOPPIN

McFarland & Company, Inc., Publishers
Jefferson, North Carolina

LIBRARY OF CONGRESS CATALOGUING-IN-PUBLICATION DATA

McCoppin, Rachel S., 1977–
    The lessons of nature in mythology / Rachel S. McCoppin.
    p.   cm.
    Includes bibliographical references and index.

    ISBN 978-1-4766-6200-8 (softcover : acid free paper) ∞
    ISBN 978-1-4766-2215-6 (ebook)

    1. Nature—Mythology.   I. Title.

BL435.M33 2015
201'.3—dc23   2015036634

BRITISH LIBRARY CATALOGUING DATA ARE AVAILABLE

Front cover: photograph of ruins at Delphi © iStock/Thinkstock

Printed in the United States of America

McFarland & Company, Inc., Publishers
    Box 611, Jefferson, North Carolina 28640
    www.mcfarlandpub.com

Dedicated to
Landon and Season

Table of Contents

Preface

This book is an introduction to many of the world's most treasured myths; it is also a detailed examination of the role nature plays within these myths.

This book addresses myths of creation, showing that myriad cultures around the world fathomed that the first human beings came directly from natural elements. It then focuses on the transition of mythic representations from the Paleolithic to Neolithic period, where many cultures moved from relying on hunter/gatherer subsistence to the advent of agriculture. Next, it defines numerous belief systems that account for divinities that were direct reproductions of the natural world and its elements. This book then looks towards the depiction of nature within mythology as a place that is unfettered and wild, but also redemptive, providing solace and even spiritual wisdom to the mythic characters who seek out the lessons of the environment. Finally, it ends with a look towards mythic representations that connect the lives of human beings to the seasons of nature, showing that birth, adulthood, and old age often are mythically portrayed as spring, summer, and fall; this portrayal in myth arguably asks audiences to contend with the inevitability of winter being connected to the necessity of death in the lives of human beings. Myths that explicitly relate nature in a prominent role often provide audiences a message that they also are inextricably connected to the natural world, and this acceptance then allows audiences to obtain wisdom connected to the environment.

This book focuses on world mythology to stress a value of multiculturalism. Though the book concentrates on similar themes related to nature within many global myths, there is no intention on assuming a connection between philosophical and religious belief systems in all world cultures. Instead, this book presents merely an emphasis on the often overlooked importance of nature, in its myriad representations, within the mythology of world cultures.

I have formally studied world mythology for over twenty years and have taught it to college students for over ten years. When I encounter myths from around the world, I am genuinely excited by the consistent appearance of nature, and to me, its symbolic representations. To see that world cultures for thousands of years repeatedly tell tales of mythic characters, who despite often struggling through their lives, find peace and knowledge through an embrace of nature, even when nature is depicted as it is, both harsh and regenerative, provides me with peace in the assurance of nature's consistent cycles. In traveling to Greece and seeing how nature dominated every sacred site I visited, it became clear to me that nature dominated the myths I held so dear. Demeter, Persephone, Orpheus, Hades, Artemis, Heracles, Poseidon, etc., were only for me distant characters of old myths, until I witnessed that they were alive and well in Greece, not in books, but in the land. Therefore, to me, nature will always be at the forefront of every myth.

I would like to express extreme gratitude to the people who aided me in writing this book. First, I want to acknowledge my family who endured my constant discussion of mythology and my incessant need to seclude myself in order to write, but also encouraged me to keep going. I would also like to thank Ioannis Kiourtsoglou and Constantinos Sfikas for revealing Greece to me, and continually teaching me the nuances of its mythology. And finally, I would like to thank Danielle Johannesen for our conversations on myths and nature, as well as Rae French, Kim Gillette, Soo-Yin Lim Thompson, Jack Geller, Barbara Keinath, Fred Wood, and the University of Minnesota–Crookston for enabling me to travel the world teaching mythology.

Introduction:
The Land Is the Myth

"Earth gives birth to all beings and after having nourished them
takes from them the fertile seed."
—Aeschylus

"If you don't know the trees you may be lost in the forest, but if you
don't know the stories you may be lost in life."
—Siberian proverb

Sitting at the Oracle of Delphi while visiting Greece, settled within vast
and jagged mountains, I watched the sunrise play off the rolling, distant hills.
I looked around at the mysterious caves that hid among the cliff walls. I
watched as bees pollinated laurel next to the Pythia's rock. I noticed the ivy
climbing steadfastly up broken pillars. There is a mysterious energy here,
and despite the crowds of people, one still feels secluded. The land whispers
to those who listen. It consistently assures you that it is sacred.

In Dion, Greece, as I traveled to a sanctuary of the goddess Demeter, I
again marveled at the natural beauty that dominated the site. The sanctuary
itself was barely there; the replica of Demeter sat beheaded on the ground,
exactly as she was found when rediscovered centuries later. It was evident
that this sanctuary, and other mythic sites around Greece, were worshipped
by ancient peoples because the natural landscape evoked awe, and myths
were created to capture this reverence. Settled at the base of Mount Olympus,
next to intertwining streams of impossible clarity, vines crawled up every
tree, until they spilled back over outstretched branches. Wildlife still
abounded within this preserved sanctuary. It became profoundly clear to me
that this place was Demeter herself, just as the sea was Poseidon. As stated
by Stange about the Greek mythological belief system, "the gods do not 'represent' or 'symbolize' elements of our world—they are our world" (qtd. in
Swan 52).

Climbing Mount Olympus the landscape dramatically changed again; everything became more intense. Gray and jagged slopes drastically sliced the landscape, as trees struggled to hold onto the surface of the mountain. Looking downward, it became apparent why Orpheus is associated with this mountain. The ravine itself could be understood as the underworld Hades, and the ascent up the peaks of the mountain would renew any climber. The sacred island of Delos in Greece also reveals why it was chosen for the birthplace of the god Apollo, as the land is harsh and sundrenched. Swan states, "The ancient Greeks spoke of the ... spirit of each place.... The landscapes we visit move us, especially when the spirit of a place is strong" (23).

Whenever we find ourselves at places that hold their own myths the land reveals itself, for those who look closely, as the myth itself. Sleeping Bear Dunes outside of Traverse City, Michigan, in the United States holds a primary dune that is shaped like a giant mother bear, as its American Indian Ojibwe myth tells. It is covered in short, hard foliage that looks from afar to be black fur, and the mound seems to have a head that looks far out towards Lake Michigan at two smaller islands, said to be the bodies of her drowned young. The great mound and the islands speak for themselves; the landscape presumably inspired awe in the Ojibwe, thus this myth was created to explain the natural topography. Devil's Tower in Wyoming demanded myths from over twenty different American Indian tribes, such as the Kiowa storyline of a giant mythic bear hunting seven sisters, until the Great Spirit raised the tower to save the sisters' lives. Loch Ness, Scotland, birthed its own mystery, just as the volcanos in Hilo, Hawaii, forced storylines of the goddess Pele. The mythic characters of Osiris and Isis must be connected to the Nile in Egypt, just as Gilgamesh requires the harsh landscape of ancient Uruk in modern Iraq.

Myths of nature-based cultures, like many of the American Indian and Aboriginal Australian legends, illuminate the role that nature plays in their most sacred myths. A connection to nature is vital to these cultures, and therefore nature's seasonal cycles became mythic messages that were meant to guide listeners in their deepest questionings of life and death.

The American Indian Cherokee have a single word for land, "eloheh." This one word represents the many facets of "history, culture, and religion" that the land holds for the Cherokee. It "emphasizes how the people conceive of themselves as inseparable to their homeland" (Zimmerman 44). For many American Indians

the Earth itself is holy, with a sacred history that explains how the first people came into being, and how each tribe came to occupy its particular place on the land. The animals on which humans depend for food and warmth have the same spiritual value as their hunters.... Every natural phenomenon—forests, mountains ... rivers ... has its spirit.... Through stories, rituals, and ceremonies, Native Americans reveal and affirm their kinship with the sacred totality [Lowenstein & Vitebsky 47].

R. Berndt and C. Berndt in speaking about Aboriginal Australian mythology state that "no traditional Aboriginal myth was told without reference to the land.... The land and all within it was irrevocably tied up with the content of the myth or story.... It is, then, the land which is really speaking" (5–6). In agreement to this view that many Aboriginal Australians hold towards their own mythology, this book contends that the land is an integral element of world mythology in more significant ways than just the obvious markers of place.

This book showcases how myths that seem removed from a clear association to nature still hold messages quite similar to those held by nature-dependent cultures. We are not so removed from our nature worshipping, agriculturally dependent ancestors, as even our contemporary narratives, heroic characters, philosophies, and religious axioms still portray some of the most basic tenets derived from viewing the cycles of nature day in and day out.

This book argues that the land is often the myth itself, and the people reflected in various mythological tales, even heroes, only reference a small, fleeting place within the larger cycles of nature. Mythic messages reflect humanity's struggles and subsequent spiritual wisdom that can be obtained from connecting oneself to the environment. The lessons of myth, therefore, are continuously repeated because they are the most simple and timeless of lessons—the lessons of nature.

The Necessity of Myth

Myths, in the ceaseless wonderings of humanity, portray the apparent mysteries of nature. Often they strive to explain a natural phenomenon, like why thunder and lightning accompany a rainstorm, or how a chipmunk got stripes down its back. Remarkably, though, world myths repeatedly show an accurate explanation to biological or evolutionary concepts of natural law. For instance, it has been scientifically confirmed that life emerged from water eons ago, and numerous creation myths from around the globe capture this accurately with their representations of life emerging from a primordial sea.

In addition, myths often portray more than explanatory lessons of what was to ancient people natural phenomenon; more often, myths incorporate a harmony between all living beings and the natural environment. We know today that plants and other photosynthesizers need carbon to survive, and then from this "the plants, and all the organisms that eat them, use this carbon to make up their tissues and to power their activities. Finally, all these organisms die, and as their remains are broken down, some of the carbon in them is released into the atmosphere. But this is not a one-way trip; sooner or later, this same carbon is likely to move back into the living world, to be made part of a tree or a mushroom or a human being once again" (Krogh 41). When this principle is conceived, it means that "human beings can no longer view themselves as something *separate* from all other living things" (Krogh 292). Myths help to capture this concept that all life is inextricably connected within the natural world.

Some myths portray creation as coming directly from natural sources, such as rotting logs, clay, or stones, and in some cases creation emerges directly from the ground. Linking the creation of all beings, including humans, to elemental agents shows a mythic conception of unity with nature. Many ancient, nature-dependent cultures saw all aspects of the environment as equal; "people thought that gods, humans, animals and nature were inextricably bound up together, subject to the same laws, and composed of the same divine substance" (Armstrong, *Short History*, 5). Without the success of the natural symbiotic system, ancient people believed their own lives would be jeopardized. Quite often there was no differentiation in thought that identified mankind as superior to nature; instead, human beings simply *were* another component of nature. Biology also supports this unity among all living beings on a cellular level, as all life is either composed of or needs cells to survive; "the fact that all cells come from cells means that each cell in your body is a link in a cellular chain the stretches back more than 3.5 billion years ago" (Krogh 64).

Krogh also states that because of the biological principle of common descent with modification, "all living things on earth ultimately are descended from a single, ancient ancestor" (292). Similarly in ancient times, the Roman Ovid speaking of the Greek Pythagoras discussed this same concept:

> Even things which we call elements, do not endure.... The everlasting universe contains four elemental parts...—earth and water—... air and—even lighter—fire.... These four elements, though far apart in space, are all derived from one another. Earth dissolves as flowing water! Water, thinned still more, departs as wind and air; and the light air, still losing weight, sparkles on high as fire. But they return, along their former way: the fire, assuming weight, is changed to air; and then, more dense, that air is changed again to water; and that water, still more dense, compacts itself again as primal earth [372–3].

The principle of evolution can affect human perception about life, not as a fixed concept, but as an ever-changing, evolving natural process, and this concept is found innumerable times in myth as well. Natural biology, when looked at through a mythological lens, can account for the myriad mythic representations of the interconnectivity of all living creatures on the planet. Myths strive to teach human beings again and again that they indeed are not removed from their biological ancestral source. Myths remind audiences that to forget their link with nature is to lose sight of themselves.

Mythology, therefore, must not be flippantly regarded as a thing of the past, but instead as a vital means of connection with humanity to the natural world. In mythically linking nature to the lives of mankind, lessons of selfhood can arguably be derived, most significant is the ultimate question of mankind—that of mortality; "the vegetable world has supplied not only the food, clothing, and shelter of man since time out of mind, but also his model of the wonder of life—in its cycle of growth and decay, blossom and seed, wherein death and life appear as transformations of a single, superordinated, indestructible force" (Campbell, *Primitive Mythology*, 137).

Humans are natural storytellers; in attempting to make sense of the world and their place within it, humanity has created countless myths that continue to fascinate, inspire, and sometimes haunt audiences. Myths are more than folktales and fairytales; myths were often an important part of the religion of ancient people. Therefore, one should not confuse folktales with mythology. Myths are often held as sacred to the people who recount them; they were often told and retold to live audiences in association with consecrated rituals. Folktales, on the other hand, hold a different position in cultural need; folktales are less serious, less sacred. Folktales can be laughed at, enjoyed, but myths, for their philosophical importance, are meant to be internalized and pondered for years to come.

As Puhvel declares, "True myth is by definition deadly serious to its originating environment. In myth are exposed the thought patterns by which a group formulates self-cognition and self-realization, attains self-knowledge and self-confidence, explains its own source and being and that of its surroundings.... By myth man has lived, died, and—all too often—killed" (2). Most myths were not believed to happen in real time, or that mythical beings, like giants, gorgons, dragons, etc., really existed; instead, these symbolic elements helped audiences of myth identify with religious and spiritual beliefs. Myths provide meaning for a community, and for the individual within a community. Nature, its cycles and phenomenons, fueled many myths, and thus nature has been a timeless means to explain to humanity their position in the cosmic cycle.

Again, nature, to early humans, was a part of every aspect of life. To attempt to separate the environment from the mythology of ancient civilizations is largely impossible. Walking in any natural location, it does not take long to see how plants and animals contribute to humanity's understanding of life. When a person stands among a virgin forest, it is unfeasible not to feel insignificant amidst the towering trees. In the deep boreal forests of the Amazon, or the harsh deserts of the Serengeti, humanity sees an explicit explanation of the natural processes of life, death, and regeneration. As Humpfrey states, "Through close contact with nature ... a profound sense of the relationship of human to plant can develop, indeed a sense of the interconnectedness of all things. Perhaps the botanical stories of human death and transfiguration that came down through the ages were first inspired by early humans' reverence and respect for, and dependence upon, plants as food, shelter, and fuel. Or perhaps these striking tales developed from the realization that a landscape's beauty is born out of the death of the beauties before it" (6). The myths of early cultures remind human beings that they too are inextricably bound to the cycles of the natural world.

The Promise of Nature—Life, Death, Rebirth

This book will reveal the important role of nature in mythology: from creation myths, myths that present the necessity of the harvest for survival, myths that tie humans to wild aspects of the environment, and finally myths that reveal the human life cycle as no different from the cycles of the seasons.

Chapter 1, "Emerging from the Earth," will describe various world myths that portray the creation of life on earth as inextricably connected to the land. Paleolithic and Neolithic man "lived out in the open[;] he was surrounded by flowers, plants and trees appealing to all of his five senses.... Man's mind became attracted to these ... beings, willingly lending themselves to his needs, giving him food and shelter" (Lehner & Lehner 11). And presumably from this observance of natural process, many creation myths portray human beings as also emerging directly from the elements. Myriad world myths recount a division of a primordial sea from habitable land, where sometimes life was sculpted from parts of a mythic creator's body, or human beings emerged directly from seeds or underground chambers within the earth. These portrayals of the creation of life as connected to nature remind audiences that humankind is intimately bound to the elements of the earth.

Chapter 2, "The Earth Goddess, the Male Seed and the Harvest," looks at numerous myths that connect seasonal change and the harvest to the lives of human beings. When a culture depends on agriculture for the production of staple crops, as it did in the Neolithic era, the change of the seasons profoundly impacts the lives of humans. As the assurance of verdant summer receded, and days began to get colder and shorter, humanity knew at the onset of autumn that a period of dormancy would always approach. In winter, food supplies became threatened, and communities often had to gather for an assurance of solidarity. Time indoors allowed one to reflect on philosophical quandaries and to hope that nature would again maintain its promise of renewal. With the annual arrival of spring, nature was witnessed as fulfilling its promise to meet the needs of its offspring. Ever since man "realized the eternal re-occurrence of nature's cyclic behavior throughout the year, he tried to coordinate his sowing and gathering of food plants in accordance with the seasonal cycle" (E. Lehner & J. Lehner 93). It is therefore not surprising that this cyclical promise of nature provided the foundation for the world's first heroic myths, but this promise was viewed to many ancient communities as coming with a price. Many Neolithic myths portray an Earth Goddess, often reflected as the earth itself, requiring first fertilization through the male seed, but then nutrition of the land through the death of a mythic male consort. These early myths often connected the cyclical death and resurrection of the crops with the annual death and resurrection of their mythic characters.

Chapter 3, "Divine Nature," discusses humanity's need to connect their belief in divinity to natural elements. The elements, changes of seasons, and physical landscapes often helped shape a people's belief in their gods and goddesses. In Egypt, for example, divine beings were often viewed as benevolent because of the predictability of the Nile; whereas, in Mesopotamia, the gods were often depicted as unpredictable and even hostile, because they were first associated as representations of the harsh landscape of the desert. Ancient humans needed to anthropomorphize nature as divine, so that they could come to an understanding of what appeared to them as natural phenomenon. To ritually perform a sacrifice to a god or goddess in order to alleviate his or her anger, and thus stop a drought, put into the hands of early humans a perceived means towards changing the hardships they faced. Creating myths that personified nature in myriad divine forms allowed human beings to come one step closer to connecting with the natural world. The divine beings often were guised in human form, so nature, as a divine being, could be worshipped in ways fitting to human conception.

Chapter 4, "Untamed Nature and the Unfettered Human," portrays nature myths that call audiences to embrace their own connection to wildness. Numerous world myths appeal to audiences to leave behind the confines of a structured society to embrace their more animalistic "wild" selves. The human alone in the wilderness presents a timeless literary device of transformation. Nature is presented as speaking to the lone transgressor, and often it is presented as educator to mythic protagonists. Numerous mythic characters learn an important lesson because of their experience in nature. Nature, though, often serves as a harsh and unforgiving teacher to its human pupils. Many mythic characters become disoriented, crazed, or even mutilated in their wilderness experience, but this encounter often conveys an important lesson to the audience of myth. In addition, this chapter portrays many myths of human contact with animals. Animals in myth have long been regarded as portents of important messages to mythic characters. Oftentimes, myths even focus on a human metamorphosing into animal form; when this occurs in myth, it is usually also indicative of a process of education for the mythic protagonist. The transformation into animal form is often viewed as a positive transformation whereby the character obtains special knowledge of nature's mysteries.

Chapter 5, "Trees of Knowledge and Botanical Metamorphosis," presents the botanical elements within the natural world as tied to the lives of human beings. Vegetation has frequently been regarded as holding mystical powers throughout world mythology. Sometimes plants serve as representations of divinities; sometimes, they hold medicinal or hallucinogenic powers, and can enable one to heal or transcend into mystical realms. Secluded nature is often portrayed in ancient stories as holding transcendent wisdom, whether nature is conceived as providing prophetic clues imagined by human transgressors, such as the ancient practice of forecasting the future by deciphering natural occurrences; for instance, a falcon dropping a snake it has just caught may signal a failure in an impending battle, or whether nature's general occurrences provide the human imagination meaning for their lives, such as witnessing a reed bend but not break in a steady stream, becoming a lesson for the onlooker that he or she too should be more willing to be flexible in times of strife. Nature throughout time has encouraged mankind to look inward, and the mythic representation of humans within nature often portray characters as obtaining wisdom because of their time with the land. This chapter looks at myths that present a mythic character's quest for knowledge by decisively seeking out a botanical source, such as a Tree of Knowledge. Plants sustain and protect mankind. In myth, they often serve to teach lessons of coexistence and even immortality through a promise of annual resurrection, as humans witness the botanical process of birth, death, and rebirth. Again, mythic characters learn lessons from their connection to botanical elements, most significantly lessons of natural resurrection as tied to the lives of human beings.

Also, sometimes mythic characters become part of nature through the means of metamorphosis into a botanical element, such as transforming into a flower or tree, and again, this is often viewed as a positive transformation.

Chapter 6, "The Seasonal Life Cycle and Myths of Destruction," shows a connection to the mythic portrayal of youth, maturity, and old age as a reflection to the natural progression of the seasons. World myth continuously shows life in a spring-like state of youth and vigor moving steadfastly to a late summer stage that allows one to reap the benefits of family life and communal responsibility, as one would reap the benefits of the harvest. But, this stage of abundance, as with the season of summer, cannot perpetually last in the lives of mortals. Men and women must move into a time of letting go; just as the leaves yellow and wither in autumn, so too must parents watch their own children grow and obtain families of their own. And finally, as vegetation decays in preparation for the dormancy of winter, so too must humans concede to the facts of mortality—old age, death, decay. The greatest of world myths repeatedly teach this message—mankind, like nature, is subject to the same seasonal laws. Myths of destruction within this chapter showcase the mythic archetype of inevitable obliteration of the known world. As myths present individual mortals living and dying, like all natural beings, so too do they represent this cyclical pattern on a larger scale. Many cultures discuss myths that present the destruction of the world, so that out of this "death" of the planet, like that of the plant, animal, and human being, the earth too "dies" in order to be reborn into a new and better world.

Myths were created because the lesson of life and inevitable death, just like we see around us each day in the natural world, is not an easy concept to internalize, but the inescapable factuality that humanity is profoundly connected to the same patterns as all plants and animals, makes this lesson one that all human beings must face. Myths remind audiences that we are forever tied to the most natural of cycles.

1

Emerging from the Earth

"A human being is a part of the whole called by us universe, a part limited in time and space. He experiences himself, his thoughts and feelings as something separated from the rest, a kind of optical delusion of his consciousness. This delusion is a kind of prison for us, restricting us to our personal desires and to affection for a few persons nearest to us. Our task must be to free ourselves from this prison by widening our circle of compassion to embrace all living creatures and the whole of nature in its beauty."
—Albert Einstein

"Is not the sky a father and the earth a mother, and are not all living things with feet or wings or roots their children?"
—Black Elk

Archeologists have found evidence of mythology as early as the Paleolithic period (20,000–8,000 BCE). In this period, before the advent of predictable agriculture, human beings existed off of a means of hunting and gathering. It is believed that Paleolithic man was "highly conscious of a spiritual dimension in their daily lives" (Armstrong, *Short History*, 13); the spiritual world was directly connected to the world in which they lived their lives each day. Therefore, "trees, stones and heavenly bodies were never objects of worship in themselves but were revered because they were epiphanies of a hidden force that could be seen powerfully at work in all natural phenomena" (Armstrong, *Short History*, 17). Nature, and humanity's place within it, was not considered something separate. Nature was a living force, and all aspects within it were inextricably connected; this is represented in Totemism, which many scholars believe may have been an existing belief system in Paleolithic cultures, which "classified all living things and natural phenomenon in a single system.... Thus the totem was the manifestation of a relationship with the entire world" (Allan, Fleming, & Kerrigan 57). Paleolithic human beings did not view themselves as superior to nature, rather they viewed themselves as stewards of the environment because their very survival depended upon their respect for the land.

Life from Water

Only water existed for eons. It is estimated that it took over three billion years "between the time life first got going (in the ancient oceans) and the time living things first came onto land (in the form of ancient plants)" (Krough 30). Astonishingly, myths often capture this evolutionary fact accurately with their portrayals of creation.

Many creation myths showcase the act of creation with a creature, usually an animal, volunteering to dive within primordial waters to bring up a piece of soil or find something whereupon earth's inhabitants can rest, such as the body of a turtle or whale. The American Indians have many versions of this type of creation myth initiated by their animal brethren; "the diver had various identities: the Cherokee of the east said it was a water beetle, their near neighbors the Chickasaw that it was a crayfish; elsewhere it was a beaver, muskrat, mink or duck" (Allan & Phillips, World, 22).

An Osage American Indian myth[1] shows their primordial beings, born of the sun and moon, going from the sky down to earth, but finding that the earth is immersed in water. The people and the animals with them are considered to be connected in this myth because both are despairing to find a way to survive. The people turn to Elk for help, so Elk throws himself into the primordial water and begins to sink. Often in these myths of early earth inhabitants pre-existing before the earth emerges out of vast waters, belief in success plays a crucial role. Elk believes that he will not die, and therefore he does not; his confidence that nature will provide the means for survival is revealed when he calls forth the wind to blow the water surrounding his body away, and thus it indeed does evaporate into mist. With Elk's action, land full of rocky soil emerges, and the animals and humans have a place to reside. But, there are still no plants, so Elk lies down on the ground, rolls his body about, and directly from the hairs on his body, plant life begins to emerge, so that the animals and humans have the nutritive means now to prosper.

This myth has multiple parts; first it tells a common theme that out of primordial waters, life emerges, as many world myths also contend, such as from the Yoruba, Greeks, Aztecs, etc. This early understanding that water is a crucial element towards creation points to an early understanding of evolution. It also shows an interconnectedness of mankind to animals and nature, as this myth portrays the necessity of all beings coming together in order for creation to be successful, most significantly in the symbolic sacrifice of Elk diving into the primordial sea and then rolling his body on the newly created land, so that his body will directly nourish the soil enough so that it may produce the means of survival for the beings of earth. This myth conveys the belief that the earth will provide for the needs of its inhabitants, but it also suggests that is can only provide if it is given a nutritive source, thus hinting at the necessity of death, through the portrayal of Elk giving a piece of his physical body—the hair on his body, to provide the enrichment needed to produce the next generation.

The American Indian Zuni tribe hold a myth of creation[2] that portrays the beginning of existence as a state of only moisture. The Creator, Awonawilona, is able to thicken this moisture, until it transforms into a primordial ocean. With the sacrifice of his own flesh, Awonawilona "fertilized the sea and green algae grew over it. The green algae produced the earth and the sky. The marriage of earth and sky and the action of the sun on the green algae produced all living things" (Bierlein 68). The accuracy of this evolutionary explanation for the beginnings of life is astounding, but mythically the legend also reveals an interconnectedness of all beings to all elements within the natural world.

The Taíno people of the Caribbean island of Hispaniola believe that creation occurred in stages.[3] In the first stage there was a supreme deity named Yaya; his son rebelled against him, so Yaya killed his son and hung up his corpse in a giant gourd. Yaya discovered to his surprise that after a few days had passed his son's corpse had transformed into many small fish that swam within the gourd. Yaya's wife, upon discovering the fish, took them, cooked, and ate them. After some time, the gourd broke open, and the waters spilled out upon the earth and became the ocean. Next the first human beings were created, and in a common mythic archetype, they were said to emerge from caves in the area. Some of the people, however, were caught by the rays of the sun that immediately made them transform into the first trees. Some of the people also metamorphosed into the first stones and birds, but still the first humans persevered, and in time they were able to fully emerge from the caves and begin a life of farming.

Another myth involving the Inuit of Tikigaq in Alaska showcases Raven braving the harshest of elements before the earth was made ready for land-dwelling inhabitants.[4] In the beginning the earth was only one vast expanse of icy water, and Raven after incessantly flying, became wearisome. He needed a place to rest, but there existed nowhere for him to land. When Raven was near death from sheer exhaustion, he finally saw that the "waters seemed to swell and sputter beneath him, and a dark form suddenly broke the surface of the sea: a mighty sea beast, its vast body extending from one horizon to the other" (Allan, Phillips, & Kerrigan 44–5). Raven at once knew what he must do, so that not only he would survive, but so that all future land-dwellers would be ensured a place to reside. When the whale surfaced once more,

Raven threw a giant harpoon at it, and after an agonizing struggle, managed to slay the giant whale, so that the whale's corpse became land.

The Sky and the Earth—The Male and the Female

Many anthropologists believe that Paleolithic cultures looking towards the sky with its "endless drama of … thunderbolts, eclipses, storms, sunsets, rainbows and meteors spoke of another endlessly active dimension" (Armstrong, *Short History,* 18), and it is out of this awe-inspiring sky that many early people may have mythically invented a belief in a Sky God. Armstrong states that "nearly every pantheon has its Sky God" (*Short History,* 20), yet the Sky God is not an accessible God; he is above the workings of mankind, inexpressible, and remote. Many early myths portray a Sky God as a creator god that exists in the cosmos, and oftentimes the Sky God must merge with a female Earth Goddess. The female divine being is represented in accordance with the earth and therefore is accessible in the daily lives of human beings. This differentiation will become highly important in myth.

Archeological evidence shows that Africa is the place where the first hominids emerged; it is also the home of the first recognizable human, Homo habilis (Allan, Fleming, & Phillips 9). Therefore, the myths of Africa may represent some of the most ancient of concepts, though because most myths in Africa were passed down through the oral tradition, as is the case with many cultures, many African myths were preserved in recorded format well after European contact and thus have modified content. Still, myths from Africa reveal an everlasting reverence for the environment, as "Africans have occupied every type of environment on their landmass: deserts and fertile river valleys, mountain-slopes and swamps, the tropical forests and the savannah grasslands … [and] it was from Africa that humans dispersed, tens of thousands of years ago, into every habitable corner of our globe" (Belcher xi–xii).

In one of the African Yoruba myths of creation,[5] Olorun is the male god of the sky, and Olokun is the female goddess of the water. Olokun is content ruling over the primordial abyss of water that holds no living beings, but Olorun's son, Obatala, feels compelled to create life. Obatala gathers a gold chain, sand in snail shells, a hen, a black cat, and a palm nut; he pours the sand from the shell, and it creates land, so he climbs down his gold chain. Once his feet touch upon the newly created earth that once was only primordial sea, he sets down his hen, which further scatters the sand around the earth, making mountains and hills. Then Obatala plants his palm nut into the ground, which produces all of the earth's plants. He then sets down the black cat as his only companion to reside with him in this new creation. He names earth Ife, and soon realizes that it is missing something—light. He asks his father, Olorun, to shed light upon the earth, so Olorun creates the sun. Obatala is then said to create the first humans from clay, a common mythic theme; his first creations are perfect, but then he gets drunk and makes humans who are, according to him, less than perfect. He sees his mistake in making some humans malformed, so out of his sadness and guilt, he vows never to drink alcohol again. Obatala then resides among these first humans, taking care of them, but after some time he tires of a life that is not filled with creating new life, so he goes back to his home in the sky.

The myth continues showing other gods who live in the sky also wanting to go down to live among the newly created human beings, so they take turns visiting earth. The portrayal of divine beings living among the Yoruba people is crucial to their understanding of mankind's connection to divinity. The people, as presented within the myth, are forever connected to nature because they came directly from the moist clay of the earth. The people are also portrayed as loved by Obatala, and the fact that he chooses to live among them, as do the other gods, places a divine importance on mankind itself; this is contrary to many other existing religious traditions.

In one of the Chinese myths of creation,[6] two distinct elements: Yin and Yang form as divinities beyond all human comprehension out of primordial chaos. Together they create the universe. Yang, representing the male essences of life, all things that are light and warm, uses his body to ascend upward creating the cosmos, and Yin representing the female, dark, cool essences of all living beings, uses her body to create the earth. Yang's hot breath creates the sun, and Yin's cold breath forms the waters; "the complex essence of Yang and Yin became the four seasons that dwell on earth in an endless cycle. And the essence of the four seasons became the ten thousand things in nature that populate the earth" (Rosenberg 326). This Taoist myth of creation explains the interconnectedness of humanity to all beings of the earth, as they are all showcased as being created from the same source.

The Polynesian creation myth[7] is similar to the Chinese creation myth just discussed. First out of chaos a singular being, Ku, begins to chant and thus separates two contrasting elements: Ao, the male force of light and sky, and Po, the female force of darkness and earth. Once separated, Ku creates Kane, who then has intercourse with many beings, and out of these unions, he creates the natural aspects of the earth, such as the plants and streams. This myth again ties creation directly to natural forces as found on the existing earth. From the secondary creator of Kane, his sexual unions create the earth's resources; linking the creation of natural elements with sexual intercourse again suggests an interconnectivity between nature and mankind, since divine beings are portrayed as creating the earth's inhabitants and resources the same way earthly beings create life.

Out of clay from the earth, Kane then crafts the first woman, Hine-hau-ona. Kane unites with Hine-hau-ona, and from this they have a daughter, Hine-titama. Kane then has sex with Hine-titama, and as a result, instead of creation resulting from this union, as happened with his other affairs, Hine-titama flees her father and goes to the Land of Po, "the world of the dead" (Bierlein 57), where she and her mother, Hine-hau-ona, reign forever. Because Kane broke "natural laws" of incest, as the myth defines it, with his coupling of Hine-titama, the legend states that his offspring, the people of the earth, are able to reside on earth, their fatherland, for a time, but all must also eventually die and return to their motherland in Po. The myth concludes further defining Po as the "creative world of night, a place of dreams, lovemaking, and the appearance of spirits" (Bierlein 57).

The myth's explanation of Po as a place of solace after negative worldly affairs is an essential part of the myth's message. The Land of Po is not only a place of desolation and death after life on earth; it is represented more as a place within the earth, a place that can heal, as it mythically does for Hine-titama. It also is represented as a place seemingly within one's own unconscious, as Po appears to humans in dreams and moments of creativity. The mythic underworld is often portrayed in world myth as a place visited for psychological purposes. The underworld, though it is depicted as a place of death, is not in many myths portrayed as an evil place. The mythic underworld most often serves as a representation of the womb of the earth, thus often tying it to female attributes, as in this case it is Hine-titama and her mother Hine-hau-ona who reign over Po, just as the Sumerian Ershkigal and the Norse Hel rule their respective underworlds. The womb-like significance of the mythic underworld, instead of the often contemporary view of a place for the sinful, is integral to myriad world myths, as it shows life, including creation, as being tied to an endless natural cycle of life, death, and rebirth.

In New Zealand, the Maoris also believe in a "great father of forests" known as Tane-Mahuta.[8] He was believed to be in the shape of a giant tree. In Maori creation, heaven and earth were connected in sexual union; their subsequent children were forced to reside trapped in darkness, until one day Tane-Mahuta stated to his siblings that they should sever their two parents. He declared that they should have their father, the sky god, remain high above them forever separated from them, but the earth should "remain close to us as our nursing mother" (Porteous 213). Tane-Mahuta then took it upon himself to continue the creation he initiated; he began to grow into his giant tree form. He grew so tall and strong that he forced his primordial parents apart.

The Earth as Mother

Anthropologists often point to Paleolithic caves as indicators of early mythology. The cave paintings of Lascaux in France and Altamira in Spain[9] present exquisite sites of early man's artistry. The inner recesses of the caves were not easily accessible, suggesting that the practice of cave painting held sacred, mythic significance. The process of crawling through the caves itself has been paralleled with the heroic and shamanic journey, and the final result of seeing the grandiose spectacle of animal and human form artistically captured as paintings on the cave walls helped initiates, taking part in what anthropologists often believe to be a ritualistic practice, to ultimately connect their own lives with the lives of animals (Armstrong, *Short History,* 32). The cave as a physical representation of the womb of the earth is also an important aspect associated with these early sacred sites. The journey back into the earth is purposely tied to the decision to render artistic creations in such remote and inaccessible places. The caves, as representational earth-wombs, may have been connected with a concept of symbolic death and rebirth, as the initiate must travel deep into the cave and then emerge from the cave in a symbolic rebirth.

In the Neolithic period (c. 8,000–4,000 BCE) with the advent of agriculture and thus civilizations, "people now made ritual contact with the sacred in the earth. Neolithic labyrinths have been discovered that are similar to Paleolithic tunnels at Lascaux.... These worshippers felt that they were entering the womb of Mother Earth, and making a mystical return to the source of all being" (Armstrong, *Short History,* 45). Campbell also concurs:

> The concept of the earth as both bearing and nourishing mother has been extremely prominent in the mythologies both of hunting societies and of planters. According to the imagery of the hunters, it is from her womb that the game animals derive.... Comparably, according to the planters, it is the mother's body that the grain is sown.... Furthermore, the idea of the earth as mother and of burial as a re-entry into the womb for rebirth appears to have recommended itself to at least some of the communities of mankind at an extremely early date [*Primitive Mythology,* 66].

This same type of belief, that creation emerges from the womb of the earth, is also evidenced in later cultures, as the Anasazi-Pueblo American Indians believed that their people emerged from the "vulva of the earth" (Leeming

& Page, *Goddess*, 31), and the Inca of the Andes Mountains in western South America believed that the first humans emerged out of caves, suggesting again creation as a birthing process. Among the Ibo people of Western Africa, Ala, the goddess of the underworld, is also the Earth Goddess who protects the harvest. Ala receives the dead, as burial is thought to be placing the dead in her womb. In her portrayal of both underworld goddess and earth womb, she also ensures renewed life by making people and animals fertile. Death when viewed in these terms in just a necessary means towards securing new life for future generations. These creation myths that identify the first inhabitants coming from the earth itself indicate a conscious connection towards humanity and nature. Ancient people acknowledged that they belonged "to the earth in the same way as rocks, rivers and trees do. They must, therefore, respect her natural rhythms" (Armstrong, *Short History*, 45).

In the Babylonian and Assyrian creation myths Ninhursag, the Earth Goddess, created humanity from clay and blood. These myths make it clear that the earth is considered divine, and that mankind is also connected to this natural divinity, as are all other aspects of the earth:

> "The goddess they called ... [the mot]her,
> The most helpful of the gods, the wise Mami:
> Though art the mother-womb,
> The one who creates mankind" [qtd. in Sproul 114].

Ninhursag's myth places her, therefore, as a goddess of the birthing process, and the ritualistic aspect of the myth "underscores the point that the holy birth of all mankind is repeated in time through the birth of each individual" (Sproul 114):

> "As the Bearing One gives birth,
> May the mo[ther of the ch[ild] bring forth by herself!" [qtd. in Sproul 115].

The Okanagan Indians of the northern United States and of British Columbia also have a myth where earth is created from a primordial woman.[10] For the Okanagan Indians, the earth is literally the body of this woman; she "lives still, but transformed so we cannot see her as the person she is. But she still has all the parts of a person—legs, arms, flesh, and bone. Her flesh is the soil; her hair is the trees and other plants. Her bones are the rocks, and her breath is the wind" (Leeming & Page, *Goddess*, 12). The primordial woman as one and the same as the earth itself allows audiences of this myth to connect themselves to nature. Just as Christians state that God created mankind in His image, here mankind is created in nature's image; this distinction is important.

The Baransana people of southeastern Columbia discuss Romi Kumu as their primordial being who initiated the creation of the universe directly from her body, and because of this she rules over the different aspects of nature, including mankind.[11] What is more is that "each night ... she becomes old and the world mourns, but every morning she is young once again" (Leeming & Page, *Goddess*, 34). This creation myth directly connects humanity to nature, but it also identifies a pattern that will be repeated often in world myth—that of death and resurrection. Similarly, another Columbian tribe, the Kagaba, believe that the earth itself is their divine mother, and humans are therefore the offspring of the earth, thus inextricably a part of nature and its cycles. It is said that the Kagaba mother will care for her people, "for we are her seed, and we belong to her only" (Leeming & Page, *Goddess*, 35).

The Hawaiian myth of the goddess Pele also showcases a divine goddess is the form of the earth itself. Pele is a massive volcano; it is through her eruptions that the islands of Hawaii were created, but she also is equally capable of causing insurmountable destruction to the inhabitants of the islands. The mythic portrayal of nature is not always pleasant, precisely because the natural world is often viewed as harsh. In Greek mythology Typhon, an offspring of the Earth Mother, Gaia, controls the winds; he is responsible for immense storms and typhoons. The Greek Poseidon was also attributed as having caused horrendous storms and earthquakes if upset. After joining in a competition with Athena to see who would be the patron divinity of Athens, Poseidon, having lost because he gave the people a spring of salt water which they could not use, as opposed to Athena's gift of an olive tree, caused such a tremendous flood that many people perished, until the Athenians placated him.

Emerging Directly from the Earth

The American Indians living throughout North and South America are represented by many diverse populations; therefore, their myths and customs vary depending on the environmental region in which they reside. The landscape vastly affects the myths that emerge from each tribe. For example, the American Indian tribes of the northwest tell tales that depict their clan founders appearing as animals, and the legends of the American Indians of the southwest depict humans as inextricably tied to agricultural cycles (Wilkinson 177). The environment has always been a central component in the lives and beliefs of the American Indians; "What inspires and unites these different groups is a view of the world as a place of sacred mystery. The native relationship with the world is rooted in a profound respect for the land, its features and life-forms.... Humans are not above creation, but a part of it, and people must forge a respectful, balanced relationship with the world around them" (Zimmerman 9).

The way that a culture explains their creation reveals a lot about their tie to the natural environment. The creation myths of many American Indian cultures identify people and animals emerging from an underworld or series of underworlds. In these stories the underworld is again portrayed as a womb in which life is nurtured or prepared until the time is right for ascension onto the earth.

Many American Indian legends recount life beginning by an emergence directly out of the land or out of the water[12]; as Zimmerman states, "Many origin stories describe native people as coming from a dark place—some emerge from beneath the ground, others from under the waters. Some experts have suggested that this dark place is an allegory for being born, of passing through the birth canal into the light" (41). Leeming and Page also discuss the archetype of emergence from the underworld found in many American Indian creation myths; "an underworld in this context can be seen as a world womb, a place in the Earth Mother where humans, plants, and animals are conceived and gradually mature from a seedlike state in darkness until they are ready to be born through a sacred opening.... The agricultural implications of the emergence creation are obvious" (*The Mythology*, 89). And as Allan and Phillips state, "For peoples who practiced burial rather than cre-mation of the dead, the Earth was also a place where the ancestors went.... As seeds are broken and give issue to shoots, so new life came from the underground realm of the dead" (*World*, 28). In addition, often American Indian myths that recount emergence as creation have a guide in female form seeing over this "birthing" process, "such as the Hopi Spider Woman, the Navajo Changing Woman, and the Keres Thinking Woman" (Leeming & Page, *The Mythology*, 90).

The Mandan American Indians tell of a myth where their people emerged from below the ground.[13] A grapevine was said to hang down into the realm of the first people; the bravest ones chose to climb it, and to their surprise they discovered that they had been living in an underworld compared to this brilliant realm. In this upper world, they found verdant flowers of every hue; this world was also teeming with resources, like wild game and fish. They called to their people still below the ground and encouraged them to climb out of their underworld, and so many more Mandan emerged onto the earth. The myth states, though, that one woman began to climb, but she got stuck, causing some people to be forced to remain in the underworld and some to live above on earth. The myth, therefore, recounts that when the Mandan die, they eventually get to be reunited with the people still below the ground. Death is stripped of negative associations in this mythic portrayal of the underworld as earth womb; life and death are instead portrayed here as only a natural event. The womb-like attribute of the Mandan underworld merely presents life and death as a natural, cyclical process; some live on earth for a time, but when they die their bodies simply reenter this underworld, so that the cycle, presented botanically, can continue.

The Hopi American Indians of Arizona believe that their people emerged from under the ground in a series of steps with the help of Grandmother Spider. The people had to climb three consecutive worlds, until they were finally at the cusp of the underworld, almost within the fourth world.[14] But once they finally emerged out of the third world into the fourth world by climbing up a reed, a child died. The chief of the people thought that sinister magic must have been to blame, but a girl finally confessed to the murder. The people, enraged, were about to throw this girl back into the third world, but she amazed the people by telling them that anyone who died in the fourth world were still alive and well in the third world, and then she proved her remark by showing the murdered child quite alive in the third world. Awed, the people let the accused girl go free, but they understood that now with her presence in their world there would always be contrary forces within the fourth world. They also saw that death, initially thought to be the worst of offenses, was something that was only an illusion, as the process of growth could seemingly be started again from the underworld womb source.

The American Indian Navajo in their telling of the five worlds[15] also recount their first people emerging from a womb-like underworld. Each world is portrayed as above one another, and First Man, First Woman, and Coyote must climb these early worlds in order to emerge from underneath the ground onto the surface of the earth. The first world was filled with darkness, and in the second world, the sun tried to have sex with First Woman, but Coyote convinced Man and Woman to continue their climb. In the third world, it was calm and beautiful, filled with majestic mountains and mountain people who welcomed the newcomers and told them they could stay as long as they liked if they left a giant, primordial serpent in peace. Coyote, though, unable to resist such things, stole the serpent's children, and subsequently caused the serpent to flood the third world in order to retrieve her children. First Man and Woman climbed up to the fourth world by piling the mountains upon one another and planting a giant reed into the ground, so that the reed grew tall enough to help them climb to their needed fourth world.

But the salvation of the fourth world also proved short-lived, as the fourth world challenged First Man and Woman, and they began to quarrel.

They tried living apart, but grew sad and unfulfilled without the presence of children, so they vowed to live together from now on. The flood waters of the third world permeated the soil of the fourth world, and the people realized that soon they would have to move on yet again. So they climbed higher in order to escape another flood. Again, the people piled the mountains on top of one another and planted their sacred reed, until it grew tall enough to let them escape to the fifth and final world, the world the people inhabit today.

This myth presents the natural cycle of life occurring within each earthly layer. First from the dark, initial underground, First Man, Woman, and Coyote emerge like seedlings, and then they come into the second world by the aid of sunlight, a clearly botanical reference. In the third world, with water, they again are connected to vegetative growth, as they grow further upwards like a mature plant stretches ever higher towards the sun. In the fourth world, they learn that they must regenerate to ensure their own survival as a species, so they can successfully enter into the final and fully developed realm of the fifth world. The myth does not end here however.

The myth's ending suggests the cyclical part of the entire process. In the fifth world, all the people are in jeopardy of being burned alive because the sun, being thrown into the sky by the people, initially does not move; it remains bound within a single spot. The chief's wife comes forward and tells the people that to ensure that the sun moves accordingly to its natural plan, a life must be sacrificed to it. To the astonishment of the people, the woman offers herself. The people mourn this terrible loss, until one day, a man looks down a hole in the earth and sees the woman there content; "Since that time, one human being has had to die each day in order to make the sun move" (Bierlein 108). The portrayal of the woman sacrificing herself for the success of her people ties to the natural cyclical aspect of the life process. As a woman, she can symbolically assure the regeneration of her people by mythically giving her body back over to the processes of nature. Instead of finding the woman contently sitting in a higher world, as the myth suggests might happen, she is found below the fifth world. This indicates that the process of emerging from within the earth, and steadfastly growing higher and higher, like vegetation with the aid of natural elements such as sunlight and water, is a cyclical process that must have an endpoint. To ensure the regeneration of her people, the myth portrays the necessity of death for all people, so the process can forever renew itself.

Similarly, the Jicarilla Apache American Indians have a myth that explains creation in the form of emergence.[16] In this version the underworld is portrayed as beneath the water; the humans, animals, and plants all resided there in a dark, aquatic habitat. Some animals, those associated with daylight hours, resented this environment, but the nocturnal plants and animals preferred it. One day there was a contest to see if a world of light or darkness would ultimately win. The creatures of the light eventually won, and as a reward they received the sun. The creatures of the day were filled with delight to see the sun illuminate their dreary sea home. Still, more light was desired, and one creature of the day looked "as the sun came to the top of the underworld ... [and] found a hole and saw a different world out there. He told the people about this other world and they all clamored to go there. So they built four mounds—one for each direction—and planted them with fruits and flowers. The mounds began to grow upward toward the hole" (Leeming & Page, *The Mythology*, 96). The people finally emerged into the upper world inhabiting all the land.

The American Indian Kiowa creation myth speaks of the first people coming from underneath the ground and ascending directly out of a rotting log.[17] Emerging from the rotting log is suggestive of the cyclical botanical process—only from decay can life begin anew. After the people emerge, a man and his wife have a baby daughter. One day the mother puts her daughter in a cradle from a tree. The baby crawls out of the cradle and up the tree to try and grasp a beautiful and mystical red bird. As she is climbing, the tree continues to grow up into the sky. Again in connection to the botanical process, the girl grows with the tree, and once she has reached the sky, she has grown into a beautiful maiden. Once in the sky, a man who is portrayed as the sun forces her to stay there and marry him. She soon loses her virginity to the sun, and while living there becomes desperate to return to earth. While the sun is away, the woman carries her newborn son upon her back and climbs down a sinew hanging from the sky to try to reach land again. The sun comes back home and sees his wife and son hanging in the air by the sinew, still far from the earth. Enraged, the sun throws a ring at his wife and kills her. Their son, though, falls to the earth and survives.

This myth also is again directly connected to themes that link humans to the botanical cycles of nature. The myth shows the woman as literally growing with the tree, reaching towards the sun as any plant must do. Once she has reached her full maidenhood, standing before the sun, she begins the next part of her life, losing her virginity and moving from maidenhood to motherhood. After proliferating, she progresses from this vegetative role into her final natural role, that of her death, which, again like a decaying plant, directly enables the growth of her son, as symbolic seed, once he hits or is symbolically planted into the earth. This myth reminds audiences that just as the first people came directly out of the earth and returned into it, so too are all humans forever intimately connected to the same natural cycles.

Growing from Seeds

Many myths also recount creation emerging from natural elements, such as water, plants, or the earth itself:

> African tradition was rich in tales of the first people emerging from plants. For the southern African Zulu and Tsonga peoples, the earliest ancestors came from a reed bed. The Herero of Namibia said that their ancestors climbed down from a tree…. The pygmy hunters of central Africa's forests recounted that the first man and woman emerged from a tree trunk…. The Keraki of New Guinea … said the primordial being Gainji discovered the first people chattering high in a palm tree [Allan & Phillips, World, 28].

Many American Indian legends also recount mankind being made from the earth. Oftentimes humanity is depicted as first being made out of an insufficient, natural element, and a subsequent series usually takes place where a divinity tries, fails, and must finally perfect the process by choosing a different resource to create the first humans, such as with the Quiches of Central America. In their myth mankind was first created out of clay, but they were weak and could be ruined by water, so then people were created out of wood, but they too were not right either. So, finally, from maize, people were created.[18]

A myth of the Yurucases of Bolivia "relates that when all mankind had been destroyed by fire, the god Tiri opened a tree and from it drew forth all the various tribes. When a sufficient number had come forth he closed up the tree" (Porteous 159). Also, among the Polynesian tribes of West Ceram, they believe that the first people emerged from clusters of bananas (Campbell, Primitive Mythology, 173). One of the Greek myths about the creation of the island of Santorini relates that the origin of the island is tied to the legend of Jason and the Argonauts, stating that one of the Argonauts, Euphemus, aboard the journey home after helping Jason fetch the Golden Fleece was given a clod of dirt. Euphemus kept the dirt next to him for several days, feeling it to be of great importance, until one night Euphemus had a dream that he began to nurse the clod of dirt with milk from his own breasts. Suddenly, Euphemus was stunned to find that the dirt turned into a beautiful woman with whom he immediately had sex. The woman told Euphemus that she was a daughter of Poseidon and ordered Euphemus to throw the dirt into the Aegean Sea, so that it would grow into an island for his descendants to live on. Euphemus obeyed the mystical woman and found that her prophecy was fulfilled. The mythic portrayal of creation coming directly from various elements of the earth solidifies the connection of mankind to all elements of nature. It stresses a philosophy of co-existence between mankind and nature as opposed to viewing humanity as elevated from the myriad aspects of the natural world.

The Australian Gagadju (Kakadu) people tell of Manamaramar[19] who one day as he walked the bush found a baby crying, "who had just emerged from the ground during the night" (Berndt & Berndt 22). Manamaramar picked the child, Dulungun-dulungul, up and using natural resources, made a shelter and a bed for the baby and hid him for the harsh elements of the bush. Manamaramar then went home and told his people to avoid the direction where he hid Dulungun-dulungul, stating that a bird might lay eggs in a nest he spotted. Manamaramar returned to the secret child the next day and proceeded in the days to come to care for him; "from the ground, the child grew rapidly; within four weeks he was running around" (Berndt & Berndt 22). Dulungun-dulungul soon became a man, and Manamaramar, honoring this rite of passage, decorated his body with natural materials, such as smearing red ochre all over his skin, adorning him with cane bangles, banyan fibers across his chest, grass beads around his neck, and crane and cockatoo feathers for his head-dress, and finally gave him small bamboo spears and a spear-thrower. Manamaramar then took Dulungun-dulungul to his camp; the people marveled at his mystical beauty, but soon word spread, and the people of a neighboring village wished to harm him. Dulungun-dulungul went to the village and joined in a fight with their best adversary, Grudbibi. After they fought using their bamboo spears, Grudbibi fatally wounded Dulungun-dulungul. Dulungun-dulungul's friends chased Grudbibi, who immediately began Dreaming and transformed himself into a rock, and told the people, "You can see me as a big rock.... At low tide you can see Grudbibi, 'along sunrise way'" (Berndt & Berndt 23). The people carried the corpse of Dulungun-dulungul back to the place where he emerged from the ground, and from his body a high hill pushed forth that can still be seen today.

Interestingly many world creation myths also recount tales where the first people emerged from seeds. This clear botanical reference to creation first in the form of a seed and then to the full fruition of maturity also ties mankind to the processes of nature. Integral to the seed portrayal of creation is the acceptance that what came from the earth will also inevitably have to go back into the earth, so that the process can be renewed.

For instance, the Zia American Indians tell of Sus'sistinako, Thinking Woman, who appears in the form of a spider. In the beginning of creation, only Sus'sistinako existed. She carried with her two bundles filled with seeds, and inside the bundles were the twin mothers who would populate the earth with all the animals and human beings. Sus'sistinako laid the bundles on the earth and sung to them, until the two women emerged, and life began.

Similarly, the Acoma American Indians believed in Tsichtinako, also Thinking Woman, who gave birth to again twin daughters. Tsichtinako gave birth to her daughters deep within the earth. The girls grew slowly in the dark underground nurtured by their mother. When Tsichtinako knew it was the right time for their emergence, she gave each daughter a basket filled with seeds and models of the different creatures that were to be born. She instructed them where to plant each seed, and "after a very long time, the seeds sprouted and one seedling, a pine, eventually grew tall enough to break a small hole through the earth above, letting in some light" (Leeming & Page, *The Mythology*, 31). The sisters found the model of Badger and told him to dig around the pine tree to make the hole bigger; they next told Locust to smooth the edges of the hole, which he did, but he snuck a peek at the upper world, and as punishment, the sisters made locusts forever doomed to die and be reborn each year. The sisters, with the help of Tsichtinako, climbed into the upper world, planted the seeds, and breathed life into their models, until all creation thrived.

The northern Andean tribes from South America also feature a creation myth where a divinity named Sibu created the first human beings and animals from seeds.[20] Sibu is told to give his sacred seeds to another god, Sura, to bury them in a designated spot. But, momentarily Sura turns his back before planting the seeds, and the trickster Jabaru comes in and steals the seeds. Jabaru then cuts Sura's throat and buries him in the place where the seeds were to be planted. Later Jabaru returns to the place of the crime and finds Sibu standing at the exact spot looking at a cacao and a calabash tree. Sibu, though, merely asks Jabaru for a drink of cacao; "Jabaru took some beans to his wives who prepared the drink, using the hard shell of the calabash fruit as a cup. When Jabaru returned Sibu insisted he drink first. Jabaru grasped the cup and drank thirstily. The fruit of Sura tasted good" (Allan, Bishop, & Phillips 31). Though Jabaru initially enjoyed the fruit of his malicious doing, the cacao caused his stomach to swell until it finally burst open, allowing Sura's seeds to be spread throughout the land. Directly from these seeds, all humans and animals emerged.

The Mande people of Mali[21] recount a myth where their creation divinity also creates mankind from seeds. The myth first tells the process of cultivating the seeds with many successes and failures. One seed, Pembra, chooses to emerge early from his pod; he tears off the surrounding material of his "placenta" and falls into nothingness, but "the piece of the placenta with him soon becomes the earth" (Leeming & Page, *God*, 65). However, because Pembra did not fully germinate, the earth is at first a barren place. Pembra tries to return to the cosmos to fully mature, but he is refused, so he steals more seeds and begins to plant them into his premature and thus barren earth. Again, though, because Pembra tries to speed up the needed growth process of the seeds, his effort is a failure, as the seeds do not have the necessary elements required for their maturation, and they wither and die. Meanwhile, the other seeds left alone in the cosmos fully germinate and grow into fish; one of the fish is called Faro. The creation divinity cut Faro into pieces "which he cast out into space. The pieces floated down through space and landed on the dry earth where they each soon grew into tall, self-seeding trees" (Leeming & Page, *God,* 67). From Faro's body, then, humanity was created.

This myth again identifies creation as a botanical process. In this myth it is the seeds that directly enable the earth itself to grow; the seeds also enable the development of the environmental elements needed for survival, and then seeds additionally create animals and humans. The act of cutting up the body of Faro is essential as well. This mythic act of mutilation appears violent, and it is one that will be repeated often in world myth, but when the cutting up of the mythic character is viewed in botanical terms, the death and mutilation of Faro is presented as a mythic sacrifice for the good of the earth. His body directly causes everything to grow and to be sustained, as any death ultimately does. The myth's connection to sacrifice is an essential one; it teaches the importance of the natural cycle of life, death, and rebirth to its audience, as from the death of Faro, and all matter, nature's cycles can be renewed resulting in the production of new life.

Moreover, The Australian Unumbal of Kimberly believe in the Wondjina,[22] the god of rain, who produces "child seeds who will implant themselves in women" (Lemming & Page, *God,* 69); they are called "child-germs." It is from these "child germs" that the people are created; therefore, when a person dies, the "child-germ" returns to the waters and waits for the next host. This concept again directly ties creation to the botanical process; it also speaks of the natural cycle of destruction, but also of rebirth because the "child-germs" can never be totally destroyed, as when a person dies within this myth, the seed is said to return to the water, from which it originated from the god of rain, and waits to grow again.

Evolving Creation

Australian Aboriginal mythology provides myriad creation accounts that showcase nature and its inhabitants being inextricably tied to one another. In Aboriginal myth, "humankind was and is inseparable ... from what happened in the Dreaming. Men and women were originally 'conceived' and born into the creative era of the Dreaming. They emerged from the womb of a mythic being or were otherwise generated or prepared from emergence" (Berndt & Berndt 17). The Australian Aboriginal people believe that through Dreaming their ancestors' spirits awoke and began creation, and after they were finished, they again entered into a deep slumber. But it is also important to note that the "Dreaming characters themselves are bounded by a kind of circularity, by what has been called sacred time, a cyclical, constantly recurring, essentially repetitive process which ensures their survival through time" (Berndt & Berndt 18). Therefore, Dreamtime is never truly finished; its cyclical pattern mimics the seasonal changes found in nature and provides mythic meaning for audiences about the necessity of creation, demise, and recreation for all living beings.

One myth from the Dieri of South Australia tells of creation starting in Perigundi Lake[23] where "incomplete creatures emerged" (Berndt & Berndt 16). This account describes creation in evolutionary terms, as these primal beings having left the water had to first stretch themselves out on the sand to become strong enough to mature from the energy of the sun's rays. These early creatures eventually became the first human beings. Showing creation as a slow and evolving process also puts the myth in botanical terms, as these first humans must evolve as a result of emerging from the water partially formed, and then progress fast into fully-developed humans from the emanations of the sun's heat. Their evolutionary success is described in vegetative terms, which serves to connect mankind to all aspects of nature.

The Australian Bandicoot people believe[24] that their creator, Karora "lay at the bottom of a soak, covered with earth" (Berndt & Berndt 16). The myth states that Karora slept in his womb-like abode within the earth, until like a seedling he emerged from the soil. He then slept in the sun, and again suggestive of the botanical process, the first people began to emerge from the navel and armpits of Karora; "they burst through the soil and sprang into life" (Berndt & Berndt 16). Karora then awoke and immediately knew the immensity of his creation. This process showcases the act of creation on the part of Karora as a passive act because it is not the creator's initiative that produces new life, but the natural, botanical process.

The landscape of the far north region in North America has inspired some of the most intriguing myths of creation. The bitter cold and unforgiving natural conditions makes the land seemingly inhospitable, yet people have lived there for thousands of years. To the people of this region, "nature ... was not seen as hostile but as working by rules which compelled humans to adapt their ways to forces which were far greater than themselves. They had to … respect the animals and environment which supported them. For help they could turn to shamans, soul voyagers who journeyed to the spirit world" (Allan, Phillips, & Kerrigan 7). To the Tagish people of the Yukon, creation involved a process where the earth had to adapt itself, so that its inhabitants could survive.[25]

The Tagish believe that in primordial time there existed ravenous, giant animals that the earth could not properly support, so the myth states that Beaver, the trickster, confronted the beasts in order to prepare for the arrival of more conducive life forms. Beaver bravely enticed a massive giant into following him as he backed up onto a mountain peak; once there Beaver killed the giant "by stabbing him in the hand—where all his strength lay. He then cut him into pieces, and scattered the scraps all about him in the forest. Each one became a harmless little rock rabbit" (Allan, Phillips, & Kerrigan 32). This mythic element of killing someone or something and cutting up the remains to spread throughout the earth again mythically explains the cycles of nature, whereby one death aids in the coming of new life. This necessary process is viewed in both hunting societies where a death of an animal allows the tribe to be sustained, and agricultural communities where the "death" of natural material fertilizes the soil allowing for new growth. Beaver then goes on many more quests where he either kills an adversary that is diminishing nature's resources or instructs the giant animals not to produce any more giant offspring and to consume only the resources that they need, like smaller plants instead of only meat sources. Beaver's creation, then, is as an act of understanding the environment and making it suitable for all its inhabitants; this suggests a mythic explanation for communal behavior within the tribe and towards the land around them.

From the Body of the Creator

Oftentimes, the mythic act of creation simply occurs naturally without a divinity or mythic character taking any initiative; this involuntary creation reminds audiences of myth that unregulated nature is the cause of the creation of the earth, its resources, and its inhabitants. Many world myths present a creator god or goddess who indirectly creates the earth and its inhabitants, like Karora of the Australian Bandicoot awakening from a deep slumber to find that human beings have emerged from his navel and armpits.

Another version of creation in Chinese mythology is represented by a belief that the earth emerged out of giant, primordial egg.[26] It is clear that the myth's framework for creation came from an act that was noticed in the natural world day in and day out; as people witnessed the seemingly miraculous occurrence of a fully formed being emerge out of an egg, they made use of this natural imagery to explain their own creation. In this myth, the primeval egg contained chaos, but over time chaos formed into the first living being, P'an Ku. Finding himself within a dark realm of nothingness, P'an Ku consciously decided to continue creation. Once he made his mind up to continue the plan set in motion by his formation, he broke free from his confinement by separating the two halves of the egg shell, so that the top half became the sky, and the bottom half became the earth. Finally, witnessing his creation, P'an Ku came to realize that no living beings would be able to survive in the environment he created because the earth and the sky were too close together, so P'an Ku voluntarily sacrificed himself by offering to hold the sky up away from the surface of the earth for eighteen thousand years. After P'an Ku's immense sacrifice, the cosmos was well above the earth, and he was assured that life could thrive on the earth he helped to create, but with this knowledge, he finally felt immensely tired. So, P'an Ku laid his immense body down upon the earth and passed away.

Directly from P'an Ku's dead body, life began to emerge without any voluntary action on his part. P'an Ku's head, feet, arms, and torso created the sacred mountains of China; his eyes became the sun and moon; his breath became the clouds; his voice transformed into thunder, and his sweat became the rain. P'an Ku's "flesh formed the soil of the earth, while his blood and his semen become the oceans and rivers that encircle it. His veins and muscles gave shape to the earth's surface. His teeth and his bones formed rocks and minerals…. From the hair on his body, came forth trees, plants, and flowers" (Rosenberg 329). And finally, from the mites that lived on his giant body, human beings were created.

The myth repeatedly demonstrates that nature is the true creator of the myth, as P'an Ku and his cosmic and earthly egg shell originated out of an indiscriminate nature, just as it is the inactive corpse of P'an Ku that passively enables life to emerge. This myth also reveals an outlook that connects the natural world with the lives of human beings; it clearly does not put humanity at an elevated position above other created beings, as human beings are portrayed here as having been created from the mites that crawl upon P'an Ku's flesh.

In addition, essential to the message of this myth is the willing sacrifice of P'an Ku. P'an Ku is portrayed as aiding creation, but only because he immediately accepts the dominant role that nature plays in the process. From nature he was indiscriminately created, and once created he never attempted to step away from the processes of nature. Upon his first act of creation came the precursor that he must begin to sacrifice himself. In contemporary times, this act of sacrifice carries with it severe importance, but this myth lacks the aspect of him lamenting over his inevitable death, and this component, that will be repeated throughout many world myths, is presented as mundane, as simply a part of the natural life process. P'an Ku unassumingly plays out his role to continue the succession of life after his own life. He easily decides to give his life, presented mythically as a constant sacrificial decision to separate the sky from the earth over thousands of years, to ensure that new life will one day thrive. When his life cycle is complete, the myth symbolically portrays this primeval giant lying down and piece by piece becoming myriad parts of the earth and cosmos. The act of his death directly producing life is tied to the cycles of vegetative growth found in the natural world; precisely out of his body, as happens with all decaying matter, new life emerges. The myth educates audiences to accept this natural part of life and envision that one lives according to the same natural processes.

The Norse, as told in Snorri Sturluson's *Prose Edda*,[27] believed in a version of creation that also used a primordial being to directly explain the creation of the world and its inhabitants. The myth recounts creation as consisting again of a primeval void filled with "windless skies," frost, and ice. This portrayal of creation reflects a connection to the landscape the Norse inhabited in winter. Eventually "mist and wind-whipped rain" (Sturluson 13) comes, and the ice begins to thaw, creating the body of a frost giant named Ymir and a primeval cow named Audhumla. Audhumla licks the ice away, which reveals another giant man named Buri; "he was beautiful, big and strong" (Sturluson 15). Buri eventually had a son, who with his wife created three sons: Odin, Vili, and Ve. The three new gods then slew the frost giant Ymir, and his blood formed the seas and lakes; his flesh made the earth; his bones formed the mountains and cliffs, and his teeth made rocks. Finally from Ymir's skull, the sky was made, and the clouds were made from Ymir's brain. The three sons also created humankind by the logs of two trees they found lying on a beach; men were created from the ash tree and women from the elm, similar to the American Indian Kiowa belief that life emerged from a rotting log. The three sons in this Norse myth are essential in completing this creation, as the first one gives them breath and life, the second "intelligence and movement," and the third "speech, hearing, and sight" (Sturluson 18). But, again, creation only happens using natural elements that were already in existence. Nature is portrayed as indiscriminately creating Ymir, Audhumla, and Buri. The three simply emerge because the natural elements produced them, and it is only from the body of Ymir that the next generation of gods can enable the successful environment needed for new life to thrive.

Creation as Decision

Oftentimes, myths portray creation as coming about through the conscious decision of a single creator or a group of creators. Instead of creation simply happening through a natural occurrence, like the bodies of P'an Ku and Ymir becoming the environment needed to produce life, a creator actively decides to create new life. Though creation is described as occurring only because a creator consciously initiates it, nature is still depicted as central to these myths, as most often the divine creator is portrayed as a mythical personification of natural elements and processes.

The Japanese creation myth of Izanagi and Izanami[28] presents creation as both happening as a result of active and conscious choice, but also as tied to natural laws. Izanagi and Izanami exist in chaos, until they together decide to create life by stirring chaos with a giant spear. This act creates land and water; after this they copulate to produce creation, first starting out small with what is to them a disappointment, the creation of leeches, until they are practiced and create everything from trees to waterfalls. Izanami then gives birth to fire, a necessary element of life, but it is this act that kills her as she is consumed by her own flames. This mythic explanation for the death of one of the creators puts nature in again a dominant role. Though Izanagi and Izanami are centrally important to initiating new life, once unleashed, nature, here presented in the form of fire, and subsequently death, holds a power of its own.

Izanami upon dying descends to the underworld, the Land of Darkness, but her husband, Izanagi, is desperate to retrieve her. This motif will become common in mythology, and often it signals a realization on the part of the living person who makes the journey into the underworld that all life initiates out of the earth, and so too all life must descend back into it, as presented earlier in this chapter with the discussion of creation emerging directly out of the ground. This kind of symbolism showcases again the mythic underworld in terms of the womb of the earth. Discussing the realm of death in terms of womb symbolism lessens the severity of the concept of death for audiences and serves as a vital part of the myth's message.

As Izanagi travels to the Land of Darkness, he must face components of death that are horrifying to him in his role as creator of life. The details of death terrify him as he reaches closer to his wife. Finally upon seeing Izanami, the culmination of his journey is realized, as she is in a state he never could have imagined. He begs her to return with him to earth, promising that a life of happiness and splendor awaits them in the land of the living, but Izanami refuses, saying it is too late because she has eaten the food of the underworld.

To Izanagi's horror, he finds that his beloved wife has begun to decay. The theme of eating the food, or fruit, of the underworld, is also a common tenet in world myth. It suggests a connection with humans and the vegetative world, as it reveals that humanity must face the inevitable ending of death— just as fruit must decay, so too will the human body. In this myth, Izanagi has been forced to realize the full force of the fact of mortality, and as is usually the case in world myths that present the living descending to the underworld, he is astonished and terrified by his realization. He sees in the decaying flesh of Izanami his own mortality; his horror, and that of his mythic underworld counterparts, comes from grasping the inevitability of his own impending death.

Terrified, Izanagi flees the underworld and leaves his wife behind forever. Infuriated by Izanagi's cruelty, Izanami sends the spirits of the Land of Darkness after Izanagi to pull him back to her domain. As the spirits chase him and finally close in, he arrives at a peach tree and as a last effort to stay alive, he throws plump, ripe peaches at them. Some versions of the myth show Izanagi throwing first grapes and then bamboo shoots at the spirits. Astounded, Izanagi realizes that the spirits flee in terror, or in some accounts forget their pursuit and stop to eat the food. Again, the tenet of the vegetative is central to the myth, as its message serves to connect audiences to the life cycles found in the natural world—just as fruit always must eventually rot to produce new growth, so too must it have its time to grow and ripen in full sunlight. The myth concludes with this same message, as still in the Land of Darkness Izanami, enraged, calls up to her husband that because of his behavior, she will ensure that all living beings on earth must eventually die, as she vows to kill one thousand beings each day, and Izanagi's only retort is that he will then ensure that one thousand, five hundred new beings will be born each day. Therefore, audiences of the myth make the connection that though life on earth has its inevitable end, it also always assures a promise that out of death, new life will continue to generate—thus representing the full natural cycle of life.

When Izanagi emerged from the underworld, he cleansed himself in a river, and from this his daughter Amaterasu and his son Susano-O were born. Amaterasu, coming from Izanagi's cleansed eyes was so bright, she had to remain in the sky. Susano-O was said to come from Izanagi's nose, and he was portrayed as oppositional. Amarterasu's warmth caused the earth to heat up enough to allow vegetation to grow, so she came down to earth and taught its inhabitants the necessities of survival, such as farming. Susano-O, initially contrary, was not the consistent helper of mankind his sister was. Susano-O shows the dualistic nature of Japanese mythology, as he, unlike Amaterasu, questions why his mother Izanami resides within the underworld, so he ventures there to see her. Amaterasu was so angered by this that she shut herself up in a cave, and without her light, the crops began to wither, and the people started to starve. Finally, though, after being tricked by the gods who shined a mirror in the cave she hid in, Amaterasu emerged towards the enticing light and continued her care of earth's inhabitants.

The Finnish *Kalevala* by Elias Lönnrot describes the creation of the earth as starting with Ilma, a primordial goddess of the air, who gives birth to a daughter named Luonnotar. Luonnotar grows lonely living amongst the clouds, which is a common mythic element in creation works, as the primordial being often longs for the yet created earth and it inhabitants. Luonnotar consciously decides to descend to the earth in order to try and alleviate her loneliness, but finds only the deep, dark ocean. This example of the divine being descending into a dark and mysterious sea is connected to the heroic journey of the living protagonist descending into the underworld; to divine beings the primordial sea is often their underworld, and this connection to the mythic hero's decent into the realm of death, reveals in creation myths, that a descent into mysterious and foreboding realms can be a positive and transformative experience, for if the creators never descended to find new possibilities, then no one would exist. Therefore, audiences of myth come to realize the possible psychological and transformative powers that their own mythic underworlds represent.

Luonnotar once descended, like the mythic hero, finds the primordial sea terrifying and lonely; here she must only face her solitary self, and after seven hundred years of anguish in this respective underworld, a duck finally arrives. The duck lands on her knee, lays eggs, and sits upon the nest. Luonnotar, having never felt the touch of an earthly being is scorched and finally after three days of torture, she can't endure the pain any more, so she turns over allowing the eggs to fall into the sea. What she doesn't realize is that the primordial ocean is fertile, and the eggs transform into the sun, moon, stars, and clouds. Luonnotar is also impregnated by the lapping of the waves, but she remained pregnant so long that by the time she gave birth to the epic's protagonist, Väinämöinin, he was already an old man. It is Väinämöinin who then mythically provides the Finnish people with the means to survive as a result of his epic journey.

Also, in India the *Brhadāranyaka Upanishad* tells of Brahman,[29] who took the form of Brahma, the Creator. Finding himself in primordial nothingness, he became conscious of his first thought, which was fear, but realizing that he was all alone, he understood that there was nothing to fear. Next, he consciously became aware of feeling the full weight of being entirely alone in the void of the universe, so he yearned for a companion, and his thoughts split his primordial body into two halves. One part was his male self, and the other part his female self. The male and female looked at each other and recognized that they were two halves of the same being, so they partook on a series of sexual unions that produced the entire world: every rock, plant, animal, human, etc. Therefore, it is believed that all things come from Brahma. This realization that all existence is inextricably tied to one another is essential to understanding much of Indian mythology. The natural world is often not viewed as separate from the lives of mankind, but forever tied as an essential component of the natural order of the universe.

Similarly, in ancient Egypt, Rê, the central sun god, emerges from a watery void, and in some variations, he emerges directly from a "primeval lotus that floated up out of the chaotic waters of Nun" (Sproul 90). Through his speech, like Brahma's conscious choice to create, all earthly beings were created. He creates air, Shu, moisture, Tefnut, and the goddess Hathor, who was to be his sight. From his sight, he began to weep, and thus in Egyptian mythology, humanity was created from Rê's tears. Again, in this version of creation, it connects all earthly beings back to one source, creating a mythic understanding that all beings are inseparably connected.

The Bambuti people from the eastern Congo tell a creation story where their creator, Khvum, lives alone in the middle of a deep forest, and one day he finds that he has grown bored, so he also takes the initiative to create life.[30] He went into the forest and collected many nkula nuts. He then called his crocodile over, and instructed it to pull his boat far out to sea. Once far away, Khvum took out the first nut "blew on it and threw it back towards the land, saying 'You shall be the first man.' The next nut he called woman, and so on until all the nuts from his bag had been sent back towards the land" (Belcher 19). When Khvum finally made it back to shore, the people of his creation were there waiting for him, and he found that he was happy.

The African myth of the Fon people of Dahomey recount a creation myth[31] of two primordial beings, the male serpent Aido-Hwedo and the female creator deity Mawu. Mawu is said to have given birth to all the gods and goddesses represented as the different elements of the earth. Then she began to create human beings out of clay. After she crafted the first people, she realized that she needed to create a place for the people to live, so she began to make the earth. She sought out Aido-Hwedo, and entered his mouth, where together they proceeded to ride amongst the surface of the earth, which created the different impressions of the landscape; as Aido-Hwedo moved throughout the land "his path created winding rivers and valleys with steep sloping land on either side … undulating like the track of a serpent" (Wilkinson 154). After Mawu and Aido-Hwedo created the landscape, they saw that it was too heavy to hold all the earth's inhabitants, so Mawu instructed Aido-Hwedo to coil himself beneath the earth to support it, which he gladly did. But, one day, the Fon people believe that Aido-Hwedo will consume his own tail, and the earth and all its inhabitants will fall into the vast sea.

Also the Fang people who live in Gabon, the Democratic Republic of the Congo and the Central African Republic describe a creation myth where a creator god again purposely starts the act of creation, but here the myth also connects with the creation stories that showcase the creator's body as producing new life. The Fang people recount their creator as voluntarily taking portions of his own body to implement creation[32] by making "a world egg by mixing his underarm hair with a pebble and part of his brain. He then anoints the egg with his seed, following which three gods hatch out of the egg, including a secondary creator who goes on to make both the land and the people" (Wilkinson 161).

The African Boshongo and Bakuba people tell a myth of creation involving Bumba[33] who existed at the beginning of time entirely alone. In what appears to be a symbolic birthing representation, Bumba one day becomes ill, and from his stomach, he involuntarily vomits up creation. In this same way, he indirectly creates the sun that dries up the waters that cover the earth, and then by still vomiting he creates the moon, stars, animals, and humans. And, contrary to Bumba's more passive act of creation, the first animals fashion similar animals out of themselves, populating the earth with its inhabitants.

Bumba is then depicted as having three sons, and it is they, not Bumba, who take the active initiative to continue creation. The first son, not at all described as a passive creator, exerts so much effort in just creating ants to inhabit the world that he dies. It is this sacrifice that causes his creation, the ants, to feel sorrow for their creator, so they bring enough sand and dirt to cover his corpse; this enables the second son to plant seeds into the dirt, thus creating plant life on earth. Bumba's third son creates the birds of the world. This depiction of the three brothers needing the actions of each other in order to perfect the natural creative act, as with innumerable creation myths, articulates the belief that all creation is intertwined.

Though Bumba did not actively create humans, he decides to take responsibility for them; he watches them and sees that that they struggle to survive in this new environment of his accidental creation and realizes that he must find within himself an active way to help them succeed in life. He then teaches the people the skills he knows. He also lives for a time among his people, declaring:

Men and women rejoice! Look at the sky above. See the sun that brightens each day.... Look at the land that lies at your feet. See the grasses that come forth from the soil. See their gifts of flowers and life-sustaining fruits, nuts, and grains.... Look at the waters that flow past your feet.... See these wonders! And let joy flood your hearts that they are yours! [Rosenberg 517].

Bumba's appreciation and awe of his own creation is central to this myth's message. It teaches audiences that nature, in its perpetual ability to exist and prosper, holds a power of its own, as even Bumba, their creator god, is powerless to initiate or control the powers of nature when they are ready to emerge. He uncontrollably vomits the beginnings of all existence and then teaches his people to always maintain his own sense of awe at the power of nature.

The Ancient Mongol people believed that creation started when Qormusta gave Sakayamuni, the Buddha, a handful of dirt and stones.[34] Sakayamuni threw the dirt into the only thing that existed at the time, a vast primordial sea, and suddenly the dirt and stones began to form the earth, but upon this creation a counter element immediately arrived in the form of a giant tortoise who stole the newly created earth. Sakayamuni knew that it was up to him to save the earth, and that the only way to do this was to kill the tortoise, but being holy, he did not want to harm any living creature. The tengri, who are the spirits that inhabit the earth, assured him that this death would allow many lives to exist, so Sakayamuni sacrificed his moral views and killed the tortoise. From the death of the tortoise, life emerged. Again, this concept of death being tied to creation is essential, as it shows that in nature, death initiates new life.

Early Turkic and Mongol people, as agriculturalists, lived in harmony with all aspects of nature, as they believed that every aspect of the environment was inhabited by sacred spirits. They attributed many natural occurrences as being caused by Mongke Tengri, the supreme sky god, or the other spirits of the land, the tengri. Wilkinson states that thunder and lightning portrayed the terrifying authority of Tengri, but his storms were also viewed as necessary for a favorable crop (99). From this belief the Mongol and Turkic people believed in Tengrism which involved the practice of shamanism in order to communicate with the spirits that resided within the natural elements of the earth. The followers of Tengrism "respected nature spirits.... If people lost their balance with the natural world due to their actions or the actions of malign spirits, the shamans would intervene to restore it" (Wilkinson 99).

The Mongol creation myth states that after earth was created, Mongke Tengri created the first man and woman and sought out the Spring of Immortality to give them everlasting life. While Mongke Tengri journeyed to the

Spring of Immortality, he asked a cat and dog to watch over the man and woman. However, when Mongke Tengri was gone, another force of opposition immediately arrived, this time in the form of Erlik Khan, the god of the underworld. Erlik Khan distracted the cat and dog and then urinated on the first man and woman, desecrating them. When Mongke Tengri returned he tried to pour the sacred water on the humans, but Erlik Khan's desecration made it impossible for human beings to be immortal. This mythic element of the underworld element of Erlik Khan again reiterates the necessity of death for the renewal of life.

Survival—The Creation of the Staple Crop

The mythic portrayal explaining the creation of a people's means towards survival is also of central importance to connecting mankind's debt to the natural world. Often myths show creators feeling responsible for their created beings, and are thus mythically represented as taking it upon themselves to teach the earth's inhabitants the means of survival, such as making fire or properly planting crops. The myths that portray the creation of the staple crop for a people remind audiences of their inextricable connection to nature, for without the staple crop the people would be forced to subsist primarily off of hunting and gathering methods and would often be in danger of starvation if conditions were not favorable for securing food. The staple crop, however, provides a predictable means for survival, and thus the myths that portray the creation of the staple crop often tie together the people themselves with the coming of the needed crop.

The Aboriginal Australians have a myth where three beings: Wadi Gudjara (Two Men), Yungga (Black Goanna), and Djimbi (White Goanna) travel throughout the bush in Dreamtime.[35] Suddenly the three characters hear voices of men, women, and children; they go to investigate and see a camp of people welcoming them, but as they approach, all the people disappear. Confused, Wadi Gudjara stomped the ground, and suddenly "wada plants (sweet potato or yam)" (Berndt & Berndt 50) emerged from the place of the encampment. Then Yungga hit the ground, and black wada grew, and lastly Djimbi does the same, and as the meaning of his name recounts, white wada grew. It is believed that "these vegetables were once men, women, girls and boys" (Berndt & Berndt 50).

The South American Maya creation epic, *The Popul Vuh*,[36] expresses the idea that again creation arose out of a dark environment of only sea and sky. The first Creators, Tepeu and Gucumatz, "existed as sun-fire powers"

(Sproul 287) "hidden in the water under green and blue feathers" (Rosenberg 596). They decide in whispers to initiate creation. They first make the animals and birds of the earth by simply proclaiming, "Let it be done!" (Rosenberg 596). They continue in this way to make the rest of the inhabitants of the earth. The Creators, though, soon grow disappointed because the animals they created cannot worship them, so they endeavor to create humans, but this act is a struggle, as stated earlier in this chapter. They first create human beings out of clay and mud, then wood, then finally from cornmeal. The explanation that mankind was first created out of cornmeal defines their survival as dependent on this staple crop.

The Polynesian have a myth about their cultural hero Maui who encounters one of his early adversaries, a massive eel named Te Tuna, meaning "the penis." Te Tuna confronts Maui because he has been having an affair with Te Tuna's wife, Hina.[37] Te Tuna sends massive ocean waves to try and drown Maui, and finally Te Tuna comes forth to swallow Maui, but Maui makes his body incredibly small and enters into the body of Te Tuna, where he tears Te Tuna's body apart from the inside. Maui proceeds to cut of Te Tuna's head and plants it near his home. Soon Maui notices "a green shoot growing from the place where Te Tuna's head had been buried" (Poignant 27). Maui's mother tells him that the sprout will become a coconut tree that will enable the people to survive. This myth directly recounts that the act of burying the head of Te Tuna is in essence planting it. Te Tuna, meaning "penis," provides associations of him, portrayed mythically here as his severed head, serving as seed to the earth, which causes the creation of the dietary staple; "the coconut tree is a great provider," as the leaves can be used for making baskets, hats, and fans; the husks can be used to make "sennit for caulking canoes" ropes and mats; the flesh and milk can be consumed; the oil can hydrate the skin (Poignant 48).

The Malagasy people of Madagascar have a myth that also discusses the creation of the staple crop of rice coming from death.[38] The myth states that a young mother who loved her daughter more than anything was out playing with her one summer day. The child spotted a grasshopper, and delighted she wanted to play with it. The mother gave her daughter the grasshopper, but it hopped away. The child screamed with the pain of her loss and mythically is described as never recovering from her disappointment, so much so that she became sick and eventually died. The mother, in agony, appealed with such ferocity to the gods, that they felt her sorrow and instructed her to bury her child's corpse in a marsh. The mother did as instructed, and when she returned to tend her daughter's grave, she found that grains unlike any anyone had ever seen had miraculously sprouted there. The gods told the mother to pick the grain, pound it, and cook it. She again did as she was told, and the people of Madagascar were provided with rice—a staple to their dietary needs.

These myths of death in order to receive the benefit of the staple crop are quite common, as again death is mythically portrayed as a necessity for the emergence of new life. When a mythic character dies in order for the people to survive, mythic audiences realize that the cyclical aspect of nature, that will one day claim their own lives, is essential in assuring their survival.

The Wik Munggan of Cape York Peninsula tell of another myth of death causing the coming of the much needed staple of the yam.[39] In this myth a man and woman fall in love; the woman becomes pregnant, but before the child is born, the man leaves her. The woman, heavy with child, finds that she cannot make herself comfortable once he leaves. Distraught, she scrapes part of her floor away and lies in the dirt; feeling comforted by the earth, she digs herself deeper into the earth. She continues to dig deeper and deeper enjoying the embrace of the earth, until an opposite sensation hits her; she suddenly feels claustrophobic being so deeply recessed within the soil. So the woman attempts over and over again to climb out and save herself and her child, but she finds that she cannot escape; "in time, she resigned herself to her imprisonment, recognizing it as a part of her reproductive function: from this hole would issue an abundance of yams for future women to cook for food" (Allan, Fleming, & Kerrigan 73).

The Jivaro of South America also account for the introduction of the staple crop of manioc by a myth of sacrifice.[40] They believe that a woman named Nunghui had a son who could produce manioc simply by stating its name. Nunghui entrusted her son to a group of tribal women to look after him while she went away. The children of the tribe, though, became jealous of Nunghui's son, so they stole into the hut and threw ashes into his eyes, which immediately caused him to die. Because he was the only one who could provide manioc, all of the people began to starve. The people turned against Nunghui, because she was the one who initially let her son out of her watchful care, so they forced her to live underground. But, Nunghui was always known and respected within the tribe because she possessed great mystical powers. Miraculously, when she retreated within the earth, she chose to save the people, though they were the ones who punished her for their own doing. Nunghui caused the staple crop of manioc to emerge each harvest by pushing it up through the soil and dancing with the roots, so they would grow strong. In addition, the tribes of the northwest Amazon discuss a similar myth that states that "manioc grew from the corpse of a white child born to a virgin, or from a maiden who asked to be buried alive" (Allan, Bishop, & Phillips 119).

Myths that present the staple crop coming by means of a sacrifice are quite prominent in world mythology. Death is mythically explained again and again as necessary to the survival of all species, and myths repeatedly teach audiences that the deaths of the mythic beings are as necessary as any other towards renewing this cycle. The myths of sacrifice to initiate the growth of a successful staple food becomes a dominant archetype in world myth beginning with the advent of agriculture in Neolithic times, as will be discussed in the next chapter.

Finally, in looking at the role that nature plays in creation myths from around the world, it becomes evident that mythic explanations for creation repeatedly accounts for humanity's debt to the natural world. Creation mythology teaches audiences of myth that they come from the same natural elements that surround them in their daily lives. Showing that mankind emerged from beneath the ground or from seeds teaches people that they are not superior to nature, but are only one part of it. Seeing creation occur slowly and often indiscriminately, sometimes killing the creator, educates audiences on the power of nature's laws. Thus, creation myths show humanity that their lives are forever forged together with the natural elements of the earth, and therefore, human beings too must succumb to the natural life cycle of such elements.

2

The Earth Goddess, the Male Seed and the Harvest

"I will tell you something about stories.... They aren't just enter-
tainment. Don't be fooled. They are all we have, you see, all we have
to fight off illness and death."
—Leslie Marmon Silko

"It takes a thousand voices to tell a single story."
—American Indian proverb

Scholars[1] look towards the Paleolithic period as indicative of the importance of sacrifice to early civilizations and myth. The practice of hunting as
a means of survival left ancient people with feelings of guilt as well as reverence for the animal giving its life to assure the continuation of the hunter
and his people. Paleolithic hunters killed prey with respect; they attributed
a sacred understanding between the animal and the human killing the animal.
They created myths and rituals that explained a belief that the animal willingly
gave its life, so that human beings could live. Out of this early justification
towards the killing of animals, myths and rituals evolved to put this same
story into more and more grandiose terms.

From the early mythic explanation that the animals willingly sacrificed
their bodies to propel the natural order of survival, came myths that displayed
the need to ritualize the process of sacrifice with the beginning of the first
civilizations and the development of agriculture in the Neolithic period (c.
8,000–4,000 BCE). The act of sacrifice became a ritualized practice performed
by priests or priestesses. As in the Paleolithic period, Neolithic myths reveal
a central tie to humanity and the natural world. As with the myths of creation,
these myths promote again a message of acceptance of one's position as only
part of a larger natural process.

44

The Mysterious Goddess of the Paleolithic Hunters

As discussed, there is much evidence to suggest that early Stone Age humans believed in an earth-based Great Mother; "This deity was, after all the great progenerative Goddess of Creation, the source of animals hunted and vegetation gathered. And she was the dark place to which both vegetation and people returned and from which they might be reborn" (Leeming & Page, *Goddess,* 9). Leonard Cottrell states that Margaret Mead, famous archeologist most well known for her work in Olduvai Gorge, and other anthropologists "have established that in the very early stages of man's development, before the secret of fecundity was understood, before coitus was associated with childbirth, the female was revered as the giver of life. Only women could produce their own kind, and man's part in the process was not as yet recognized" (qtd. in Stone 11). Thus, "it was not surprising that metaphors for the deity were found in the mysterious generative and nurturing processes of the female body. The woman was the apparent source of human life, the producer of milk that fed the young, and the instrument of power that attracted others to her body" (Leeming & Page, *Goddess,* 10). In addition, it is important to note that "the word *religion* is probably misleading when applied to Goddess worship in the Paleolithic period. It seems likely that worship as we know it would have been unnecessary for a people who were not separate from their source, who—like the trees, the animals, and everything else on earth—were emanations of Goddess" (Leeming & Page, *Goddess,* 10).

Archeologists and scholars have dated the worship of the Great Mother in her many representations from late Paleolithic cultures of about 25,000 BCE to Neolithic communities (Stone 10) based in part on countless statues that reveal the Great Mother in her myriad representations; "these small female figures, made of stone and bone and clay and often referred to as *Venus figures,* have been found in areas where small settled communities once lived…. These statues of women, some seemingly pregnant, have been found throughout the widespread Gravettian-Augrignacian sites in areas as far apart as Spain, France, Germany, Austria, Czechoslovakia and Russia" (Stone 13). Burkert also notes that these female figurines may carry with them a religious significance; "they are small terracotta or occasionally stone figures which mostly represent naked women, often with an exaggerated emphasis on the belly, buttocks, and sexual organs. They have forbears as early as the Paleolithic and persist in varying forms into the high civilizations" (Burkert 11–2). Though there remains inconsistency in how one interprets these findings, since they have no accompanying texts, many scholars debate their meaning. Some research points to them as being representations of a central belief in a Great Mother who is a representation of nature, but many scholars still contend that there is not enough evidence to confirm this hypothesis. Burkert, for example, remains skeptical, as he states, "Specialist research lays emphasis on the peculiarities of each individual area, and the minimal opportunities for communication in the Stone Age would lead one to expect fragmentation rather than spiritual unity. And indeed among the Sesklo statuettes there are a number of male figures shown seated on a throne, whereas the female figures stand or cower ... the ithyphallic male statuettes and simple phalloi may signify fertility, but they may equally serve for the apotropaic demarcation of territory; in no way can this be decided" (12). Still, many researchers do point to a belief that these myriad female figurines, found from the Paleolithic period in high numbers, propose a strong belief system in divine females being connected to both nature and fertility within many communities.

The Neolithic Age of the Supreme Goddess

The practice of grain agriculture and domesticated stock-breeding began in the Near East in the Neolithic period and "spread eastward and westward from this center ... displacing the earlier, much more precariously supported hunting and food-collecting cultures, until both the Pacific coast of Asia and the Atlantic coasts of Europe and Africa were attained by about 2,500 BC[E]" (Campbell, *Primitive Mythology,* 135). Women are believed to be the first who discovered the vegetative growth process by learning to systematically save and replant seeds from successful harvests. Therefore, women continued in Neolithic times to be represented mythically as central to the regenerative processes of nature.

The Neolithic period continued to place high importance on a clear connection between humanity and nature, but nature now became largely conceptualized in terms of the controlled harvest. For the agriculturalists of the Neolithic period "the crop was an epiphany, a revelation of divine energy, and when farmers cultivated the land and brought forth food for their community, they felt that they had entered a sacred realm and participated in this miraculous abundance. The earth seemed to sustain all creatures—the plants, animals, and humans—as in a living womb" (Armstrong, *Short History,* 42). Farming, because it assured the survival of a people, became a sacred practice, and many of the first recorded myths and rituals created to capture this sacredness repeatedly portrayed a people's desire to feel they had a role in maintaining the assurance of the harvest. Most often, the myths and rituals meant to secure a successful harvest were aimed at a representational Mother

Earth Goddess who could help assure the survival of humanity if appeased and honored properly. As Allan and Phillips state:

> With the coming of agriculture, human hopes and fears turned on harvesting the crops, and the seasons assumed a central importance both in real life and in the myths that were its reflection. Seminal legends arose around the endless cycles of growth, death and regeneration, seeking to explain why the world comes alive in spring and dies in the winter.... Inextricably linked with the notion of restored fertility was the age-old belief in a female principle in nature that expressed itself in the worship of the Great Goddess [*World*, 45].

To understand the role of the Mother Earth Goddess within the myths and lives of Neolithic peoples, one must look again at the goddess figurines that were still created well after the Paleolithic era into the Neolithic period and come from the civilizations where agricultural subsistence first appeared, the "Fertile Crescent between Iran and Jericho and its diffusion ... via Asia Minor" (Burkert 11). By 4,000 BCE Neolithic Goddess figurines began to appear at Ur and Uruk, modern day Iraq and in the Badarian and Amratian cultures of Egypt (Stone 18), and it is clear that in the Neolithic era the figurines most assuredly carried with them some religious significance. Campbell, speaking of these numerous artifacts, states that they present the Goddess "standing pregnant, squatting as though in childbirth, holding an infant to her breast, clutching her breasts with her two hands ... or ... we may see her endowed with the head of a cow, bearing in her arms a bull-headed child; standing naked on a back of a lion; or flanked by animals.... Her arms may be opened to the sides, as though to receive us, or extended, holding flowers, holding serpents" (*Primitive Mythology*, 140).

Excavations at Çatal Hüyük revealed a small figurine that "perfectly illustrates the mythic role" of the Mother Earth Goddess; "She is shown back-to-back with herself, in one aspect embracing an adult male and in the other, holding a child. She receives the seed of the past and through the magic of her body transmutes it into the future" (Campbell, *Goddesses*, xviii). Burkert also states that "the most intriguing, most impressive and most unambiguous discoveries are those from Çatal Hüyük. The Early Neolithic town here contains a series of sanctuaries ... secondary burials of the dead, cattle horns set into benches, figurative wall paintings and, most strikingly, wall reliefs of a Great Goddess with uplifted arms and straddled legs—clearly the birth-giving mother of the animals and of life itself" (12). Another Mother Goddess figurine from Çatal Hüyük shows her "enthroned, giving birth, flanked and supported by lions" or leopards and men hunting a bull; the depiction of similar images would be carried on to even Rome six millennia later with the portrayal of Cybele, the same Anatolian Goddess (Campbell, *Goddesses*, xviii).

Burkett supports Campbell's assertion by stating that "the association with the Asia Minor Great Mother of historical times, with her leopards or lions … and with the society of men and bull sacrifice is irresistible. Here we have overwhelmingly clear proof of religious continuity of more than five millennia" (Burkert 13).

Burkert and Campbell connect the findings at Çatal Hüyük with a continuation of the worship of the Goddess in surrounding areas, such as Anatolia, Egypt, Crete, Greece, and Rome. For instance, the similarity of the portrayal of the bull shape both in Çatal Hüyük and in Minoan Crete is undeniable; the artifacts found at the Palace of Knossos on Crete show that there are numerous depictions of bull horns adorning the entire compound, similar to those found at Çatal Hüyük. Portrayals of a "human figure with hands raised in the epiphany gesture" are also found in both Çatal Hüyük and Minoan and Mycenaean cultures (Burkert 13). Burkert and Campbell contend that Mycenaean culture, from which most well-known Greek myths arose, was founded upon centers that had contact with the great agrarian civilizations and their mythic structures; "forces of continuity have always reasserted themselves, and probably nowhere as much as in the sphere of religion" (Burkert 13). Therefore, evidence supports the idea that cultural diffusion may have led to instances of lasting similarity in the mythology of the Neolithic period.

As these first mighty civilizations continued, the invention of writing in about 3,000 BCE allowed the portrayal of the Goddess to finally be revealed in her mythic form, though "many centuries of transformation had undoubtedly changed the religion in various ways" (Stone 18). What is preserved through early written material reveals the Goddess in her important role to the community. The Mother Goddess was often portrayed as the primary divine being, as her role encapsulated all of nature and its life cycles; it is the "religion of a supreme Goddess that existed and flourished in the Near and Middle East for thousands of years" before the arrival of patriarchal societies with a belief in male superior divinities, such as sky gods (Stone 9).

As discussed, in Paleolithic times, women were thought to be held in high regard because of their mysterious connections to fertility; they could create life of both sexes within their bodies and also create the food to sustain infants, and so in Neolithic times, "the Mother Goddess fused with the Great Mother of the hunting societies" (Armstrong, *Short History,* 46). This portrayal of women as the producers and nurturers of life accounts for the depiction of the earth as a female Goddess; "more than a mother goddess or fertility goddess, she appears to have been earth and nature itself, an immense organic, ecological, and conscious whole" (Leeming & Page, *Goddess,* 7). The Mother

Goddess then is viewed in a more elevated form than the average woman's ability to mysteriously produce new life within her body, as the Mother Goddess can produce all life within her earth womb. Also, just as a mortal woman can produce the necessary food for her infant, the elevated representation of the earth as Goddess also is viewed as providing all of the needed nutrients for the survival of her offspring—all of earth's inhabitants. In addition, the Mother Goddess, as a representation of nature, holds another mysterious quality, as she resides over death as well as birth. The Goddess is associated as the great provider; from her all life is created and nurtured, but she is also portrayed as destructive; as conversely, everything that lives must die; therefore, the Goddess was portrayed as both the giver and taker of life. Since all of earth's inhabitants are viewed as coming from the Goddess, they all too are witnessed as eventually going back into the womb of the Goddess upon their deaths. Mythically, then, the Goddess holds the power over all birth, subsistence, and death, as all are necessary for her continued productivity.

As Burkert discusses, cultural diffusion in many civilizations led to a widespread belief in a central Mother Goddess, therefore, the Goddess was identified by varying names in different civilizations. Leeming and Page contend that the Mother Goddess "took the familiar forms such as Inanna, Cybele, and Hathor" (*God*, 58). The Derveni Papyrus found in the fourth century BCE in Greece also discusses the concept of a Mother Goddess figure who is known by multiple names, and also continues well into the Olympic pantheon portrayal of the goddesses Hera and Demeter as divided forms of the same primary Goddess: "Ge, Meter, Rhea, and Hera are the same one. She was called Ge (Earth) by convention—Ge and Gaia according to each one's dialect, and Meter (Mother) because all things are born from her. And she was named Demeter, as if it were Ge Meter, one name from both; for it was the same" (Archeological Museum of Thessaloniki, Greece). The Roman author Apuleius in the mid-second century CE in his *Golden Ass* succinctly notes the widespread worship of the Goddess into Roman times:

> I am Nature, the universal Mother, mistress of all elements, primordial child of time, sovereign of all things spiritual, queen of the dead, queen also of the immortals, the single manifestation of all gods and goddesses that are.... Though I am worshipped in many aspects, known by countless names ... yet the whole round earth venerates me. The primeval Phrygians call me Pessinuntica, Mother of the gods; the Athenians ... call me Artemis, for the islanders of Cyprus I am Aphrodite; for the archers of Crete, I am Dictynna; for the Sicilians, Persephone; and for the Eleusinians their ancient Mother of Corn ... the Egyptians who excel in ancient learning worship me with ceremonies proper to my godhead, call me by my true name, namely Queen Isis [197–8].

The sacred agricultural methods to produce a bountiful harvest provided the foundations by which Neolithic peoples found meaning in their own lives. Jensen continues that the transition from Paleolithic to Neolithic cultures provided "'in some measure, a new field of illumination. For the plants were continually being killed through the gathering of their fruits, yet the death was extraordinarily quickly overcome by their new life. Thus there was made available to man a synthesizing insight, relating his own destiny to that of the animals, the plants, and the moon'" (qtd. in Campbell, *Primitive Mythologies,* 178). This advancement of agriculture allowed mythology to help people see that their own lives and deaths were also tied to the natural processes of the harvest; this was not viewed in negative terms but gave people a spiritual understanding that as life inevitably ended for all living beings, it would also be renewed as with the cyclical nature of the harvest—from the womb-like earth everything emerged: plants, animals, and humanity, but also back into the earth would everything eventually go, so that it could emerge again as new growth.

Sacrifice for Survival

The respect for the natural agricultural processes that provided the means of survival mythically came to be understood as something that required sacrifice, and "rituals were designed to replenish the power lest it exhaust itself; the first seeds were 'thrown away' as offerings, and the first fruits of the harvests were left unpicked, as a way of recycling these sacred energies" (Armstrong, *Short History,* 42). There is some evidence that Paleolithic practices involving sacrifice may have been continued in the Near East and Mediterranean, such as the sacrifice of pigs; "clay pigs studded with grains of corn" found throughout Greece and the Balkans immediately points to the connection of sacrifice being tied to the fertility of the earth (Burkert 13). Just as Paleolithic man first revered the animal killed as prey in terms of a willing sacrifice, so too did Neolithic peoples perform sacrifices to the Goddess to assure the continuation of natural vegetative propagation. Armstrong states that two principles were integral to these rites:

> First ... in order to receive, you had to give something back. Second was a holistic vision of reality. The sacred was not felt to be a metaphysical reality, beyond the natural world. It could only be encountered in the earth and its products, which were in themselves sacred. Gods, human beings, animals and plants all shared the same nature, and could, therefore, invigorate and replenish one another [*Short History,* 43].

Many world myths identify a human being as playing a crucial role in aiding the agricultural cycles of nature, and often the requirement for a bountiful harvest was either a physical sacrifice of a living being or a ritualized symbolic sacrifice.

The identification of male and female roles in agriculture became integral to the first recorded myths of the Goddess. As farming technology further developed, men were needed less in the role of hunter, and more in the role of farmer; "The men plowed the body of the Great Mother so that she could be filled with the seeds of last year's dying plants and by some strange mystery the Great Mother gave off new plants" (Leeming & Page, *God*, 71). From the early understanding of agriculture the archetype of the Earth Goddess and the male consort was mythically created; "though at first the Goddess appears to have reigned alone, at some yet unknown point in time She acquired a … consort" (Stone 19). In this period, the myths of the Mother Goddess portray the necessary sacrifice of her male consort. The Goddess "was the source of the food supply, which she might withhold at will by raising storms, causing floods, or sending disease" (Armstrong, *Short History*, 47), and it was important to appease her through rituals. The Goddess remains constant, but the mythic males are portrayed as expendable because the Goddess is the earth itself, and the male is the means towards seeding the earth. The male momentarily dies, often through sacrifice, to assure the proliferation of the next generation; "the seed must be sacrificed—planted—buried—before it can give forth fruit as the new son of the Mother" (Leeming & Page, *God*,76). The male consort is identified in various representations as "Damuzi, Tammuz, Attis, Adonis, Osiris, or Baal; this consort died in his youth, causing an annual period of grief and lamentation among those who paid homage to the Goddess" (Stone 20). These annual rituals involving the Earth Goddess and her male consort took place in Egypt, Sumer, Babylon, Anatolia, Canaan, Greece, and pre–Christian Rome.

What is important to remember is that the myths involving a portrayal of the sacrifice of the male consort carries with them a message that links human life to the natural cycles of the earth—most specifically in these myths, the harsh reality of the harvest cycle. The male consorts of the Mother Goddess in myth "are all nearly torn apart, dismembered, brutally mutilated, and killed before they can rise again, with the crops, to new life" (Armstrong, *Short History*, 47–8). Frazer contends that the killing and subsequent resurrection of the representative male has carried over from "the hunting and pastoral stage of society, when the slain god was an animal, and survived into the agricultural stage, when the slain god was the corn or a human being representing the corn" (253), as was seen in Egypt when ancient practice demanded mourning for Osiris when the first grain crop was harvested. Frazer states that the fact that there are so many violent deaths of the male consort comes from an ancient preference for this as opposed to an extended natural death from old age (216). As the concept of death was viewed as essential in bringing upon regeneration of the crop, it makes sense that the death of a young consort as opposed to an enfeebled, elderly man, produces a more healthy and vigorous, renewed crop:

> The divine life, incarnate in a material and mortal body, is liable to be tainted and corrupted by the weakness of the frail medium in which it is for a time enshrined; and if it is to be saved from the increasing enfeeblement which it must necessarily share with its human incarnation as he advances in years, it must be detached from him before, or at least as soon as, he exhibits signs of decay, in order to be transferred to a vigorous successor.... The killing of the god, that is, of his human incarnation, is, therefore, only a necessary step to his revival or resurrection in a better form [Frazer 248].

The role of the king in many ancient civilizations often mimics the role of the male consort in early myth. For instance, "amongst the Antaymours of Madagascar the king is responsible for the growth of the crops and for every misfortune that befalls the people" (Frazer 46); if it does not rain, for instance, the people hold the king responsible. Frazer states that "it appears to be assumed that the king's power over nature, like that over his subjects or slaves, is exerted through definite acts of will; and therefore if drought, famine, pestilence, or storms arise, the people attribute the misfortune to the negligence of the king, and punish him accordingly with stripes and bonds, or, if he remains obdurate, with deposition and death" (109).

Often human sexual encounters were deemed as necessary to initiate the fertility of the harvest, so initiates would sometimes engage in sexual rituals along with the planting of the crops (Armstrong, *Short History,* 43). This belief that ritualized sex initiated the harvest cycle also connects to the myths of the male consort being essential for the continuation of the success of the crops. As discussed in chapter 1 of this book, there are many world myths that showcase mythic characters being sacrificed to create the much-needed staple food for a people, such as the severed head of the Polynesian Te Tuna producing the coconut tree; the phallic reference of Te Tuna's name shows the connection between sexual intercourse and crop success. The myths involving the Earth Goddess and her male consort resulting "from her mating rituals are among the most extraordinary and persistently popular the world has known, primarily the great vegetation-year myths of the Fertile Crescent and the Myths of the Mother and her sacrificial victim-king-lover. They are the myths of ... the king as sacred seed planted in the Goddess's vulva, which is the earth, the death-seed buried, without which there can be no procreation, no regeneration, no life" (Leeming & Page, *Goddess*, 60).

It is important to note that "Neolithic myths continued to force people to face up to the reality of death. They were not pastoral idylls, and the Mother Goddess was not a gentle, consoling deity, because agriculture was not experienced as a peaceful, contemplative occupation. It was a constant battle, a desperate struggle, against sterility, drought, famine and the violent forces of nature, which were also manifestations of divine power" (Armstrong, *Short History*, 46–7). This is why in Neolithic times the mythology that represents the process of producing the food staple is often portrayed as a harsh experience. In early myths of agriculturally dependent civilizations, "food is produced only by a constant warfare against the sacred forces of death and destruction. The seed has to go down into the earth and die in order to bring forth its fruit, and its death is painful and traumatic" (Armstrong, *Short History*, 47). This is why archetypically myths portray characters who suffer similar fates; a human life is similarly full of struggle, and to reap reward, one must abide by natural laws.

The Goddess

The Sumerian myth of Inanna and Dumuzi perhaps best showcases the connection of the Earth Goddess with her male consort, as Inanna is portrayed as immortal, and Dumuzi is a mortal shepherd. Inanna is ready to marry, and so she begins to search for a husband, first assuming her brother Utu will marry her, but he reveals to her that her husband will be mortal. At first Inanna resists this union, stating that Dumuzi has insolently brought grain, flax, and barley into her sacred store houses, but she realizes upon meeting Dumuzi that indeed their union is essential. As an Earth Goddess, Inanna needs the male mortal Dumuzi to assure her success at reproduction, thus assuring survival of the people. This myth shows that their subsequent sexual union is directly tied to the assurance of the harvest. Inanna reveals the importance of their sexual act; she states that this act must be told to the sacred bards, so that it may be preserved for generations as a guide to assure crop fertility. Inanna declares[2] that her "vulva"

> is full of eagerness like the young moon.
> My untilled land lies fallow.
> As for me, Inanna,
> Who will plow my vulva? [Wolsktein & Kramer 30].

Dumuzi replies that he will "plow" Inanna's "vulva," and as a result of their sexual union

> plants grew high by their side.
> Grains grew high by their side.
> Gardens flourished luxuriantly [Wolkstein & Kramer 30].

Inanna's and Dumuzi's sexual acts are continually connected to the regenerative success of the harvest. In the myth Inanna's body is described quite literally as the earth itself, the field that must be fertilized and plowed, and it is Dumuzi's role as her mortal lover to contribute to this process. Dumuzi's function is vital, but as a mortal male, he is only a passing part of the greater process of the natural cycle.

The myth makes it clear that Inanna, as Earth Goddess, is the superior of Dumuzi, as it is Inanna who decrees "the fate of Dumuzi":

> "You, the chosen shepherd of the holy shrine,
> You, the king, the faithful provider of Uruk...
> In all ways you are fit" [Wolkstein & Kramer 31].

Inanna, as a representation of the earth, will continue indefinitely, but Dumuzi is fated to die, as the natural cycle demands of all mortal beings. Dumuzi is essential to the act of fertility, but he must accept that his time on earth is limited. The myth suggests that Dumuzi, and therefore all humankind, is inextricably linked to the natural life cycle:

> As the farmer, let him make the fields fertile,
> As the shepherd, let him make the sheepfolds multiply...
> Under his reign let there be rich grain....
> In the palace may there be long life [Wolkstein & Kramer 31].

The myth portrays Dumuzi's role within the natural life cycle as highly verdant; in his prime, as in the prime of mankind, he is to reap the benefits of the harvest. But, the end of the myth foreshadows another stage of his life cycle—his necessary death. Dumuzi pleads to Inanna: "Set me free, my sister, set me free," but Inanna only states:

> "Dumuzi-abzu, your allure was sweet.
> My fearless one,
> My holy statue...
> How sweet was your allure" [Wolkstein & Kramer 32].

In stating the past tense when referring to Dumuzi, it indicates that the sexual union between Inanna and Dumuzi has served its purpose. The harvest, successfully fertilized and tilled, must concede to its next stage, that of decay and dormancy. Dumuzi, in stating "set me free" understands his limited role.

In a later myth of Inanna, transitioning to the name of Ishtar for the Akkadians, Ishtar, the "Queen of Heaven," descends into the underworld to face her sister Ershkigal, ruler of the underworld. This myth, "Descent of the

Goddess Ishtar into the Lower World"[3] again recounts the lesson of the natural components of mortality. Ishtar, in an act of self-righteousness, demands to be let into Ershkigal's realm of the underworld. Ishtar knocks on the gates of the underworld and commands to be admitted:

> "If thou openest not the gate to let me enter,
> I will break the door, I will wrench the lock,
> I will smash the door-posts, I will force the doors.
> I will bring up the dead to eat the living.
> And the dead will outnumber the living."[4]

Ishtar's tone upon demanding to be let in to this domain of the dead identifies her as not yet understanding the role that death must play within the natural life cycle. Her audacious demeanor suggests that she, as the ruler of the earth, feels that she may be capable of ruling the realm of the underworld as well, but her self-conceit is soon proven ridiculous when she must face the terrifying fact of death through the lessons her sister Ershkigal has in store for her.

Upon being let in to the underworld, the myth systematically takes away every quality that allowed Ishtar to rule over life, as well as every attribute that allowed her to live any semblance of a happy life. She is stripped of each jewel she is adorned with and every piece of clothing she wears, until she stands before Ershkigal naked and vulnerable. There Ershkigal gives Ishtar every imaginable disease that human beings must face, and talks to her about what it truly means to be mortal and die or lose a loved one. Then Ishtar must face death by being turned into a decaying corpse and hung upon a hook. Therefore, in the underworld, Ishtar is forced to face the reality of death, the cost of all life.

The myth shows Ishtar's vital connection to life on earth because as she is not among the living on earth, all life ceases to propagate, which of course will eventually cause the final destruction of all living beings:

> After the lady Ishtar had gone down into the land of no return,
> The bull did not mount the cow, the ass approached not the she-ass,
> To the maid in the street, no man drew near
> The man slept in his apartment,
> The maid slept by herself.[5]

The people begin to panic as the propagation of nature falls into stagnancy, and all life is threatened with starvation and demise. Without Ishtar in her Earth Goddess capacity, life on earth is endangered, but the format of the myth shows audiences that even Ishtar's transgression into the underworld is wholly natural. She must, to fully realize her role as Earth Goddess, experience and then accept that death is essential to regenerate new life. The myth teaches Ishtar, a divinity without a sense of mortality, what it means to be mortal. This mythic pattern also identifies that humanity is tied to this same natural cycle that Ishtar must undergo.

The myth continues to further its message of the natural cycle of life and death through again the character of Dumuzi, now transformed into the name Tammuz. Ershkigal demands that a life be conceded to her before she will allow Ishtar to ascend from her symbolic death, and in maintaining the ancient mythic archetype of the Goddess with her male consort, Ishtar gives Ershkigal Tammuz to assure her own resurrection.

As stated this pattern is popular in world mythology; quite often, the male consort serves a timely purpose. He is a vital part of the Earth Goddess' process of fertilization and harvest, but he, like all mortals, must concede to death. Though the myth may depict Ishtar as severe for handing over her lover Tammuz, myths that portray this process are not depicted as necessarily brutal, as they are again meant to be representations of the natural cycles of life and death—as the crops are fertilized and grow, they must wither and die, but they are assured to grow again out of the earth. As portrayed in the Inanna and Dumuzi myth, Tammuz here serves in his role as male consort to show that his physical body literally serves as the necessary seed that must submerge into the earth. Tammuz also assures the regenerating of Ishtar's powers an Earth Goddess by his physical death and descent into the underworld, as his body nourishes the earth, and the natural cycle is thus promised to be renewed. The myth makes it clear that if Ishtar remains in the underworld, all of the natural cycles of the earth will cease. It is fundamental that Tummuz be sacrificed, just as it is vital that all biological beings meet the requirements of the natural cycle. In Tummuz descending into the underworld in the place of Ishtar, it replicates the necessity of death to humans. In Ishtar ascending out of the underworld, she becomes the new growth of the harvest, now armed with humanity's understanding of the painful cost of the natural cycle, so as to perceivably better commiserate with her worshippers.

Myths that recount the male consort being sacrificed, as Tammuz is here, reveal a lesson for audiences of the myth, that like Tammuz, all earthly creatures, including human beings, will eventually die, decay, and serve as fertilization for the earth to renew its resources. However, Tammuz is portrayed as being allowed to also ascend out of the underworld on an annual basis, again serving to show audiences that the process of nature may be a harsh concept to embrace, but with it there persists a cyclical promise of rebirth. Tammuz remains locked within the underworld for only half of the year, and then each spring he is free to spout forth into the land of life. This mythic portrayal of the annual death and resurrection of a protagonist is also common in world mythology.

Tammuz's resurrection was ritually enacted by Sumerian and Akkadian initiates; "through sexual union, in the new year's festival in spring or autumn, with this fearfully potent Goddess, who took the form of a temple priestess in a bed chamber atop the city ziggurat, a king of Sumer, in the role of her husband, the annually dying god Dumuzi (Akkadian Tammuz), might each year renew the imperiled fertility of his land" (Torrance 82). Tammuz's mythic resurrection provided a clear representation of the cycles of the harvest as being tied to the lives of human beings.

From the city of Ugarit, the Canaanite myth of Anat, the Mother Goddess, and her brother and husband Baal, the storm god, also reflects the mythic explanation of natural cycles. Baal one day sends a confrontational invitation to Mot, "the god of death, sterility and drought, who constantly threatens to turn the earth into a desolate wilderness" (Armstrong, *Short History*, 48). Mot takes the invitation, but also puts Baal back in his place by stating, "'My appetite is that of lions in the desert, or the longing of dolphins in the sea! So Baal, you have summoned me to eat food and drink wine! Ah, if only you would descend down my throat and into the abyss of my entrails'" (Kerrigan, Lothian, & Vitebsky 104). Baal immediately knows that he should fear Mot, and different from his normal behavior, concedes to Mot's authority, as the Lord of the Underworld. Mot then consumes Baal, and forces him into the realm of death. When Mot consumes Baal, he takes within himself all the powers that Baal held: his own ability to bring forth rain, along with his "assistants: Clouds, Rain, Thunder and Lightning, as well as his daughters Mist and Dew" (Kerrigan, Lothian, & Vitebsky 105). The world, subsequently, falls into a state of severe drought. Forced to stay within the underworld, Baal cannot produce his normal functioning of providing rain for the people of the earth, and without the rain, the crops fail, and the people begin to starve, as they did in the Akkadian myth of Ishtar when Ishtar remained in the underworld.

El, the high god, was so distraught to hear of Baal's death, that he sat in the drought-ridden fields, poured dust upon himself and cut deep furrows in his own flesh. Baal's sister and wife Anat upon hearing the news, wept and also "ploughed her flesh with her nails" (Kerrigan, Lothian, & Vitebsky 105). This natural imagery used to connect the deities with the suffering of earth is significant to their representational nature roles within Canaanite belief. Anat and the goddess of the sun take it upon themselves to journey into the underworld to rescue Baal, whereas El, as high god, seems unable to take this action upon himself. It is significant that El is ineffective at saving his son Baal when he hears that he has died, as the only effective agents towards resuming the earth's natural processes are the females Anat and the sun goddess.

The female representations of the earth, Anat and the sun goddess, find Baal's body, carry it out of the underworld, and bury it on his mountain of Zaphon. The earth is still described as being in a state of drought, and El tries to replace Baal's role as rainmaker by finding someone else who might serve the purpose, but no one is adequate. Anat, though, knows that she holds the power to bring her brother and husband back to life. Armstrong describes Anat, in searching for Baal, as being "as fierce and beyond control as an animal when its young are in danger" (*Short History,* 49). Anat finds Baal, but seeks more than reunion with him; she seeks Mot, death itself; "her heart beating for him like a cow's heart for her calf, she went down a second time to Mot's realm and seized the dark lord by his cloak, screaming, 'Give me back my brother!' But Mot replied, 'What do you want of me, Anat? Yes, I swallow people up. I crunched the mighty Baal like a lamb in my jaws. That's how it is'" (Kerrigan, Lothian, &Vitebsky 105). Mot's words to Anat, "'Yes, I swallow people up.... That's how it is,'" shows the vital role he, as a representation of death, serves within the natural life cycle.

Anat, as Mother Goddess, though, also reveals her natural role in her treatment of Mot; "At these words the enraged Anat took hold of Mot. She cut him with a blade, winnowed him with a winnowing fan, parched him with fire, ground him with a millstone and finally scattered him in the fields for the birds to eat" (Kerrigan, Lothian, & Vitebsky 105). The reference here to the treatment of the body of Baal is clearly aligned again to the techniques associated with agricultural practice; Anat treats Mot "in exactly the same way as a farmer treats his grain" (Armstrong, *Short History,* 49–50), as was the initial references to the reaction of El and Anat upon hearing about the death of Baal. To prepare for the harvest, the fields require ploughing, as the two deities literally do to their own flesh in their sorrow, and in order to bring the land "back to life," like Baal needs to have done to him, the field must be prepared. The mythic text of Baal and Anat does not capture how Anat is able to use her magical powers to resurrect Baal, but the myth makes it clear that she does indeed hold the power to do this miraculous endeavor, as do many other Mother Goddesses in mythology, such as the Egyptian Isis resurrecting Osiris. Baal, once resurrected, is portrayed as sexually uniting again with Anat, and this union assures the return of the harvest for the survival of the people.

This myth portrays the process between Mot, Baal, and Anat as never-ending because they are mythic representations of nature, none of them can ever truly die, and each of them will always be resurrected. Mot, as death, is presented as a cyclical figure. Mot must kill Baal to ensure the fertilization of Anat, and Anat must kill and work over Mot to entice the natural cycle to indefinitely continue. Anat, as Mother Earth Goddess, is the only one who possesses the knowledge of how to not completely conquer death, but how to encourage the earth to renew its promised cycles. Baal represents the male seed that is needed annually to invigorate the earth, presented mythically here as the Goddess Anat. Yet in Anat's role as Earth Goddess, she always must help Baal be reborn, just as the earth accepts the seed into the dirt and annually produces a newly sprouted seedling. Anat, as Mother Goddess, knows that death if worked over properly, always initiates new life.

Annually, like the Sumerian and Akkadian ritualistic enactment of the Inanna/Ishtar and Dumuzi/Tammuz myths, the Canaanites reenacted this myth between Anat, Baal, and Mot; this ritualistic acknowledgement of the mythic lesson was also believed to assure the renewal of the harvest each year.

In the Akkadian myth of "Enki and the Island of Dilmun,"[6] an island thought to be the modern Bahrain, the deity Enki, the craftsman of the gods, possesses the ability to nurture earth's inhabitants through sexual intercourse. Enki is shown as wishing to enrich the island of Dilmun, which was at that time completely barren. Enki goes on a series of quests to populate the island with plants, animals, and human beings, but in order to do this, he must have sex with many figures. First, he slept with Ninhursag, the goddess of motherhood, and impregnated her, so that in nine days, she gave birth to the goddess Ninsar. After Ninsar grew, Enki impregnated her, and after nine days, she too gave birth to Ninkurra, Mistress of the Mountains. Enki then slept with her and produced Ninimma, Lady Vulva; he followed up by having sex with Ninimma, and they produced Uttu. This time, "Uttu's great-grandmother Ninhursag warned her not to yield to Enki's advances unless he brought her the fruits of irrigated gardening such as cucumbers, apples and grapes.... When Enki presented the gifts to Uttu she let him make love to her" (Kerrigan, Lothian, & Vitebsky 29). When they were having sex, Enki's semen is said to have spilled out of Uttu, which made her cry out. Her great-grandmother Ninhursag, in her role as Mother Goddess, resolved the issue by coming to her aid and wiped the spilled semen from the body of Uttu and planted it in the soil; "This time, instead of creating a daughter, Enki's semen sprouted into eight different kinds of plant" (Kerrigan, Lothian, & Vitebsky 29). Upon seeing these strange plants, and not knowing they came from his own body, Enki ate the plants and grew quite ill. Ninhursag, described as being fed up with Enki's inability to more effectively create life, almost gave up on him, but the text states that she instead slept again with him, which immediately cured him; she then gave birth to eight deities that helped humanity exist in what became the verdant island of Dilmun. Ninhursag's role, as a Mother Goddess, shows Enki as a mere male consort; instead of being successful at creation, he gives way to only sexual impulses. His lack of understanding of the process of natural creation shows that at every stage he must be guided by Ninhursag.

It is important to acknowledge the debt owed to the myths coming from the Middle East; as Kerrigan, Lothian, and Vitebsky state:

> It is scarcely an exaggeration to claim that almost every myth and legend found around the Mediterranean world has some kind of Akkadian or Sumerian parallel.... Individual gods and goddesses appear to undergo a gentle transformation as they move across from one culture to the next. Thus Inanna ... clearly shares similar characteristics with Ashtart and Anat, who in turn are associated with the Greek Pallas Athene.... Indeed, the Hebrew Bible itself, the great excoriator of the idolaters, owes something to the Mesopotamian world [136–7].

As discussed, many Near Eastern myths include the Mother Goddess linked with mythical scenes that some view as overtly sexual, and this later contrasted with the coming of new faiths that sought to teach a lesson that female sexuality should be stifled. In these Near Eastern myths, the sexual act, as with Inanna and Dumuzi, represented a means to revitalize the crops, and so it was viewed as highly sacred and necessary; in addition, the represented sexual acts were portrayed as simply a natural process, connecting humans deeply with the processes of nature of which they were forever bound. As such, often rituals involved "priestesses who served as sacred prostitutes and male hierophants who may in early times have been ritually killed after the love-making" (Allan & Phillips, *World,* 64). Religious opposition later intervened with the practices of the worship of the Earth Goddess, but still these rituals continued into Greek and Roman times with orgiastic rites where initiates openly practiced sexual acts, and sometimes, as with the followers of the Phrygian Cybele male members would castrate themselves to serve the Goddess. Later mythologies and religious systems changed to represent the new faiths arriving to various regions in large part because of unrest due to the Goddess cults' overt sexuality, but more importantly, over disdain for the messages of resurrection in Goddess myths.

The Phrygian Goddess, Cybele, from Anatolia, modern day Turkey, is portrayed again as an Earth Goddess; she gives birth to Agdistis, a hermaphrodite who is represented as wild. The gods fear Agdistis for his unruly nature, so they castrate him. From his genitals sprouts an almond tree. A nymph comes upon the tree and eats of its bounty, becoming pregnant; she leaves her infant to the elements, but the infant's grandmother, Cybele, seeing his beauty falls deeply in love with him. The infant, Attis, grew into an extremely handsome youth. He eventually found love with a young woman, but Cybele became enraged with his lack of affection for her and turned Attis insane. Attis then roamed the wilderness in this altered state, until he castrated himself and then committed suicide.

Attis' birth is important, as it portrays him as a representation of fertility. The fact that he comes from the genitals of his father, who represents both sexes immediately also identifies him with fertility. In addition, Attis is created directly from a representation of nature, with Agdistis' genitals becoming an almond tree that serves to produce Attis through his mother's ingestion of its bounty. Cybele's punishment of Attis also connects him as an embodiment of nature, as divine madness and exile into the wilderness are often represented in myth as elements leading to a spiritual transformation of the protagonist, a stripping away of the self. Attis' decision to castrate himself, joining him to his father, reveals him as another succession of the male consort myth, as both Agdistis and Attis are represented as dying after their sexual productivity is eliminated. In addition, like other male consorts from the Neolithic era, Attis is identified as being connected to the harvest, as he is said to have castrated himself with a harvesting sickle. The representation of Attis' castration provides symbolism of the testicles serving as symbolic seed to the earth's regenerative processes. The testicles, clearly associated with fertility, secure the continued regeneration of the earth when sacrificed to nature, just as the Polynesian Te Tuna, meaning penis, died to secure the staple crop, and the Greek Uranus' castration caused his offspring the freedom to finally reign, as well as the birth of Aphrodite. The sacrifice of the testicles in myth, therefore, clearly aligns with the role of the male consort within the myths of the steady Earth Goddess; when the male is castrated in myth it is an equal representation to when the male consort is physically killed in myth, as both sacrifices serve the same purpose of regenerating the success of the earth's bounty. Upon his death, Attis is also said to have transformed into a pine tree, which again connects him to his father, Agdistis, and to the recursive patterns of nature by showing that both Agdistis' and Attis' death allowed for the continuation of nature.

Attis becomes another mythic representation of the "the eternal seed made flesh—the rising sun, the emerging plant of the spring who continues the essence of our human sense of the new beginning.... But he is the inevitable victim, the corn god one day to be harvested, the sun that must set, the metaphor for our necessary journey back to our Mother of Being" (Leeming & Page, *God,* 89). In celebration of Attis, it is said that "at the spring equinox ... a pine-tree was cut in the woods and brought into the sanctuary of Cybele, where it was treated as a divinity.... The high priest drew blood from his arms and presented it as an offering"; an effigy of Attis was mourned and buried, and on "the fourth day ... was the Festival of Joy (*Hilaria*), at which the resurrection of Attis was probably celebrated" (Frazer 297). The myth of Cybele and Attis again serves to educate audiences on their own connection to the role mortals must play in the greater natural order—humans are similar then to the male consorts, like Attis, but they are also, like Attis, assured continuality, through the consistency of the Earth representation of Cybele.

A Greek myth of Aphrodite has similar Goddess/male consort themes. Aphrodite is said to have grown jealous of a young mortal woman named Myrrha, so she tricks her and her father, King Cinyrus of Cyprus, into having sex with each other; Myrrha then becomes pregnant. When the king finds out what happened, he chases Myrrha in order to kill both her and her unborn child. Aphrodite seeing what has resulted because of her meddling, decides to transform Myrrha into a myrrh tree. Already this myth has elements that suggest a more ancient connection. Aphrodite, a goddess who has been identified as an ancient Earth Goddess indicative in her creation myth from the severed genitals of the Sky god Uranus, here reveals her power to both create and destroy life. Her transformation of Myrrha into a tree that after nine months produced an infant child, again her own future lover Adonis, suggests a connection to the Neolithic myths of the Goddess with her male consort as a reflection of the agricultural process, as the myth of Adonis is said to have come to Greece from Syria.

The myth continues to show Aphrodite taking the newly born Adonis to the underworld, so that Persephone, wife of Hades, the god of the underworld, can help to keep the baby safe, but when Persephone saw Adonis, she immediately refused to give him back because of his stunning beauty. Here Aphrodite and Persephone represent in separate forms the two parts of the traditional Mother Goddess—one of love and life and the other of death. The myth presents Aphrodite and Persephone arguing over who should care for Adonis, until Zeus intervenes and declares that Persephone should have him for a portion of the year, the months of winter, and Aphrodite should have him for the months of spring and summer. This tie to the myth of Persephone herself is interesting. Persephone too was said to mythically descend each winter to Hades and then become resurrected each spring back to the land of the living to be with her mother Demeter, goddess of the harvest. Adonis here dies, like Persephone herself, an annual death, and is then mythically resurrected, like Persephone, each year.

Some versions of the myth continues to show Adonis as a grown man disregarding Aphrodite's warning to hunt forest animals that appeared fearless. Adonis is said to have gone deep into the unchartered wilderness to pursue a ferocious boar; the god Ares spotted Adonis showing his audacity to enter the realm of pure nature, so Ares transforms himself into a boar and tears Adonis' body apart. Aphrodite hears Adonis' cries and rushes to him, but finding him dead, she transforms Adonis forever into a flower, the anemone. In this version of the myth Adonis is still portrayed as a representation of humanity dying and resurrecting again with the botanical cycle in the symbolic form of a flower. As with the Middle Eastern traditions, Adonis' death "was annually lamented with a bitter wailing, chiefly by women; images of him, dressed to resemble corpses, were carried out as to burial and then thrown into the sea or into springs, and in some places his revival was celebrated the following day" (Frazer 279).

Again, the mythic patterns set forth from Neolithic myths of the Goddess and her male consort serve to show audiences a vital lesson—that human beings are subject to the laws of the natural world. As the male consort must die in order to renew life, so too must each mythic listener. The archetypes of Neolithic myth appear to have become so embedded in the human psyche that countless myths and stories, even in contemporary times, continue to make use of them. One may ask why seemingly remote concepts left over from the first civilizations, such as sacrifice for agricultural security, have remained an integral part of storytelling for thousands of years. Perhaps, the answer lies in dissecting the concepts presented in Neolithic myth.

Myths from the advent of farming hold nature as supreme. Their ultimate goal is to teach audiences that human beings are merely a part of a greater natural system. With the death of a protagonist, either presented in Neolithic myth or contemporary film, human beings must wrestle with their own inevitable mortality. When a character is sacrificed for the betterment of a people, especially when the character willingly steps forth into the sacrifice, such as the Neolithic male consort, audiences are renewed because the willing mythic sacrifice shows people the promise of the Earth Goddess—that of recursive natural immortality. Death as presented through the Goddess and male consort is removed of fear because the Goddess is merely a representation of the nature human beings all reside in, and the consort is ourselves.

When humanity accepts, like the consort, that life will eventually end, they accept too that it will continue. This acceptance of nature holding the key to immortality remains a vital component of storytelling. Spirituality, in ancient through contemporary times, has often been defined as being found within nature; the myths of the Goddess and her male consort merely present us the first tales of this lesson. When one lets go of the self, as the consort accepts his sacrifice, and steps forth into the natural order of life, presented mythically as the realm of the Goddess, then one is often identified in terms of having found spirituality. Though the myths of the Goddess will forego a great transformation, the archetypes and basic messages of the myths arguably withstand the test of time, as will be discussed in the proceeding chapters.

Demotion of the Goddess

It is generally believed that the influx of Indo-European cultures over centuries modified and sometimes transformed the existing cultures of many civilizations; a common proto-language can be traced throughout parts of Asia and Europe for instance. With the Indo-European invaders in the late Neolithic and Iron Ages, conceptions of male divinity began to take on a domineering role to that of the Mother Earth Goddess; "as male power on earth, embodied in the invading warriors, took precedence over the female power of the agricultural mysteries, it was inevitable that a mythological struggle would take place to reflect that loss of balance" (Leeming & Page, *God,* 123). Male divinity began to be represented most often in the form of a sky god, and "the mysteries of the Earth were somehow a threat to male dominance.... Goddess power was mysterious; its source was in the depths of the Earth itself—the world represented by the sacred cave-temples and the mysteries of germination" (Leeming & Page, *God,* 123). During these times of conquest, the mythology was transformed to account for this new role of supremacy. The resulting myths of the Indo-European invaders serves to dispel the Goddess of her supreme role and demote her to a lesser position, as presented in many myths portraying female divinities being overtaken by male mythic figures.

The resulting myths therefore exhibit the mythic demotion of traditional earth-based worship to that of a new faith. As Leeming and Page state, "Female power was no longer seen primarily as a nurturing force but as an aberration from the frightening depths, one that must be conquered or destroyed. Where Goddess had once been all things, she was now associated with darkness and chaos" (*God,* 123). And over time, "the cult of virility took precedence over that of fertility and union. The dark was separated from the light; death was opposed to life rather than a part of it" (Leeming & Page, *Goddess,* 88).

It should be stated that there is disagreement in scholarly circles as to the impact of the Indo-Europeans on existing cultures. Many imagine that

war-like Indo-Europeans invaded Neolithic civilizations bringing their patriarchal systems of government and religion, and to an extent most scholars
believe this to be true, though of course there are exceptions to this, as each
cultural infusion is unique. In Greece, for example, Burkert contends that
they remained more indebted to "Neolithic-Anatolian urban culture than to
Indo-European nomads" (18). Though many sources stand firm in separating
a clear distinction between early Neolithic cultures being transformed and
dominated by Indo-European concepts, it should always be remembered that
little is known about Neolithic mythological and religious beliefs, so much
of what is stated is mere conjecture; "quite clearly our access is to only an
amalgam of the migration period which it is not easy to analyze either lin-
guistically or mythicologically.... Relations with the Ancient Near Eastern,
Anatolian, and Semitic traditions demonstrate that the polarity of the Indo-
European and Mediterranean unduly curtails the historical diversity. Greek
religion certainly bears the stamp of its prehistory, but of a prehistory that is
an infinitely involved network of interrelations" (Burkert 19). For instance,
many scholars wish to differentiate a quasi-historical time of pre-invasion by
Indo-Europeans as nature-based, Goddess-oriented, matriarchal societies
that are violently uprooted by male, patriarchal systems of belief. To an extent,
some of this is true, as certain mythology points to a shift from Goddess
superiority to God dominance, but it should always be maintained that no
one entirely knows the content of the mythology and religion of early
Neolithic societies; no one knows for sure if, when, or why shifts in dominance of divine power occurred. Perhaps instead of arguing over female
divine power being disrupted and replaced by male dominance, it may be
helpful to look towards a culture's view on the shifting conception and value
of the natural world.

Early civilizations conceive of nature and its functionings differently
than later cultures, and so therefore, their myths and religious belief systems
shift. Once existing mythology was altered, social structures also transformed;
the position of women decreased, and the crucial tie of nature to the lives of
individuals lessened. With this loss of a close kinship with nature, philosophical and spiritual views were also renovated. Once this shift occurred, the
mythic messages of the healing and regenerative themes found in nature
myths became largely hidden within later myths. The transformation of the
nature-based Goddess mythology to a mythology of male superiority may
also have been in large part political rather than religious; many of these new
myths were believed to have been written by priests within invading tribes
who held the intent of tying the supremacy of the new invading king to existing agricultural communities (Stone 67).

The protagonist of this next stage of myth often is now presented as most often male, and usually his quest involves defeating a female. The female, assuredly a characterization of the traditional Earth Goddess, is often presented as a formidable opponent, but she appears now as a natural force that must be tamed or completely destroyed in order for life to thrive. These myths sought to demote the power the Goddess traditionally was believed to hold, and thus transfer her power to new hands. However, when the Goddess, as a representation of an intrinsic tie with nature, is demoted, or even savagely killed, this new mythic act of incessantly defeating nature, now puts mankind at an odd and clearly unnatural place.

To an increasing degree people did not look solely towards the earth when attempting to understand the meaning of their existence; instead, they began to look beyond the earth to a largely abstract male divinity. Myths began to present male protagonists as less willing to be sacrificed for the continuation of the earth's cycles. Quite often the myths present mythic male characters who savagely mutilate the Goddess representation in an effort to declare an end to the need for sacrifice. It is easy to see why one might wish to fight against myths that continuously call for annual sacrifice, as no one wants to conceive of death as necessary. But, again, in brutally resisting the Goddess figure, many mythic protagonists resist the facts of life. Some myths present a strong male character killing a female opponent, such as the Babylonian Marduk and Tiamat, and then moving on to live a fulfilling and powerful life having declared humanity's dominance over the natural environment. But, still, the most lasting of myths present complex contradictions that wrestle with the loss of the Goddess, which again, is the loss of humanity's role within a dominant nature. Losing sight of nature as primary may have led to belief systems that allow for the rampant destruction of the environment found in contemporary times.

Though the Mother Earth Goddesses are transformed after the patriarchal societies move in with their myths of supreme male deities that hold less focus on the importance of the natural world, the Goddess still remains a powerful mythic tenet; "even long after the patriarchal pantheons of Babylon, Egypt, India, and elsewhere, Goddess and her son lover remained a pervasive force in the religions and lives of peoples who practiced the arts of agriculture and animal domestications" (Lemming & Page, *God,* 59). The Goddess became represented in many later myths in symbolic form. When analyzing myths closely, one sees that the Goddess may have been demoted, but the mythic message of the Neolithic Goddess myths arguably still resides powerfully in world storytelling even to this day.

The Goddess was, and continued to be, a representation of nature and its life cycles. Though the mythology may have changed and even promoted a message contrary to the Goddesses' authority, her role was not easily eradicated. She still continued to be a part of countless myths, and though she oftentimes appears to be destroyed, most often than not, her mysterious and natural qualities keep her from being entirely abandoned. Historically, when one culture takes over another culture, as with Christianity in Celtic Europe, countless individuals maintain their traditional beliefs though appearing to adopt the new faith. Many myths suggest that this was happening with conceptions of the Goddess in expanding cultures. But on a broader level, because the Goddess is a representation of the earth itself with its assurance of life, death, and renewal, her role can never be fully eradicated and thus remains well past its Paleolithic and Neolithic origins into today.

Wrestling with Nature

The Near Eastern text the *Enuma Elish*[7] is one of the best depictions showcasing the determined message to mythically defeat an older belief system involving an Earth Goddess. Marduk is first portrayed as a lesser deity, but the *Enuma Elish* shows him rising beyond this initial inferior status to take his superior place in the Babylonian pantheon. In order to claim his elevated divine role, he must slay the existing owner of the superior position held by the primordial, female serpent of the sea, Tiamat.

The *Enuma Elish* begins by telling the Babylonian creation story that first Apsu, the ocean, and Tiamat, primordial water, lay together and eventually created the natural elements of silt and slime, the sky and the earth, and the waters of the earth. The epic soon reveals that these divine and natural offspring rebelled and wanted their own supremacy, but Apsu and Tiamat, angered by their offspring's insubordination, tried to reassert their own power by attempting to kill the younger elements; "the plan failed, however, as Tiamat withdrew out of motherly concern," and one of their offspring succeeded in killing Apsu, and after his death "presumably [his] waters were contained for purposes of irrigation in the first stage of Mesopotamian civilization (Sproul 91). Tiamat, now determined to finish what Apsu and herself attempted to do, gave birth to monsters to bring an end to her revolting offspring, but the myth shows how Marduk rose to the head of the pantheon by his ability to slay Tiamat.

The myth's recitation of the death of Tiamat is brutal; it clearly shows a message of domination of the natural elements by a male divinity. Marduk "took his route towards the rising sound of Tiamat's rage, and all the gods besides, the fathers of the gods pressed in around him, and the lord approached Tiamat.... But Tiamat without turning her neck roared, spitting defiance from bitter lips" (Sproul 101). Marduk, though, is described as undeterred by Tiamat's enormous primal ferocity; he throws his net around her, heeds the wind to enter into her body, which causes her stomach to explode. Marduk then "cut her womb" and "straddles the carcass" (Sproul 101). Hence, all the gods and the later Babylonian citizens pay homage to Marduk. The symbolism of this scene shows the pitiless takeover of nature, and again, it is vital to see the gender distinction of an earlier primal Goddess, represented as Tiamat, being utterly destroyed by the next generation of the younger male divinity.

One of the African Yoruba myths of creation, discussed in chapter 1 shows the division of sky god, Olorun, and primordial water/earth Goddess, Olokun. As discussed in chapter 1, Obatala creates land and life on earth, but the myth continues to show the primal Goddess, Olokun, as angry that some of her power may have been perceived to have been diminished or forgotten after creation, so to remind the inhabitants of earth of her power, she creates a great flood. Obatala's brother, Orunmila, who has by now learned to live with the new people, goes to earth and stops the flood, and this of course angers Olokun even more. The gods soon learn that the only way to save the earth and its inhabitants is to challenge Olokun to a contest, but what is revealing is that the gods realize that they must cheat in order to defeat her, as they concede that her power is greater than theirs.

Olokun challenges the sky god, Olorun, to a weaving contest, but Olorun admits that "'Olokun is a far better weaver than I am. However, I cannot give her the satisfaction of knowing that she is superior to me in anything. If I do, she will exert her powers in other ways as well, and that will disrupt the order that now exists throughout the universe. Somehow I must appear to accept her challenge and yet avoid participating in her contest'" (Rosenberg 514). So Olorun decides, through treachery, to send a chameleon down to earth to be the judge of this weaving contest. As predicted by Olorun, the chameleon changes color each time Olokun creates a new pattern, so that it looks like Olorun is able to match Olokun's skill in weaving. Olokun begrudgingly then admits defeat; she states, "'Tell your master that the ruler of the sea sends her greetings to the ruler of the sky. Tell him that I acknowledge his superiority in weaving and in all other pursuits as well. Olorun is indeed the greatest of the gods!'" (Rosenberg 514). The fact that the myth admits that Olokun is indeed superior, as she is only tricked by Olorun into thinking she is inferior to him, is quite telling. As stated many myths were created and adopted to counter existing traditional myths, and this myth certainly suggests that an older female-driven view of natural authority must concede to a more abstract male divine order that can rule using wit and structure to counterbalance the perceived chaos of unfettered nature.

Similarly, the Lakota American Indians identify a creation story that also involves a primordial female water monster, named Uncegila.[8] She emerges from the vast sea and floods the land, but the Thunderbird, Wakinyan, is angered by this. He worries that the inhabitants of earth will no longer be able to worship him, so he creates a massive storm by furiously flapping his wings. The wind from the storm dries up the flooded land, and a lightning bolt strikes and kills Uncegila. Her bones became the land known today in North and South Dakota as the Badlands. In addition, the South American myth of Quetzalcoatl and Tezcatlipoca show them killing the goddess of the primordial waters and carving up her body to make the earth.

Goddess Divided

Even as civilizations transformed, and new mythologies were introduced with invading power systems, the Goddess still remained essential to many world pantheons, though in a revised role. Oftentimes the primary Mother Earth Goddess was divided up into many mythic representations. In dividing one Goddess into several less dominant goddesses, her power lessened and could be mythically guarded by other male members of a given pantheon. For example, Athena, Artemis, Demeter, Hestia, Hera, and Aphrodite in the Greek Olympian pantheon are perceived as representing parts of an earlier Mother Earth Goddess. Though in looking at the many representations of goddesses within pantheons, one can see remnants of the power the central Mother Goddess once was believed to possess.

In Greece, the pantheon of the Olympians is represented as only part of a sequential history of divinity; "Creation, according to the Greeks, moves from a mother-dominated society, in which the most important divinities are female, to a father-dominated society, in which the most important divinities are male" (Rosenberg 2). Gaia is represented as Mother Earth, and as such she is the Great Goddess. She was worshipped for centuries by agriculturally dependent communities; the Neolithic people of Greece "drew a connection between a woman's ability to give birth to children and the earth's ability to 'give birth' to all plants. Therefore the earth spirit was feminine, and the principal divinities that the early Greeks worshipped were also feminine" (Rosenberg 3–4).

Greek mythology offers several accounts of creation. One version, that famous Greek mythologist Robert Graves[9] believed may have had Neolithic origins, explains that out of chaos came existence in the form of the goddess Eurynome, who Graves refers to as "the Goddess of All Things" (1). Eurynome, as Earth Goddess, danced within chaos and the winds of her movements produced a giant male serpent, named Orphion, who coupled with Eurynome. The Goddess Eurynome then transformed herself into a dove and laid an enormous "Universal Egg" (Graves 1). Eurynome commanded Orphion to curl himself around the egg to keep it warm and assure that it would hatch. Once the egg hatched, all things in nature emerged: "Uranus, the sky; Ourea, the mountains; Pontus, the sea; and all the stars and planets. Gaia, the Earth, and her mountains and rivers emerged at the same time" (Wilkinson 14). After creation both Eurynome and Orphion went to Mount Olympus to settle down, but Orphion began taking all the credit for creation, which enraged Eurynome, who possessed the power to first kick Orphion in the face, knocking out his fangs, and then force him down to the caves of the underworld forever in punishment.[10] This version of creation, though some scholars debate Graves' interpretation of its Neolithic origins,[11] still presents the archetype of a great initial Goddess possessing the power to initiate life. It also shows the powerful role of Eurynome in having the ability to punish her male counterpart by imprisoning him in the underworld.

In Hesiod's Archaic-era *Theogony,* creation is again a vast nothingness in which Gaia, the Mother Earth Goddess, emerges. Gaia gives birth to Uranus, who becomes her husband. The Greek pantheon is, again, portrayed as mythically overriding a dominant feminine rule with male divine superiority, when as part of creation, Uranus is viewed as ruler. Gaia and Uranus give birth to the first beings: three Hundred-handed Giants and three Cyclopes. Uranus fears that his children will one day overthrow him, which is biologically the natural order, so unnaturally he hurls his offspring deep into Gaia's being. Gaia is ready to give birth to thirteen Titans, but Uranus also forces them to remain within her womb; in agony, Gaia seeks help from her in-utero children to gain revenge upon Uranus. Her son, Cronus, agrees to help Gaia overthrow Uranus. When Uranus sexually enters Gaia, Cronus, waiting with a sickle, dismembers Uranus' genitals. When Uranus' semen falls into the sea, the foam it creates on contact with the water produces the Goddess of Love, Aphrodite. This creation of Aphrodite, a goddess portrayed as older than Zeus and the other members of the Olympian pantheon, is important. This birth of Aphrodite may serve as a reminder of an older Greek belief system that connects the Goddess to her natural role. Furthermore, the same mythic patterns presented here are seen in other agricultural myths:

When Uranus becomes ruler of the world, his son, Cronus, dismembers him—just as priestesses of the Great Goddess or Mother Goddess in the female-oriented religion dismembered the sacred king. They used his blood, which they considered to be a prime source of fertility, to fertilize the soil so that it would produce an abundance of crops.... When Cronus becomes ruler of the world, the divine family is in transition from the mother-dominated society to the father-dominated society that will follow under the rule of Zeus [Rosenberg 4].

Wilkinson also discusses Cronus as initially being worshipped as a harvest god, which the inclusion of the sickle as the agent of virile demotion suggests (15). It is interesting to note that Cronus, "despite his violence to his own children ... [was] often seen as a gentle, just, and kind ruler of the Golden Age" (Wilkinson 23), pointing to a possibility that his demotion through castration may have been initially a representation of the ancient practice of the sacrifice of the male consort. The political components of power transference within the myth may reference a later revised ideology portrayed artistically in the Archaic and Classical periods.

The myth continues to show Cronus and his siblings, the Titans, emerge from their mother Gaia and proceed to take over domination. However, Cronus eventually acts just like his father. He marries his sister Rhea, but upon her giving birth to the original members of the Olympian pantheon: Hades, Poseidon, Demeter, Hestia, and Hera, he swallows them whole refusing to give them the chance to overtake his power, thus again disrupting the natural order. Rhea, distraught, and having consulted her mother Gaia for advice, gives Cronus a rock wrapped in a baby's swaddling cloth, so that he, without looking, mistakenly thinks the rock is Zeus and swallows it whole.

Again, myths are often created by the civilizations that needed them to justify transference of power. Zeus has many connections to Minoan culture, as scholars believe that Zeus may have originated in a lesser divine form on the island of Crete, and in his Olympian pantheon mythic portrayal, he is still shown as hiding as an infant in a mountain cave on Crete, a previously well-documented place of Mother Goddess worship, and is nursed by the goat Amalthea, a possible direct reference to goddess worship. This Archaic and Classical period creation myth continues by having Zeus eventually leave Crete and come back to the mainland of Greece where he tricks his father, Cronus, into swallowing a poison that causes him to purge his other five siblings. Zeus then gets the Hundred-handers and the Cyclopes together to help him wage war on Cronus and the Titans. The Olympians eventually win dominance, and Zeus takes his place as central deity. Leeming and Page point out the demotion of Earth Goddess that takes place when Zeus becomes conceptualized as the central deity; "One of the best known versions of the dysfunctional marriage is the whole Zeus-Hera cycle, in which an archaic Earth Goddess, whose temples were said to have been the largest in prepatriarchal Crete and Greece, is demoted to the status of a nagging wife constantly punishing her philandering husband" (*Goddess*, 98).

Leeming and Page also recount Zeus' rape of Hera as a stark example of mythology presenting a justification of oppression over former power (*Goddess* 98). Leeming and Page state that "Hera was raised by the four seasons and inherited the mantle of the Great Mother of all" as daughter of the Titan Rhea and granddaughter of Gaia. Hera aided Zeus in obtaining his role of power, along with her siblings (*Goddess*, 98). However, the myths of Zeus' and Hera's subsequent relationship shows the overthrow of power structures quite clearly. The myth states that Hera goes to Crete, again a seeming connection to Hera returning to the Mother Goddess worship long attached to Crete, in order to rest after helping to achieve victory for the Olympian pantheon. Zeus interrupts Hera's respite by coming to Crete wanting to have sex with her. Hera refuses him, but he tricks her by transforming himself into an injured bird; Hera seeing the bird felt bad for it and brought it to her chest to console it, but the bird changed quickly into Zeus; "Before Hera could even so much as protest, Zeus threw her down and spent his passions on her, leaving her exhausted and humiliated on the ground. So ashamed was Hera that she agreed to take the unusual step not only of marrying her brother, but of promising to stay only with him" (Leeming & Page, *Goddess*, 99).

Leeming and Page also point to another rape scene involving Zeus and his mother Rhea, also often portrayed as an Earth Goddess. Rhea is said to have grown concerned at the singular power that Zeus was obtaining in his new role among the divine pantheon, and she also disdained his uncontrollable lust, so she sought him out and tried to refuse him the right to marry Hera. Earth Goddesses, like Rhea, are known for being highly sexual. As Earth Goddesses, they are connected to the fertility of the earth, so to assure continued fertility, sexual intercourse is paramount; therefore, traditionally Earth Goddesses are known for taking many partners, like the Mesopotamian Inanna/Ishtar, the Norse Freyja, and the Greek goddess of love Aphrodite, again coming into creation before any of the other Olympians in a way clearly tied to fertility. To squelch the Goddesses' right to sexually intermingle with many male partners takes power away from the female divinity and places a higher degree of power into male hands, who were once, in many myths, dispensable. Therefore, when Rhea tries to forbid Zeus from marrying Hera, she is attempting to maintain power for Hera. Zeus reacts, though, by stating that he intends to immediately rape Rhea. In showing her more ancient strength, in what is often an archetypal representation of the Earth Goddess, Rhea transforms herself into a giant serpent. However, Zeus, in this mythic rendition of male power superseding female authority, also transforms himself into a massive serpent; "Not to be outdone or thwarted in his revenge, Zeus too turned into a serpent and coiled about his mother with such muscular power that she could no longer move. When she was finally still, he fulfilled his threat, raping her and leaving her with none of her former powers but that of seeing into the future" (Leeming & Page, *Goddess*, 99–100).

The myth of the birth of Athena, like Aphrodite's birth, is also telling. Athena's mother, Metis, was a Titaness who encouraged Zeus that it was indeed possible to free his brothers and sisters from the innards of his father Cronus. Metis is the one who gave Zeus the poison needed to induce vomiting in Cronus which freed what was to become the Olympian pantheon. Later Zeus had sex with Metis, but he immediately regarded this as a mistake, as it was prophesized that a child by Metis would one day overthrow him. So, Zeus swallowed Metis. After a period, though, Zeus found that he could not escape the power of Metis, as he was overcome by an excruciating headache. Hephaestus hit Zeus upon the head to relieve his headache, and from Zeus' head emerged a fully grown Athena. This myth is remarkably similar to the creation of Aphrodite with both goddesses possibly serving as representations of an older pantheon in their renditions of their mystical creation. It is Metis who assures the success of Zeus; without her, he would be unable to reign; this also is significant in its statement of the transference of power. Athena is often portrayed as being consistently at Zeus' side, ready to act in all matters, perhaps as a mythical reminder of an older belief in Goddess worship to counterbalance the power of Zeus.

Athena was worshiped as a strong divine figure to the ancient Greeks; as the goddess of wisdom and strategic warfare, she was the patron goddess of Athens, defeating even Poseidon for power over the city. She was also said to be a favorite of Zeus. Athena was once courted by Hephaestus, who fell in love with her; he gained Zeus' approval for their marriage if Athena conceded, but Athena declared that she wished to remain a virgin. Athena's virginity, and that found in other Greek goddesses, like Artemis, attests to an intermediary position from the more ancient belief system that the Earth Goddess need not marry any one particular man, as marriage, as seen with the myths of Zeus and Hera, often signaled a demotion in strength and power. Artemis is the divinity of the unfettered wilderness and its wild animals because she maintains her power through holding onto her virginity. Athena too remains the formidable goddess she is because she holds firm onto her autonomy and self-sufficiency. Though Athena appears as a goddess of the well-developed Classical Olympian pantheon, some of her myths suggest older roots. For instance, when Athena refused to marry Hephaestus, he tried to rape her, but Athena possessed such strength that she was able to push him away from her causing his semen to fall to the ground, and "the seed fertilized Gaia (Mother Earth) and Erichthonius was created" (Wilkinson 31). Athena then agreed to raise this child of her grandmother. In addition, there is a myth that states that the prophet Tiresias once caught sight of Athena bathing, and because he witnessed what no man should see, he became blind but obtained incredible insight into the future.

The Greek myth of the creation of mankind out of clay by Prometheus, only to have Zeus send Prometheus to Mount Caucasus to have his liver eaten each day by a massive eagle as punishment for trying to assure man's survival with the gift of fire, also may portray the transference of power to justify male superiority. As additional punishment to Prometheus and his creation, Zeus sent man the first woman, Pandora, who mythically is explained as causing all of the world's ills by opening her box, given to her by Zeus, which contained, disease, pain, drought, hunger, and death. This mythic representation of punishment to mankind in the form of a woman is also seen in the Hebrew creation story of Adam and Eve. Yahweh creates Adam to live in a paradise of nature, but finds that Adam is unhappy alone, so from Adam's rib, Eve is created. But the story continues to show Eve as detrimental to man, as she is portrayed as weak in spirit because she listens to what the story states is Satan in the form of a serpent. The archetype of the serpent in the Hebrew story of creation is used to explain the enticement of Eve with an apple from the Tree of Knowledge, which suggests that Eve has overstepped her bounds in wanting divine knowledge. Eve is portrayed as wrong, weak-spirited, and thus in need of punishment with a perpetual status of inferiority to male authority, yet the depiction of the serpent offering Eve the seduction of wisdom, found in the natural portrayal of a Tree of Knowledge, suggests there is a historical reference behind the symbols within this myth.

The archetype of the snake in world myth may have Neolithic origins. Serpents are often seen in connection to the portrayal of Earth Goddesses. Snake goddess figures found in the compound at the palace of Knossos on Crete most certainly represent goddess worship. This connection of Earth Goddesses and serpents may be explained because of the attributes connected to snakes. Snakes live close to the earth, easily passing between the upper and underworld, as they often live in dens, caves, and crevices. Venomous snakes also sometimes have the ability to cause almost instantaneous death. In addition, snakes possess an odd characteristic in that they have the ability to shed their skin, which often makes them appear in myths as symbolic representations of rebirth.

However, in later mythologies, many myths present serpents in horrific form. Mythic serpents, that are usually female, are often identified as monstrous creatures that threaten the safety of a people. Many myths showcase these female serpents being defeated by a male figure, like Marduk killing the primordial sea serpent Tiamat. The Greek myth of Perseus also thrusts Perseus to the role of a hero because he slays the snake-ridden gorgon, Medusa, and then saves the helpless Andromeda from sacrifice to an enormous water serpent. The Greek Apollo must first slay the Delphic python of Gaia, the Mother Goddess, before he can rule over the Oracle. Interestingly, though, the word "python" in Greek means "to rot," and this may reveal more about the connection of Neolithic Earth Goddesses to the mythic serpent. In slaying the python of the Mother Goddess Gaia, the Greeks may have lost touch of the lesson of the more ancient Delphi—that in nature rotting is a necessary occurrence that aids in the rebirth of natural elements. Therefore, mythically connecting snakes to Earth Goddesses may serve as a symbolic representation of the processes of nature in the guise of a central Goddess. Earth Goddesses, like Gaia, can seem to be the cause of death and decay, but like Gaia's Delphic python that sheds its old skin to enable its new self to emerge, Earth Goddesses offer a perpetual cycle of rebirth from the cessation of life they demand—presenting a mythic message that in nature's cycles, there is no death. Mythically portraying male heroes who annihilate massive, often female, serpents reveals an attempt to eradicate the power of the Earth Goddess. The monstrous, mythic serpents are often terrifying, and many myths make it seem like the honorable thing to do is to rid the world of the bothersome creature, but when the mythic serpents are brutally murdered, their symbolic representation of nature's cycles are also eradicated. When an Earth Goddess in any form—malevolent or benevolent—is annihilated, the wisdom found in nature, that the Goddess embodied, is viewed as less important than newly introduced ideologies. Therefore, connecting the Hebrew Eve to a serpent to prove her as immoral for wanting knowledge reveals a message that women and a worship of nature as dominant must no longer be acceptable.

In an early Indian myth[12] the god Indra slays the giant female serpent Vritra and starts a new world order, but Indra's initial pride at dominance is short-lived, as the god Vishnu sends a young boy to teach Indra a lesson in humility. The boy tells Indra that there have been many Indras before him, and they have all been demoted back to the level of an ant; "'each ant in the greater procession was once an Indra whose noble and reverent deeds elevated him to the rank of King of the Gods. But each, through many births into this world, has become again an ant. See the army of former Indras, now crawling in dumb obedience across your floor.... Death masters all'" (Leeming & Page, *God*, 151–2). Indra upon hearing this learns to play "his proper role in the endless turning of the wheel of life" (Leeming & Page, *God*, 152). The fact that this myth begins with one era being replaced by another, as Indra slays Vritra, suggests too that Indra will also fall. The shifting of power is part of the cycle of life; therefore, it is part of the representation of the Goddess. This myth focuses on an element that lessens the importance of this power shift. Here, the Goddess was subjected to the natural cycle as well, just as her successor will be, but it also maintains that the cycle is endless, and a return to what the Goddess represents is eminent.

As with the example of Indra, world myth repeatedly shows that the death and demotion of the Mother Earth Goddess is just one stage in an endless natural cycle. In nature, everything must die so that the greater cycle can continue. Therefore, mythically Indra had to kill off the serpent to initiate the next stage of life, just as his counterparts Marduk and Apollo had to kill their respective serpents. Even the Goddess, representing nature, must die in order to resurrect, and resurrect she assuredly will.

Once the Mother Goddess, and her often serpent representations are destroyed, the lesson of nature's cycles—life, death, rebirth—becomes increasingly removed from people's psyches. If one embraces the Earth Goddess and her mythic serpents, as depicted with the figurine from Crete that depicts a female holding two snakes in her outstretched hands as she stands entranced with seemingly spiritual knowledge, then one learns the lessons of nature. This handling of snakes is certainly a dangerous endeavor, but encounters with the mythic Goddess, as with nature itself, seldom provide only situations of comfortable safety. Embracing the serpent suggests that the Hebrew Eve or any mythic character brave enough to face the terrifying and destructive elements of nature are partaking of divine wisdom.

3

Divine Nature

"Man models himself on earth,
Earth on heaven,
Heaven on the way,
And the way on that which is natural."
                                        —Lao Tzu

"The happiest man is he who learns from nature the lesson of worship."
                                        —Ralph Waldo Emerson

As long as mythology has existed, so too has the association that divine beings are connected to nature. Early humans connected the majesty, and sometimes the horror, of the natural world to spiritual beliefs. Transfiguring natural aspects to divine roles was a common occurrence; "the very existence of the gods was inseparable from that of a storm, a sea, a river" (Armstrong, *Short History,* 5–6). As discussed in the creation myths of chapter 1, nature was often personified and attributed as forming the basis for life on earth. Sometimes divinities appear as primordial beings whose very body is used to create life, and sometimes they are representations of natural occurrences or the environment itself. As civilizations arose in the Neolithic era, divine personifications of nature were designed to meet the needs of assuring a plentiful harvest each year, and female and male roles were assigned to divinities as their functions suggested when witnessing natural reproductive processes. Environmental predictability in agriculture was attributed to defining gods and goddess as benevolent or malevolent.

In the period of early civilizations (c. 4,000–800 BCE), mankind shifted again its focus from agricultural subsistence to what appears to resemble in many ways modern understandings of civilization, and again, with this shift, as seen from the Paleolithic to the Neolithic period, the mythology changes. In this new era gods and goddesses became redefined. As stated in chapter 2, male divine beings in large part took over control of mythic pantheons, and goddesses became demoted through most often a dividing up of her personifications; this demotion of a central female divinity into many lesser divinities can also be understood as devaluing the reverence for nature. As civilizations advanced technologically, nature began to play a secondary role in the daily lives of human beings, and with this their portrayal of mythic divinities became more complex, as they often no longer appeared directly connected with the cycles of the earth. Still, though, even with these newly defined pantheons, there is evidence that reverence for nature, even as a personified female earth or as divinities symbolic of environmental elements, remained as a central component of many ancient belief systems. It also is important to note that in many communities that remained directly dependent on the environment, there can be viewed a consistent mythological reverence for nature as sacred. Whether civilizations appeared removed from nature or not, the natural archetypes that shaped our earliest myths were so embedded in our storytelling techniques, and in our envisioning of life on earth, that it is not hard to see a continuation of divine nature even in works from contemporary times.

Throughout the Paleolithic, Neolithic, and certainly into later eras, myriad world myths portray the importance of appeasing divine beings as representations of nature, as angry nature divinities, such as early versions of the Roman god Vulcan or the Polynesian goddess Pele, could erupt when angered, killing all earthly inhabitants in their vicinity. Also, in world myth, there are many accounts of disappointed or wrathful gods sending environmental disasters such as immense floods to wipe out whole communities. Conversely, often nature divinities are also mythically portrayed as educators to audiences, similar to how Neolithic nature divinities instructed ritual initiates the proper techniques of a successful crop.

The Sacred Earth

Multiple civilizations recount myths that view the earth itself as being alive, and as has been stated, it is often conceived of as a divine female. Hymn XII.I, "A Hymn of Prayer or Praise to Deified Earth" from the Indian *Hymns of the Atharva Veda*[1] reveals this conception:

> May Earth...
>
> pour out for us delicious nectar, may she bedew us
> with a flood of splendor....
>
> On whom the running universal waters flow day and night with
> never-ceasing motion,

May she with many streams pour milk to feed us, may she
bedew us with a flood of splendour....

May Earth pour out her milk for us, a mother unto me her son.

Similarly, in "To Nature" from the Greek *Hymns of Orpheus*,[2] nature is also
described as divine:

Nature, all parent, ancient, divine,
O much-mechanic mother, art is thine;
Heav'nly, abundant, venerable queen,
In ev'ry part of thy dominions seen.
Untam'd, all-taming, ever splendid light,...
Finite and infinite alike you shine;
To all things common and in all things known,
Yet incommunicable and alone.
Without a father of thy wondrous frame,
Thyself a father whence thy essence came....
Immortal, Providence, the world is thine,
And thou art all things, architect divine.

Many ancient belief systems, like traditional Japanese Shintoism and
African and American Indian religion attributed spirituality to all aspects of
nature, so that every mountain, stream, and animal for example, possessed
a spirit. Parts of nature also have been mythically defined as divine for thousands of years, such as the sky and rain. The most prominent divinities in
many ancient pantheons are portrayed as natural elements; for example, many
civilizations portray the sun and moon as divine. The divine sun in a multi-
tude of cultural myths often disappears, "depriving the world of food and
warmth," and conversely in Chinese and African myth there are tales where
there exists too much sunlight, and so the divinity must be partially overcome,
so the inhabitants of earth may thrive (Wilkinson 8–9).

Occupants of the Arctic region also believe that the land is divine; "Not
just animals and plants ... but every mountain and snowstorm had what the
Inuit call *inua*, or in-dwelling beings. The word comes from the same root
as 'Inuit'—'man' or 'inhabitant'—itself, a mark of the continuity this people
saw between man and nature. No superiority set ... the human apart" (Allan,
Phillips, & Kerrigan 53). In the cultures existing in the Arctic, the land is
believed to possess

an elemental life-force, it ... resonates with myriad associations of myth.... For
every aspect of life and culture is reflected in the environment.... Arctic-dwellers
know each mountain, each promontory or inlet by its own name.... Thus
enshrined in the Arctic landscape are multifarious clues as to its effective use,
but the scene also serves as an anthology of stories.... Knowing their own native

region as a "memoryscape," Arctic-dwellers orientate themselves both geographically and psychologically [Allan, Phillips, & Kerrigan 45].

With severe weather conditions and limited natural resources, the people of the Arctic must respect the environment in which they live. Out of this endurance comes a deep respect for nature. The inhabitants of the Arctic learn a great deal from observing the animals around them, and often this observation of wildlife becomes tied to spirituality; "a great Dene shaman Yamoria once spent a year as a beaver, living in a lake in his native northwestern Canada" (Allan, Phillips, & Kerrigan 68). Yamoria felt that he learned a great deal by watching the productivity of the beavers in the summer as they prepared for the long winter ahead. He asked the beavers why they never slowed their pace, or why they sought the trees far away instead of the ones close at hand. The beavers stated that they were capable of going far away to get trees for their protective lodge in the summer, and since they knew they would be unable to do this in the approaching winter, they worked harder now to protect their beaver community in the future. Yamoria learned techniques from the beavers that would help his own people survive the severe conditions of their environment (Allan, Phillips, & Kerrigan 68).

In India, it is believed that before the invasion of the Indo-Europeans, people of the Indus Valley worshipped a Mother Goddess figure. In their close kinship with the land for survival, they worshipped the earth in this divine female form. Later, as belief systems became modified, this central Mother Goddess was said to take on many forms, as often happened in many world mythologies, like in the Greek Olympian pantheon. In India "all the goddesses are considered aspects of one great female deity" (Phillips, Kerrigan, & Gould 93). Her worship did not die out with the coming of new male deities, as in Hinduism "no Hindu god can function without his female consort, and the thousands of local folk deities found throughout the Indian countryside are mostly female" (Phillips, Kerrigan, & Gould 114). Even in modern times, there are many devotees of Shakti as a representation of the Mother Goddess who "is the mother of everything," and "at the end of each age, or *yuga,* it is Shakti who withdraws the manifested universe back into her being and in the dark night between creations all that exists lies and rests in her" (Phillips, Kerrigan, & Gould 93). Today "in rural areas of India, people rely on the land as much as they did in 3,000 BC[E], and folk religion remains focused on keeping the land fertile. The goddess, bringer of fertility, can be worshipped anywhere: in the land itself, in mountains, rocks, fields, plants, trees, and rivers (Phillips, Kerrigan, & Gould 112).

Russian and Slavic communities, dependent upon agriculture for subsistence, held the earth as "holy and wise.... The ancestors of the first Slavs on the Russian plains almost certainly worshipped the earth in the form of an Earth Mother fertility goddess" (Phillips & Kerrigan 54). The earth (*zemlya*) is worshipped as a female divinity:

> To an agricultural community, in particular, earth is the moist and fertile provider of crops, into which the seeds of future life are sown.... There is a strong sense, in Russian beliefs and customs associated with the earth, of a living entity whose good will must be earned and whose feelings must be respected. Those who worked the land entered into a delicate personal relationship with it [Warner 28–9].

This Slavic Earth Mother was named "Mati Syra Zemlya (Damp Mother Earth). Normally she was not given a specific form, but her spirit was said to be embodied in the fertile earth.... Even though she usually lacked a shape, she was seen as vibrantly alive and, therefore, helped everything in the soil to come to life.... People worship her by digging a hole in the ground and putting in offerings of bread and wine" (Wilkinson 89).

Many early Russian customs indicate this respect for the divinity of the earth, such as consuming a bit of earth when one makes a solemn vow, as with marriage (Phillips & Kerrigan 54) or providing a gift of salt to the earth after the harvest. In many Russian myths the earth is portrayed as sleeping in the winter months; sometimes the Mother Earth principle described the earth as being pregnant in its period of winter dormancy, so that in winter "it was considered inadvisable to harm it by invasive acts such as ploughing, digging or knocking in stakes for the construction of fences" (Warner 29). Only upon the earth's waking up in spring, would such work be permitted.

The early Slavs also believed in many other deities who were embodied in the natural elements of the earth. They believed in their sky god, Svarog, as their central deity; Svarog had two sons named Dazhbog and Svarozhich, who represented the sun and fire. In addition, Perun, the thunder god, Stribog, god of winds, and the Rozhanitsy "a pair of fertility goddesses [who] ... presided over ... the harvest" were also important divinities in the Slav pantheon who represented natural elements (Wilkinson 82). All of these Slavic divine beings were deeply connected to nature. Perun, the thunder god, was feared by the people for his immense ferocity, but he was also a god who was revered by the people because he was known for tearing apart any cloud that hid the sun's light from allowing a successful growing season. Again, like the Greek god Dionysus, the Slavs also had a god associated with the grape harvest and the making of wine; their god was named Kurent, and in some festivals celebrating the arrival of spring in Slovenia, they still wear masks made of sheepskin to celebrate Kurent. Cultures of Central and Eastern Europe also have many myths that recount mythical beings or spirits living in or embodied as natural environments. It is from the Czech Republic that the Christian tradition of decorating Easter eggs can be traced back to pre–Christian times where the egg was recognized as a fertility symbol associated with rebirth (Wilkinson 83). Images of the egg also representing fertility are seen in ancient civilizations such as the statue depicting Diana of Ephesus in Anatolia.

In addition, the earth as a divine figure often was connected to a belief in death in Russian and East Slavonic mythology. If a plague hit the community, "a ritual furrow was ploughed around the village. In a reversal of normal agricultural practice the participants in this magical act, whose purpose was the release of the generative and therefore death and disease-defying forces of the earth, were not men but exclusively women" (Wilkinson 29). In this sacred ritual women ploughed the earth to drive out death and entice the female generative forces the earth held to resume its cycle back towards the production of new life. If a man ever even witnessed this secret ritual, he could be killed by his community.

Many American Indian tribes also identify the earth as both feminine and divine; "Mother Earth takes many forms. She provides everything to sustain life and more: she is the nurturer. She is a point of origin and a point of completion. As the Ojibwe say: 'Woman is forever, eternal: man comes from woman and to woman he returns'" (Zimmerman 25). Belief in the earth as mother accounts for a collectivity between all of the inhabitants of the earth; the American Indian Earth Mother has "many faces, as numerous as her divine landscapes, and all of her children affirm their kinship with her" (Lowenstein & Vitebsky 48). The Peruvians believe in a Mother Goddess who is the earth itself; "she is the mother of everything, absorbing her children back into her body when they die, and according to herbalists it is her blood that flows through plants and gives them their healing powers" (Allan, Bishop, & Phillips 96). Many American Indian people also believe in the concept of the Great Spirit, in which "permeates all people, animals, places, and phenomena" (Lowenstein & Vitebsky 30).

Place within the environment is a key component to American Indian worship. In order to maintain sustainability, American Indians developed close ties with the landscape around them, and thus their mythology records the importance of the meaning of the various topography they live amongst. For example, "sites can become important because of their unusual appearance, as with the skull-shaped Blood Rock" in northwestern Canada where the Dogrib Indians believe their cultural hero Yomosh was born (Zimmerman 27); "places at a high altitude are closer to the juncture of earth and sky, and it is therefore thought that certain spirits may be more accessible here.... Some places become intertwined with oral tradition and tribal myth because 'history,' and thus the tribe's 'character,' is thought to have originated there. Wind Cave in the southern Black Hills is where the Lakota people were tricked by the spider Iktomi into emerging" (Zimmerman 27). And, Niagara Falls was believed by the Iroquois to be the voice of an immense Thunder Being represented as the spirit of the water (Zimmerman 36). The elements within nature, like rain storms or blizzards, were also believed to possess awareness, and sometimes could be influenced through ceremony.

The Aboriginal Australians identify a sacred energy that they believe resonates through all nature called djang; "the creative energy by which the world was originally formed, djang, is literally as old as the hills. The Dreamtime stories tell how spirit beings metamorphosed into things which remain in the landscape" (Allan, Fleming, & Kerrigan 25). Djang is a force that the Aboriginals believe they can tap into through reverence of nature, bringing sun or rain when needed.

The Divine Elements of Nature

The deification of the sun and moon was centrally important to the creation of many cultures' divine pantheons and mythologies. The Egyptians defined the Sun as Rê; the Inca believed in Inti as their sun god, and in Japan, the sun was the goddess Amaterasu. The principle of natural balance found with the transference of day to night and night to day was central to the beliefs of many ancient cultures upon viewing the daily cycles of the natural world; "in early times the existence of the two great heavenly bodies, one visible by day, the other by night, led people to speculate that the universe was ordered by contrasting principles, with pairs of opposites regulating life's flow" (Allan & Phillips, *World,* 41). Both qualities of the sun and of its mythic opposite the moon was viewed as vitally important for the continuation of all life; "the nurturing, life-giving qualities of sunlight were fundamental to agriculture, while the lunar cycle emphasized the predictable, recurring rhythms of life, death and rebirth" (Allan & Phillips, *World,* 41).

A Chinese myth, "Archer Hou Yi and Chang-O,"[3] recounts how there was initially ten suns, all of which were divine brothers. One day, instead of rotating shifts, they decide that they all want to burn bright day in and day out; this causes the earth to enter into severe drought, and many people begin to die or develop burned skin and bones. The Heavenly Emperor Di Jun, who was the father of the ten suns, regretfully asks that the Archer Hou Yi come and shoot down some of his sons. Hou Yi is successful, and this explains why today there is only one sun left to warm the earth.

Mountains were also highly revered in world mythology for the grandiose effect they played on human imagination. Oftentimes, cultures believed that their divine beings resided atop of high mountain peaks, like the Greek Mount Olympus being considered the home of the Olympian pantheon. Many civilizations worshipped the high peaks of their environment; the Incas felt that mountains allowed them to get closer to their gods, so this is where they chose to make their sacrificial offerings. In addition, Mount Alburz in Iran was said to be the home of the sun god Mithra; Mount Kailash in western Tibet is sacred to Hindus, Buddhists, and the indigenous Tibetan Bon religion, and Mount Kunlun in China was also venerated for "linking earth and sky" (Allan & Phillips, *World,* 23).

Caves were also revered in many cultures. Very often caves signified the entrance to the underworld, thought also to be the womb of the earth, so caves to many civilizations were considered consecrated. Priestesses of Minoan culture in Crete would conduct their sacred rituals within caves, as would the Inca of what is now Peru. In Crete, the worship of caves has been documented; clay vessels, grains, and animal bones have all been found within or near separate caves on the island, as has "double-axes, some made of gold, hundreds of long, thin swords, daggers and knives, and also bronze [and clay] figurines" (Burkert 25). The cave of Eileithyia at Amnisos shows Minoan period worship as

> not far from the entrance is an oval elevation like a belly with a navel, and at the back of the cave is a seated figure; at the very centre [sic] of the cave is a stalagmite resembling a female figure ... the figure is surrounded by a low wall and has an altar-like stone block pushed in front of it; the stalagmite seems to have been touched, smoothed, and polished by countless human hands. Pools of mineral water from which water was obviously drawn are found at the very back of the cave. Here people must have come to seek help in contact with the mysterious powers. Eileithyia is the Greek goddess of birth [Burkert 26].

In addition, rocks were respected as worthy of worship in many ancient communities. Significant rock formations inspired awe in ancient people, and because of this, mythic explanations evolved to account for them. Also on Crete, the site of Phaistos suggests the worship of rocks as sacred, as there are many carved images in stone still preserved at the site. A conical shaped rock, known as the omphalos of the earth, was worshipped at the holy site of Delphi in Greece. In fear of defeat by the Carthaginians, the Romans took the advice of the Cumaean Sybil and sought a meteorite from Anatolia that was believed to be the mountain goddess Cybele; they carried this meteorite back in their ship to Rome and erected a temple to Cybele, the Great Mother, on Palatine Hill where the meteorite served as the face of the Goddess. The Inca, Aboriginal Australians, and American Indians were also known to venerate rocks as representations of their ancient ancestors.

Many cultures also viewed volcanoes as possessing divinity. The Polynesian goddess Pele is the goddess of volcanoes. Many myths describe her impetuous temperament; one moment she may be docile and content, but if someone or something angers her, she spews forth fiery vengeance. Oftentimes, her wrath, that is of course accompanied by "thunder and lightning, earthquake[s], and streams of burning, steaming lava" (Andersen 268), is seemingly unjustified in her myths. Her anger and subsequent destruction occurs without cause; this aspect, portrayed mythically as a divine goddess, explains the unpredictable and apparently indifferent wrath of nature.

In one of her myths, Pele is described as being associated with death. As a nature goddess, she moves easily between forms; she poses as an old woman or a young maiden depending on her mood; she can also transform from tangible form to that of a spirit. Lured by the sound of drumming, Pele, asleep, followed the sound in her spirit form until she found a young prince named Lohiau. Seeing him, she fell in love with him and changed her spirit form into a young and beautiful maiden; he, knowing nothing of the divinity of this alluring stranger, also fell in love with her and shortly married her. But, Pele had to return to her home in Hawaii as mistress of volcanoes, so she left her love behind. Lohiau was so distraught that he died mysteriously of grief. Pele, who never thought she would think again of Lohiau found that she too began to miss him, so she launched a plot to have her sister, Hiiaká, find him. Hiiaká traveled to the underworld, found him, and eventually fell in love with him herself though. Lohiau briefly was brought back to life. Pele, upon Hiiaká's and Lohiau's return, was so outraged that she again killed Lohiau by burning him to ash. Hiiaká, fully in love with Lohiau, allowed herself to also descend into death. Seemingly without cause, Pele, "in one of her sudden and unpredictable revulsion of feeling" (Andersen 276), then enticed both Hiiaká and Lohiau to come back to life and granted them her blessing for their united happiness.

The myth recounts Pele as unpredictable because she represents a force that to ancient Polynesians was viewed as instantaneously harsh and unforgiving, and then just as immediately, calm and regretful. The myth also discusses the connection of love of the natural world. Lohiau falls passionately in love with the mysterious divine Pele, but he cannot simply continue an existence where he only loves her without knowing her. To know and embrace nature, one must accept the realistic, harsher sides of nature. Pele is benevolent, but she also must be malevolent; this is why she is impelled, though she loves Lohiau, to return to Hawaii to maintain her duty as goddess of the volcanoes. Lohiau's death at the loss of Pele is significant as well; often in nature myths, as discussed in chapter 2, death is an integral part of the myth's message. In nature, death appears as a momentary stage; it is a necessary time of destruction that enables regeneration. Lohiau in learning who his bride really is must face death, but like nature, he is mythically portrayed as being resurrected with the help of Pele's divine sister Hiiaká. The myth splits the portrayal of the goddess at this point; Pele now remains only harsh, and Hiiaká takes the role of benevolent nurturer who rescues and resurrects Lohiau from the underworld. Pele, in her volcanic wrath, slowly kills him again, but then abruptly takes on her full Earth Goddess role again and grants both Lohiau and Hiiaká forgiveness. Lohiau, as the mortal of the story, learns that nature comes with both ferocity and sublimity; he must love both to fully live.

As a needed life-giving force to plants, animals, and humans alike, many cultures viewed water as also sacred. The Ganges River in India is viewed as sanctified; "according to the myth, the Ganges flows from Vishnu's toes through heaven, earth, and the underworld" (Phillips, Kerrigan, & Gould 51). Oftentimes, as with the Slavs and Celts, people made offerings to rivers, lakes, or springs, believing them to be divine. A common mythic belief was that water held mystical healing qualities; "In France the source of the Seine … was the centre [sic] of a temple complex in Roman times, while in Britain people came from all parts to visit the site the Romans called Aquae Sulis, the water of the god Sulis, which later became the city of Bath" (Allan & Phillips, *World,* 48). For the Slavic people, springs or pools held "wondrous healing powers…. By a tradition still alive in the nineteenth century, sick people seeking healing would visit the sacred spring, cast a piece of bread into it and ask forgiveness of the water mother or spirit. The ancient midsummer rites of Kupala, which involved ritual bathing and offerings to the water, preserved the cult of water spirits" (Phillips & Kerrigan 49). This mythical explanation for the renewing power of water is often represented in world myth, as it was even portrayed in the conquistador Ponce de León's belief that there existed a Fountain of Youth.

The American Indian Iroquois present a myth of the healing powers found in water.[4] The protagonist of the myth, Nekumonta, and his people first encountered a winter so harsh that it left his people weak, and then what followed threatened to decimate the Iroquois Nation. A great plague hit, and Nekumonta had to watch as his parents, all his siblings, and his own children succumbed to the plague. Finally, he realized that his wife too was near death, and he vowed to go in search of the great Manitou to see where he "had planted His healing herbs" (Ferguson 155). As he partook of his quest, he stopped and asked the animals of the forest for assistance, but they simply looked away knowing that his mission was futile. Finally, Nekumonta fell down upon the earth exhausted, and the same animals gathered around him and watched him while he was sleeping; "Each one of them had known Nekumonta to be a sympathetic man—a compassionate hunter, a protector of the flowers and the trees" (Ferguson 156). The animals all raised their voices in unison to the Great Manitou, and hearing this connected voice, the Manitou acknowledged their cry.

The Manitou gave Nekumonta a dream; in it he saw his wife singing, and then replacing her image, he saw a clear and beautiful spring. He awoke but saw no water; suddenly he felt that he must begin to dig into the earth to find the water he knew would heal his wife. Here again, this myth expounds on the belief that new life is obtained from within the earth; the element of pure spring water residing within the ground adds to its belief in holding healing properties.

The digging into the earth for Nekumonta must be an intense undertaking, as with most myths, he must prove himself worthy of finding the source of the healing water. He is portrayed as digging and digging, scraping the frozen ground with a piece of flint, until he finally finds what he has been searching for. When Nekumonta finds the coveted source of healing, he immediately knows that his instincts to ceaselessly search were worthwhile; the spring is surrounded by abundant and verdant life, and he lays his whole body within the pool. The water immediately heals Nekumonta physically and spiritually. After thanking the Manitou, he makes a jar from the clay of the earth, hardens it in fire, and pours the water into it, so that he may heal the sole survivor of his family.

Nekumonta returns to his people with the boon of his journey; he tells the sick where to find the spring of the Manitou and proceeds to help his wife drink from the cup of life. She falls into slumber and awakens renewed. Again, this myth follows archetypes seen in many myths associated with nature. Nekumonta is permitted to search for the renewing aspects that nature provides; though no one believes he can do it, he continues his journey. His quest becomes a psychological one, where he internally knows, through believing his dream, where to find the natural source that will give new life to his wife, thus assuring his own renewed life. The myth follows the same pattern of life and death discussed in many myths thus far, but it also shows that out of the earth, new life can be sought and attained; Nekumonta knows this natural wisdom, and so he succeeds in his quest.

Nature Represented as World Divinities

In Egyptian mythology there are many divine representations of nature and its processes, as again agricultural sustenance depended on a close examination of the cycles of the seasons. The predictable flooding of the Nile each summer allowed Egyptians the means to survive as the receding waters created ideal farm land; if however, the Nile failed to comply to its predictable pattern, then "people would starve in the thousands ... the waters were regarded as a miracle from above—proof that there was an order to the universe and that the Egyptians were its deserving beneficiaries" (Fleming & Lothian 8). In fact, the Egyptian belief of an afterlife stemmed from their perception of the Nile and its regenerative power to both destroy and bring forth new life.

Some versions of Egyptian creation describe Maat as a goddess that is the earth itself. Other versions describe creation coming from the Egyptian serpent goddess Ua Zit who "was the world rising from a fiery island of the Nile, the womb that arose from the reeds of the delta, the Cobra Goddess who spread her hood so that the future would be known. Born again from each shedding of her skin, she was known as the third eye, the all-seeing eye in the holy forehead, and she spat forth her venomous and fiery spells of wisdom" (Leeming & Page, *Goddess,* 45). The Egyptian gods and goddesses regarded Ua Zit as a force of balance; she was the source of knowledge, as for them creation was said to have come from a formless abyss, known as Nuu. And from Nuu birthed Rê, the sun. It is Rê who created all beings. And from his thoughts, he is said to have created Shu and Tefênet, the upper and lower air, and from their union came Oêb and Nut, the earth and sky; once the earth and sky formed a union, they produced Osiris and Isis and their siblings: Thout, Nephthys, and Sêth (Colum 1). In time Rê "exerted such a strong influence that most other significant gods were eventually subsumed into the sun cult by the process of syncretism ... for example, Rê was combined with the two major creation deities, Atum and Amun, to produce the hybrid entities, Atum-Re and Amun-Re. Thus the sun god came to be worshipped as the creator" (Fleming & Lothian 34).

Leeming and Page state:

> The greatest and most powerful of the matrilineal cultures of the Neolithic Near East was that of Egypt, where goddess had first reigned supreme, probably in the predynastic period (before 3,000 BCE), as Nut, as the great snake Ua Zit, as the more abstract Maat, and as Hathor. Hathor is the Eye of the Universe and the carrier of the ankh—the Egyptian looped cross that symbolizes life. She is also the sacred Cow of Heaven who can become the Great Serpent [*Goddess,* 43].

Hathor is also identified with fertility and the underworld. Hathor was "often depicted as welcoming souls into the underworld with the beneficent gifts of refreshing food and drink.... [She] was customarily depicted as a cow leaving the arid desert, where most pharaonic burials took place, to drink from the papyrus marshes" (Fleming & Lothian 60). In Hathor's creation myth, she as the sacred Cow of Heaven, waits in the sanctified sycamore tree. Her representation of her cow form speaks towards her ability to provide a food staple to her people—the milk of life. She waits in her tree in order to welcome "back those exhausted by life on earth"; as they ascend to her realm.

Though Hathor is a benevolent goddess, like most representations of early Earth Goddesses, she too can be a vicious goddess, becoming known as another of her forms—Sekhmet (Colum 5). When she discovers that some of her offspring, the people of the earth, try to overthrow the power of the sun god Rê, she turns herself into Sekhmet, portrayed as a lioness, and pursues the men, killing them. As she does this task, she finds that she enjoys it and continues to slaughter the people of the earth for their insolence; "Was not, she raged, all humankind unworthy of the life she had given them" (Leeming & Page, *Goddess,* 44). She must be reminded by Rê that enough bloodshed has occurred, as he begins to see that the world suffers from starvation without the benevolence of Hathor. This myth shows the dualistic side of nature. With the several representations that Hathor can transform into, she is a representation of the earth, and if the people forget the power of nature, she certainly reminds them.

Isis is one of the most renowned and enduring of Egyptian divinities; she too probably "evolved from an early fertility goddess. Archaeological evidence has shown that the Egyptians worshipped a goddess ... [who] clearly demonstrated her fecundity" (Fleming & Lothian 58). Many myths of Isis show her in quite a powerful role; she possesses mystical wisdom, formidable enough to raise the dead, much like many of her other Earth Goddess counterparts. Within one myth, Isis is portrayed as lacking one thing however—the power that comes from receiving the true name of the sun god Rê. Rê is shown at this point in the myth as an old man, asleep and drooling, barely able to move about. Isis came to him and stole some of his saliva. Using her magical powers, she mixed the saliva with clay and formed a poisonous serpent; she then, as she often does in her myths, breathed life into the snake. Knowing that each day Rê went for a walk, she placed the serpent in his path, so that eventually Rê was bitten by the snake. In agony Rê begged the other gods and goddesses for assistance, but the myth shows that they do not possess the ability to save the sun god; they can only lament at the loss of life that will soon follow if the sun dies. Isis, though, stepped forth and told Rê that if he tells her his true name, she will cure him. Often in myth, the true name or form of a god or goddess is viewed as a factor that carries with it the power of the divine being. Whoever learns the truth of the deity's identity will hold the wisdom and power of that particular being, if they can survive the onslaught of divine truth, as the Greek mother of Dionysus, Semele, could not when she was consumed by flames upon seeing the true form of Zeus. Similarly, the Hebrew Moses had to view Yahweh in the muted form of a burning bush in order to learn his true name, Elohim, as presumably the full sight of Yahweh would destroy Moses. Rê, after trying to defy Isis' request, eventually could not stand the agony of the venom surging through his body, so he revealed his true name to her. Isis was mythically represented then as obtaining the last bit of power she desired, the true name of Rê. Isis used the new found power of Rê to cure him. Mythically she is presented here as dominant over the central deity of Egyptian mythology, an indication of the vital role Isis held in the Egyptian pantheon.

The myth of Isis and Osiris is the most well-known of Egyptian myths. The myth conceptualizes death for its audiences in natural terms, and it relates how both Isis and Osiris, and the other divinities in the myth, are representations of natural occurrences. Again, Osiris and Isis are said to have come from the same mother, the Goddess Nut, along with Thout, Nephthys, and Sêth. Osiris eventually rules on earth, but he is only one dimensional, as during Osiris' rule, there is no death for earthly inhabitants. The myth recounts how death comes to the earth with the death of Osiris himself. Osiris is described as a god who educates humanity on the skills needed for survival, which is a common mythic archetype—the god/goddess who serves to teach people how to exist in the realm created by nature divinities. It is said that it was he "who first planted the vine ... [and] showed men how and when to sow grain, how to plant and tend the fruit-trees; he caused them to rejoice in the flowers also" (Colum 1). It is clear that Osiris is viewed here as a nature divinity whose role is to educate humanity on how to live in accordance with nature's balance.

Sêth is mythically described as being synonymous with the barren desert; ruling this domain he grows jealous of Osiris, who invigorates continuous new life to grow in abundance wherever he walks. Before the season of drought, it is said that Sêth invited all his siblings to a feast. There he fashioned a wooden box with the exact measurements of Osiris' body; he welcomed each of his siblings to try lying in the box to see if it fit them, stating that whoever fit perfectly would get to keep the box as a gift. They all try and of course do not fit, until Osiris lies within the box. Finding that it is a perfect fit, Osiris looks up to see his brother Sêth enclosing him in the box and nailing it shut. Osiris, as a god associated with verdant life, must learn of death, as this is an archetype seen in myths around the world where the god or goddess who represents life must face human mortality, as Inanna/Ishtar had to do.

Sêth then places Osiris in his wooden chamber into the Nile and lets it float away. Isis takes it upon herself to partake on a journey to find her dead brother/husband. She searches everywhere along the Nile with no success. This representation of the goddess that must endeavor upon a journey to seek out a lost deceased loved one is also a common theme in world myth. As discussed Anat must search for the dead Baal, as the Greek Demeter also must search for her deceased Persephone. This concept of searching out the dead requires time, and mythically it is portrayed as connecting to the progression of the seasons; new life takes time to emerge from the decayed matter of the dead, so the goddess in searching high and low throughout the land is representative of the time of seasonal dormancy.

In the Greek Plutarch's version of this Egyptian myth, which may not accurately represent the original Egyptian version, but still is mythically revealing for its connection to divinity and nature, the box holding the corpse of Osiris eventually nestles between a patch of growing trees; "a tree, growing, had lifted it up. The branches of the tree wrapped themselves around it; the bark of the tree spread itself around it; at last the tree grew there, covering the chest with its bark" (Colum 3). Isis eventually hears of this enormous tree that the King of Byblos has placed within his castle, and seeking it out, she finds upon seeing it that it is the tree that harbors the secret of life within it. Osiris' symbolic immersion into a tree clearly indicates his tie to the natural cycles of life, as Osiris, having died, floats enclosed in a seed-like vessel, until he grows ready to emerge again within the burgeoning tree. His dead corpse resides inside this natural vegetative element, signaling to mythic audiences the natural assurance that always out of death comes new life.

Isis then enters into the palace of the King of Byblos and becomes a nursemaid to the king's child. Isis nurses the royal couple's infant child and then decides to make this infant immortal by placing the child within a sacred fire until his morality is burned off of him. The mother of the child, however, sees this action taking place, and fails to understand it as a divine act, so she rescues her child. This scene is quite similar to the scene of Demeter searching for her daughter Persephone and shows components of both Egyptian and Greek culture as represented by the Greek Plutarch's understanding of the myth. As they partake on their journeys to find their dead loved ones, the earth is described as barren, for without Osiris and Persephone, Isis and Demeter do not promote growth and life sustenance. They both come upon infants, and try to remove the mortality from the children, as they are under the pain of experiencing the loss of a loved one. They strive to mystically remove death, but both fail, and here the myths teach audiences that death cannot be overcome so easily with magic. Yet, both myths do continue to show that physical death can be symbolically overcome through accepting one's role in the natural cycles of life. Though Plutarch may have misrepresented some of the elements of the myth in an effort to connect the Egyptian myth to his own Greek ideology, Plutarch's version still maintains the vital connection between nature's necessary cycles of life and death and the divine representation of Isis and Osiris.

Discovered by the infant's mother, Isis abandons her attempt at making the infant immortal and instead reveals her divinity to the queen. The queen allows Isis to cut down the tree the harbors Osiris, and finding him there, she carries his corpse with her back into Egypt. Once there, the myth presents the same aspects found within the original Egyptian myth that discuss Isis hiding within the remote wilderness with Osiris' body and breathing "into his mouth, and, with the motion of her wings (for Isis, being divine, could assume wings), she brought life back to Osiris" (Colum 4). Again, as with the myth where Isis shows her mystical superiority over Rê, Isis here reveals herself to be a representation of nature. Most Egyptian versions of this myth also describe Isis and Osiris living together hidden away for a time, until another quintessential mythic element serves to remind the audience that life and death are an essential process; therefore, the idyllic ending of Isis bringing Osiris back to life cannot last. Sêth eventually finds them both and once more kills Osiris, tearing his body to pieces and scattering his remains throughout the land of Egypt. This act of the immortal being or hero being torn into pieces is one of the earliest representations of this mythic process, but it is a theme that will appear again and again in world myth; for instance, it is the fate of the Greek Dionysus, Orpheus, and even Jason who is cut up and resurrected by Medea, a priestess of the underworld goddess Hecate in some versions of the myth of Jason and the Golden Fleece. This example of Osiris helps one make sense out of this apparently odd mythic archetype. Osiris has repeatedly been connected to the renewal of life within nature; he teaches his people about the processes of nature and agriculture, and to teach mythic audiences that they too are part of this natural process of growth, harvest, decay, and new growth, he becomes part of this most primal of processes. His body is cut up, and as seeds, he is spread throughout the land; here the myth shows that through death, one nourishes the land, causing an ever-abundance of new growth—in this way all people become like Osiris himself.

The myth reveals that before Osiris there was no death, and after he dies, all earthly inhabitants must experience death, but in his death, people learn that they too can undergo the same process that he experienced, which allows mankind to also become the progenitor of everlasting new life. Wherever Osiris walked nature abounded, and similarly, humanity, in accepting the natural cycles of life and death, assures this same process. This is why the myth ends with the earth becoming barren again, jeopardizing all living beings in the era of Sêth the desert. But again Isis, as Earth Goddess, finds each piece of her husband, with the exclusion of his penis, and uses her magic to, momentarily this time, resurrect him, so she can fulfill her role in nature's process. She constructs a penis out of the natural element of clay, has sex with Osiris before he dies again, so that she can become a mother to the next generation, producing the next heir to oversee humanity—Horus.

Horus, once grown wishes to avenge his father's death and seeks to kill Sêth, but Isis steps in and will not allow it. Shockingly Horus then chops off Isis' head for intervening, but she replaces it with the head of a cow. Isis, again as Earth Goddess, knows that there will always be a time of drought and death, and as the myth teaches, this time is essential in assuring the resurrection of new life that comes each spring. Isis then makes "seed-like models of Osiris's missing part" and "went about the land planting them in the earth, and in every spot she so blessed, the river pulsed and flooded, bringing rich silt in which maize, wheat, and other crops came to life and grew" (Leeming & Page, Goddess, 81). The myth explains why death must happen to all, but it also articulates the regenerative promise of new life that comes with an acceptance of death. It teaches one to not strive for ways to avoid the time of drought and death, but to live life fully when alive. This is why the myth relates to the Egyptian belief in the afterlife where Osiris now serves as the judge of the mortal souls that enter the underworld. The combination of Osiris being the god associated with fertility and the underworld "led him to be identified with resurrection" (Fleming & Lothian 103).

Some myths recount Anat and Astarte, both Semitic goddesses as being the "foreign daughters of Rê." The influx of many neighboring cultures during the mid-second millennium BCE created assimilation of myths and their predominant figures (Fleming & Lothian 65). Both Anat and Astarte were viewed as similar to Egyptian counterparts, so their figures became represented next to similar Egyptian deities, as Anat was often linked with Hathor. In one myth combing the Middle Eastern Anat with Egyptian mythology, Sêth was said to have spotted Anat while she was bathing; he took the form of a bull and proceeded to rape her.[5] Being divine, though, Anat was only able to become pregnant by divine fire, "so her body expelled his semen with such force that it struck him in the forehead, making him dangerously ill" (Fleming

& Lothian 64). The Greeks and later Romans also heavily identified with Egyptian myths, so the assimilation of Egyptian deities into their own mythological narratives and worship was commonplace, as evidenced by the Greek Plutarch's rendition of the Isis and Osiris myth and the Roman Apuleius' novel, *The Golden Ass*, where Isis is revered as the Mother Goddess of all civilizations.

The Hittites of Anatolia, modern day Turkey, embraced a myth of Telepinu that perfectly accounts for the representation of natural cycles being tied to divinity. Wilkinson discusses that the people of West and Central Asia worshipped sky deities because their survival depended on their ability to predict the harsh weather conditions of their region, such as "the heat of the sun and … infrequent rains," in relation to crop growth (111). As a Hittite deity, Telepinu is directly connected to the fertility of the earth. In his myth, for precarious reasons, he becomes angry; the myth states that he becomes furious because he put his shoes on the wrong feet. Enraged, Telepinu retreats to seclude himself in a hidden cave where he falls asleep. His anger arriving, seemingly for no reason, allows Telepinu to align with the unpredictability of nature. While secluded in the cave Telepinu's absence makes the environment barren, as the earth falls into a state where nothing grows. Telepinu's rage upset the

> entire world of nature…. Corn, wheat, and barley no longer grew in the fields. All vegetation withered and died. Without moisture, the mountains and hills dried up…. The pastures became parched, and the springs became evaporated. Famine arose in the land; both human beings and gods feared that they would all die of starvation [Rosenberg 178].

What is more, the animals and the people could no longer conceive or give birth, as the fertility of the environment in myth is often tied to the fertility of the people.

Again, as with the myth of Hathor, the gods eventually become alarmed at the state of deprivation the people must face, so they intervene. What is interesting is that the gods also find that they are in jeopardy as well, as when they sit down to feast, they discover that without Telepinu, all that they eat does not make them full, and all that they drink does not quench their thirst. The storm god Taru decides to send an eagle to search for Telepinu, but to no avail. Finally, Taru's father, the great sun god, demands that Taru find Telepinu, so Taru, afraid for his life, goes to the Mother Goddess, Nintu. She instructs Taru to send a bee to Telepinu. Taru is skeptical that a creature as small as a bee can find and also convince Telepinu to return, but Nintu insists that her scheme will work.

It is significant that all the male deities are ineffective at finding Telepinu, and Nintu, the Mother Goddess, is the only one capable of finding him; this again connects the role of a Mother Goddess to the continuation of the natural cycles of the seasons. Nintu mythically educates audiences on not only the laws of the natural world, like pollination, but also her advice helps tie the message of the myth to the lives of man. The bee, the smallest of creatures, is essential in continuing the cycles of nature; this is a fairly common mythic element as well where small creatures overcome powerful adversaries, such as the American Indian Lakota legend where a mouse outsmarts a buffalo. This aspect in myth validates even the smallest contributors to the continuation and success of the ecosystem.

The bee successfully finds Telepinu, stings him, and causes him to awaken. The bee then, as instructed by the Mother Goddess Nintu, takes some of his wax and wipes Telepinu's eyes and his feet in order to purify him. Telepinu is outraged, and because of his rude awakening, he causes further devastation, described within the myth as natural disasters to the surrounding area. The only thing that will quell Telepinu's rage is the arrival of the healing goddess who speaks words of magic and reminds Telepinu of his natural duty:

> Then the goddess of healing and magic chanted: "Oh, Telepinu, here lies sweet and soothing essence of cedar. Let what has been deprived be restored! Here is sap to purify you.... Here lies an ear of corn. Let it attract your heart and your soul!.... When Telepinu was angry, his heart and his soul burned like brushwood. So let his rage, anger, wrath, and fury burn themselves out!" [Rosenberg 180].

The magical chant of the healing goddess again connects the myth to the archetypes of the Earth Goddess enticing nature of its promise of continuation. Similarly, the role of the Goddess is to induce growth after dormancy; just as Anat and Isis assist their male counterparts in resurrecting so that nature can become renewed, so too, in this myth, does the Goddess figure of Nintu assist Telepinu is fulfilling his annual role.

In addition to the healing goddess, a mortal man is also essential in convincing Telepinu to leave behind his wrath. The mortal is the only one who can speak to Telepinu about the toll his absence makes on mankind; he states, "'Oh, Telepinu, when you left the tree on a summer day, the crops became diseased. Oh Telepinu, stop your rage, anger, wrath, and fury!'" (Rosenberg 181). The mortal man is essential in finally purifying the divine Telepinu; this connection of a mortal being an essential component in revivifying Telepinu reveals the message of the myth. In order for the man to purify Telepinu, he tells Telepinu that his anger must go into the underworld; "'the doorkeeper has unlocked the seven bolts and opened the seven doors of the underworld'"

(Rosenberg 180–1). This statement to Telepinu reveals that the mortal man has fully learned that in order for nature to become renewed, as portrayed by the divine Telepinu, first it must experience death, just as mortals are also required to follow these same natural laws. Once this lesson is imparted to the mythic audience, Telepinu's anger vanishes as quickly as it arrived, and he returns to his benevolent role of provider. With Telepinu's mythic rebirth, the land is renewed from dormancy, and the people are said to multiply and prosper once more; "it signified fruitful breezes and fertility for every living thing" (Rosenberg 181). The ancient Hittites would reenact this mythological episode annually to assure the continuation of the cycles of nature, again as was seen with the Babylonian, Egyptian, and Greek counterparts.

In India the *Rig Veda* records the earliest known deities of the culture. These Vedic divinities are also portrayed as being closely aligned with natural elements. The most prominent Vedic deity was first Indra, the god of thunder and rain. The god Surya was thought to be a sun deity, and as other solar gods, he was associated with bringing knowledge to mankind. Surya travelled "across the sky in a chariot with a single wheel, signifying the cycle of the seasons" (Wilkinson 116). Surya's heat was so pronounced that his son was responsible for shielding its powerful rays from the earth's inhabitants in the morning. Surya's wife, Sanjana, also could not withstand Surya's powerful heat, so she mythically would transform herself into a horse and hide deep within the relief of dense forests. Surya was said to find his wife hiding because of his immense heat, so he promised to lessen his strength, so that she may sit beside him in the heavens.

Vayu was the Vedic god of the wind. The *Rig Veda* portrays Vayu as responsible for giving breath to primal man, Parusha. Agni was the god of fire, which was vital for the survival of mankind. Because of Agni's significance to aid in the survival of earth's inhabitants, he was also directly associated with ritual fire. Agni transported prayers from human beings to the gods, "his smoke indicating where sacrifices were being made" (Wilkinson 117). In this role, Agni represented the importance of sacrifice to adherents of the Vedas, as his creation myth shows the belief in the necessity of sacrificing to the gods for an assurance of the prosperous continuation of nature. Agni was said to be born three times: the first time was from water, then from air as lightning, and lastly from the earth in the form of fire; "he was so hungry that he ate his parents, and then grew tongues to lap the ghee (clarified butter) offered at altars" (Wilkinson 117).

As part of and on the periphery of the Greek Olympian pantheon were the chthonic deities who were associated with the underworld: Hecate, Demeter, Persephone, Hades, Hermes, Dionysus, the Titans, etc. The term "chthonic" refers to the earth, and a tie to the earth and the underworld signals the role these divinities played as representations of nature and its ceaseless cycles. Demeter, as goddess of the harvest, and her daughter Persephone, who by venturing annually in and out of the underworld, both represent critical aspects of the Greek conception of nature as divine. Their myth, which will be discussed in chapter 6, shows a vital connection to mankind accepting the cycles of nature. The god of the sea, Poseidon, also allowed the Greeks to conceive of the unpredictability of the sea as caused by divine interference.

In addition, virginal goddesses are often associated with nature in Greek mythology. Artemis, and her Roman counterpart Diana, for example hold great importance in their respective pantheons, as virginal goddesses of the hunt. As the twin sister of Apollo, Artemis resides in the most remote and wild of places. Many scholars point to the ancient beginnings of the goddess Artemis, the Mistress of Animals, as Armstrong states, Artemis was "a huntress and a patron of untamed nature [and] may also be a Paleolithic figure" (*Short History*, 38). Her perpetual virginity also connects her to a powerful sense of autonomy. In one myth Actaeon, a herdsman, spies Artemis bathing, and as a punishment for just seeing her nude flesh, associated with a transgression of her virginal status, she transforms him into a stag, so that his own hunting dogs tear him to pieces, perhaps reflective of the Neolithic role between Earth Goddess and her male consort.

Greek nymphs are also associated with both virginity and nature. The myth of Daphne and Apollo portrays the nymph Daphne at home in the wild recesses of nature, when Apollo catches sight of her and immediately falls in love. He pursues her without mercy, so that the gods save her by transforming her into a tree. This myth identifies the sacred connection of Daphne to both her virginity and nature, so much so that even the divine Apollo cannot breach this attachment.

The Phrygian goddess Cybele, as discussed in chapter 2 with her myth of Attis, represented another Mother Earth figure from around the 6th century BCE. She was often depicted as enthroned with her drum and accompanied by ferocious beasts, such as lions. Cybele also was connected with the mountains. The worship of Cybele spread throughout Asia Minor and into parts of south-eastern Europe. In Thrace, Cybele became welcomed in Greek mythology but often remained a mysterious and exotic divinity of nature. In Greece, her worship, often connected to other cultic activity like the followers of Dionysus, often involved celebrations of ecstasy. Cybele's and Dionysus' cults were said to share many characteristics, and both were sometimes viewed with suspicion, as often the throngs of celebrants were rowdy, ecstatic, inebriated, and composed of the lower classes. In addition, festivities to both Cybele and Dionysus involved women being allowed to celebrate outside the strict confines of their social position.

Even in Rome, Sybil was worshipped as a Mother Goddess figure. In Roman myth the Sibyls were always women who could prophesize; prophetic vision is often a mythic archetype given to women even after they have undergone a mythic demotion away from a portrayal of the Mother Goddess, such as the Pythia of Delphi in Greece, attaining prophetic vision after Apollo slays Gaia's python. In Roman myth, the Sibyls resided at the places where the earth and the underworld met (Wilkinson 55). In Italy, the Cumaean Sibyl was a beautiful maiden who Apollo fell in love with. Apollo offered her any gift she desired if she would sexually please him; she asked for immortality, and then proceeded to refuse Apollo his lustful desire. Apollo in retaliation granted the immortality he promised, but punished her by not giving her eternal youth as well, so that she would continue to age her entire life, until one day in the distant future she would have grown so old that she would have shrunk to an imperceptible size and finally disappeared. In Virgil's *Aeneid* the Cumaean Sybil, who at that time was said to be over seven hundred years old, must be consulted to determine the course of action for Aeneas. It is the Sybil who accompanies Aeneas on his journey into the underworld, so that he may become successful in his fated mission to save the Trojan culture by founding Rome. In addition, Rome adopted many gods and goddesses from Greece, but they also maintained some of their own from the ancient Etruscans; for instance, the goddesses Vesta, goddess of the hearth, is believed to be an older goddess that became assimilated into adopting the characteristics of the Greek Hestia.

The Celts were a group of separate tribes, most likely coming from Central Europe and expanding across the continent in the 5th to 3rd centuries BCE; "there were Celtic settlements in areas as far apart as Spain and Turkey, and at many places in between" (Wilkinson 71). With the expansion of the Roman Empire, the Celtic people moved into the areas of Wales, Ireland, Scotland, and western France, where they are most identified today. Because the Celts left behind no written accounts of their myths, much of what has been deciphered about the Celts is taken from archeological finds of the period, Roman conquerors, as well as from accounts written by monks in Wales and Ireland between the eleventh and fourteenth centuries CE, well after the destruction or incorporation of most traditional Celtic belief systems. Still, from what remains, one can see that nature played a crucial role in the religion of the Celts; "for the Celts, life was a fragile matter and nature a harsh reality. The powers of darkness brought to the northern countries an early, freezing winter, long months when crops could not grow, and the risk of early death from illness, starvation, or harsh weather" (Rosenberg 275).

The Celts believed that every aspect of nature was imbued with divinity; "nature, with its endless permutations of mountains, rivers, lakes, forests, trees, and animals, its boundless earth, and never ending sky, was sanctified by the Celts, and as a result, became the focus of important Celtic ritual" (Wood 27). When the Celts saw how the Greeks and Romans worshipped their divinities, in often large stone sanctuaries with myriad representations of divine beings in human form, the Celts thought this odd, as "the Celts worshipped the forces of nature and did not initially envisage deities in anthropomorphic terms" (Wood 28). The Celts, for the most part, worshipped in open, natural settings, providing few permanent structures of worship. Often the Celts held sacred rituals near springs, lakes, or groves.

The Celtic people also venerated a Mother Goddess; she was thought to be the "most widely-known female deity" (Wood 42) among the Celts. The Mother Goddess, as with many other cultures, was worshipped as a representation of the earth itself and was also connected to the assurance of fertility and abundance in nature:

> Earlier in the history of northern Europe, we hear of a goddess who was carried round in a wagon to bring fertility to men. Tacitus knew of such a goddess in Denmark, called Nerthus.... She represented *Terra Mater*, "Mother Earth," he tells us, and had the power to intervene in the affairs of men. She visited her people in a sacred wagon.... Everywhere Nerthus was warmly welcomed by the people [Davidson 94–5].

Also found throughout Germany, Holland, and Britain there are inscriptions that honor "mother" deities as nature-oriented deities (Davidson 112). Common to the worship of Earth Mother Goddesses, the Celts worshipped her under many names and forms. As Wood comments "the goddess Aveta was one of several deities worshipped at Trier, the capital of the Treveri in northeastern Gaul. Pilgrims to her shrines left small votive images of a maternal goddess holding symbols of prosperity and plenty, such as fruit, lapdogs, and babies" (42). In Celtic mythology the Tuatha De Danann are described as the tribes of the goddess Danu; she is the "goddess of many names" (Campbell, *Primitive Mythology*, 431). Danu is "Anu, a goddess of plenty," as well as "Brigit, the goddess of knowledge, poetry, and the arts" (Campbell, *Primitive Mythology*, 431). There are "two hills that overlook a valley to west of Killarney in Co. Kerry" that were given the name "De Chich Anann (the 'Paps' [breasts] of Danu)" (Wood 46), showing the role of Danu as one and the same with the earth itself. Epona, another Mother Goddess figure, was associated as the horse goddess and was highly venerated in Celtic circles and even in Rome.

The goddess Epona "was often depicted riding on a mare, perhaps accompanied by a foal, dispensing the earth's bounty of bread, grain, or fruit; or she might appear bearing a key and followed by a human figure, an image believed to represent the souls of the dead being conducted to the gates of the Otherworld" (Wood 135). There are also depictions of triple goddesses, who often together represent a unified Mother Goddess in Celtic mythology.

In addition, many Celtic people worshipped the nature god, Dagda, as a god of fertility, life, and death; he serves as a figure that connects the abundance of fertility with the reality that accompanies it—death. Dagda "brought forth the seasons, each in its proper order, by playing his harp. He also owned a wonderful bronze Cauldron of Plenty, which fed each person the amount of food he or she deserved yet satisfied the hunger of each. Dagda also owned a grove of fruit trees whose fruit was always ripe. And he had two wonderful pigs; at any time one was cooking in order to be eaten, and the other was living, waiting its turn to be cooked" (Rosenberg 285).

Various Celtic people, especially in Gaul and Britain, revered Sucellos as a deity of agriculture and forests. Not much is known about Sucellos, but it clear that his tie to fertility in nature was important, as he, like the Greek Dionysus, was represented by the grape harvest. The Celts also worshiped Cernunnos, the horned god, who had the horns and sometimes the hooves of a deer. Cernunnos was apparently worshiped all throughout Europe as a wild god, similar to the Greek Pan; "his horns suggest that he was a symbol of fertility, and to emphasize this point, he was associated with symbols such as the cornucopia (horn of plenty), with fruit, and with containers of grain. This function probably encompassed both sexual fertility and the fecundity of the fields" (Wilkinson 72). Taranis was a sky god in Britain; the Celts were believed to make "sacrifices to Taranis, with the offerings sometimes including humans who were burned alive in wooden boats or left to drown in bogs" (Wilkinson 73). Taranis, like the Greek Zeus and Roman Jupiter, was often depicted wielding a lightning bolt. Belenus, or Bel, was the Celtic god of light and the sun and was worshipped as far away as Austria and Italy; he also was often associated with the Greek god Apollo. Many of the shrines to Belenus were constructed near springs, much like Apollo's Oracle of Delphi. Wilkinson states that the Celtic springtime festival of Beltane, where people light fires to mark the lengthening of the days after winter, may be connected to the god Belenus.

The Celts performed many festivals at times associated with the harvest; "among the Celts of ancient Gaul a feast and sacrifice were offered for every animal taken in the chase, to a goddess whom the Romans associated with Diana [Greek Artemis], who was thought of as rushing through the forest...."

In a bronze statuette this same goddess of the Celts is shown riding a wild boar, 'her symbol,' as MacCulloch tells us, 'and, like herself, a creature of the forest, but at an earliest time itself a divinity of whom the goddess became the anthropomorphic form'" (Campbell, *Primitive Mythology*, 432).

In Ireland, between its conversion to Christianity in the fifth century CE and the arrival of the Vikings in the eighth century CE, it remained an anomaly, even a haven of independence as it was able to remain secluded from much of the turmoil of the rest of Europe at this time. This autonomy allowed for an interesting incorporation of Celtic and Christian beliefs to emerge. Many manuscripts of older Celtic epics began to be recorded that enabled them to be preserved; the traditional bard "had retained much of the prestige of his druid heritage, and now he was joined by monks and hermits who not only copied Latin manuscripts but also composed lyric Irish poems in their native Irish Gaelic" (Torrance 608). In the ancient poem "The Mystery" from Kathleen Hoagland's *1000 Years of Irish Poetry* (1953), one gets a sense of the unique connection of older Celtic belief within a burgeoning belief in Christianity: "I am the wind ... the wave of the ocean ... the vulture upon the rocks.... I am the God who created in the head the fire" (qtd. in Torrance 609). The poem connects the more ancient Celtic reverence for the divinity of the natural world with a presumably Christian-influenced singular divine conception of "God." As Rosenberg states of the divine Tuatha De Danann, "The great gods of the past continue to live in Ireland and will remain there as long as mortals walk the earth. The spirits dwell within the hills and beneath the earth" (284), as quite often Celtic religion and Christianity merged spiritual concepts and practices.

The Norse maintained a belief in nature divinities as well; "land spirts were thought to dwell in features of the landscape such as rocks, hills or rivers" (Auerbach & Simpson 59). The Aesir, of which Odin dominated, are generally thought of as a later addition to an older worship of nature-based fertility divinities known as the Vanir. Scholars point to first a mythic war between the two pantheons, the Vanir and Aesir, and then the co-existence of a belief in the Vanir as evidence of this belief; "Those gods who determined the course of war and sent thunder from heaven were essentially powers of destruction.... Other powers were said to dwell in Asgard with Odin and Thor whose province was of a different kind, since their sphere of influence was over the peace and fertility of the inhabited earth. These were called the Vanir ... the chief figures among them were the twin deities Freyr and Freyja" (Davidson 92). Snorri Sturulson presents Odin as declaring war against the Vanir, but after much bloodshed, both sides tired and agreed to a truce where they exchanged hostages, so that members of each pantheon had representatives in each compound; "it has also been suggested that the myth embodies a memory of a time when a warrior cult battled with a fertility cult for supremacy, and the two religions eventually fused" (Auerbach & Simpson 59). The Vanir were believed to be made up of various fertility divinities holding many names in the different localities of northern Europe. In addition, considering the harsh landscape of the northern Europeans, favor from the Vanir held a superior need, as one should consider "the grudging soil of the northern lands and the bitter winters and long nights" (Davidson 125). Davidson also holds that "behind the goddesses of the Vanir is the conception of the Earth Mother, the Great Goddess who gives shelter to us all" (126–7).The worship of the Vanir had ancient roots, and the continuation of their ritualized worship continued for centuries; the festivals surrounding the religion looked like other nature-based fertility celebrations in other civilizations, like the Greek cults of Dionysus:

> The religion of the Vanir was bound to include orgies, ecstasies, and sacrificial rites. In these, and in the turning of the earth and the dead, whose blessing would help to bring the harvest ... there seem to have been many who worshipped them with fervor and devotion, finding their cult nearer, more rewarding and comforting than that of the sky god and the willful god of war. The friendship of the Vanir had none of the treacherous, sliding quality of Odin's favours [sic], and it extended, like his, beyond the grave [Davidson 126].

The Vanir, as nature divinities were connected with death and the underworld as well; "the distant kingdom of the sky is not their concern" (Davidson 126) as this was the domain of the Aesir.

As part of the Vanir, Freyr was considered the "god of the world" or earth; he, in the poem *Skírnismál,* was said to journey to the underworld to try to get the maiden Gerd to marry him (Davidson 92). This pattern of a fertility god/goddess descending to the underworld is common to world mythology, as discussed in the previous chapter, and here too it may represent "the marriage of the god of the sky with the goddess of the fruitful earth, resulting in a rich harvest" (Davidson 93). In addition, Davidson contends that this journey to the underworld to initiate the nuptials of fertility divinities shows evidence that "implies the idea of a divine marriage formed an essential part of Freyr's cult. Just as it formed a part of the worship of the fertility gods of the Near East" (93).

In addition, when Snorri Sturulson introduces the Vanir goddess Freyja, he states that "she was the most renowned of the goddesses, and that she alone of the gods yet lived. This implies that he knew something of her worship continuing into his own day in Scandinavia.... The impressive list of places called after Freyja, especially in south Sweden and southwest Norway, shows that Snorri's estimate was no idle one" (Davidson 144–5). Freyja also is said to have had many names depending on the region in which she was worshipped, which is another trait common of Mother Earth Goddess figures. And like other Goddesses, Freyja was thought to be able to take on the shape of a bird or falcon at whim. She was also attributed as holding magical powers as well as the gift of prophecy; Freyja:

> was especially adept in the type of sorcery which in the Viking world was most similar to shamanism. *Seid,* as this was known, could be used in pre–Christian Scandinavia for divination, and although a man might conduct the rites, it was usually a woman known as a *volva* or seeress, who did so. The seeress carried a staff, and is described in one account as wearing a special costume from the skins of animals and from the feathers of birds, all of which represented spirits from the animal world who assisted her on her spiritual journey. During the ceremony, the seeress sat on a high platform, and incantations were sung to summon spirits who would reveal occult knowledge to her. This enabled her to enter into a trance, and descend into the netherworld [Auerbach & Simpson 73].

Freyja was often portrayed pulling a chariot drawn by cats; Davidson explains that cats were among the animals that the Norse considered sacred and capable of leading one on a spirit journey. The Norse believed these female seeresses would travel alone or in companies in consecrated wagons going "round to farms in Norway and Iceland," and this may have been "the final representatives of the fertility goddess in the north, the deity who, according to Snorri, survived last of all of the gods" (Davidson 121).

Freyja was said to have had sexual intercourse with her brother, fertility god Freyr, which is common for fertility divinities, consider Isis and Osiris for instance. She also was often associated with being amorous with many divine beings and humans alike, similar to Aphrodite or Ishtar. Freyja also had a connection with death and the underworld, which again, viewing her in terms of cyclical nature, is a common archetype for a fertility/nature divinity. Of the Norse warriors who die in battle, it is said that "whenever she rides into battle, half of the slain belong to her. Odin takes the other half" (Sturluson 35).

In Finnish mythology, nature spirits are said to reside in every aspect of the natural world as well; "with its deep lakes and dense forests, Finland presents a dramatic and sometimes harsh landscape. Its early ... storytellers responded to this environment by imagining a host of nature spirits who represented the character of their land" (Wilkinson 66). The Finnish god Tapio was said to have a beard made of trees and eyes made of lakes. Pellervoinen was a Finnish spirit of fertility who was responsible for planting the seeds of all the trees in Finland's forests. In Elias Lönnrot's Finnish epic the *Kalevala,*

Aino, a maiden drowns herself instead of marrying her elderly suitor, the protagonist Väinämöinin. After being born to his goddess mother Luonnotar, who became impregnated by the sea, Väinämöinin makes his way to Finland, and because of a mystical contest with a giant, won the right to marry Aino, but she doesn't want to marry the old Väinämöinin, so she decides to drown herself. Aino's death scene is depicted as "evasive, dreamlike" (Bosley xxxi) because her death is viewed less in terms of a tragedy, and more in terms of her union back into the water in which she seemingly came from; "As she dies, Aino identifies herself with the lake—the waters are her blood, the fish her flesh—turning back to inanimate nature is often found in Finnish folk poems about death" (Bosley xxxi).

In the next canto, Aino appears to the forlorn and still unmarried Väinämöinin as a mermaid, and with renewed power and authority in this transformation, she tells him that he is unworthy of her. As Väinämöinin is about to cut up what he thinks is a salmon, she in her new form speaks to him; "'O you old Väinämöinin! / I was not to be a salmon for you to cut up / a fish for you to divide.... I was not a sea salmon / a perch of the deep billow; / I was a girl, a young maid ... who you hunted all your days / throughout your lifetime longed for. / You wretched old man / you foolish Väinämöinin / for you knew no way to keep the Wave-wife's watery maid'" (Lönnrot 56–7). Though he is connected deeply to his role as a possible sea god, or at least a shaman, he is yet unable to comprehend the natural power that this maiden holds at this early point of the text.

The *Kalevala* continues to teach Väinämöinin the power of nature and the connection women hold within this power. For instance, the mother of the young and overly confident Lemminkäinen resurrects him after he has been cut up into many pieces and thrown into the river. She finds the pieces of her son, assembles them, and then proceeds to resurrect him, as discussed a mythological task that myriad goddesses have performed. In addition, much of the *Kalevala* portrays Väinämöinin journeying to Pohjola, the Northland, to find another bride, but there he encounters Louhi, a female leader of Pohjola, who possesses powerful and mystical talents that often overcome the abilities of Väinämöinin. Louhi is a force to be reckoned with because in many ways she is nature itself. The epic finally culminates in explaining, mythically, how Väinämöinin provides the Finnish people the components needed for survival, such as staple foods, livestock, and hunting and farming implements, as his task in order to win the daughter of Louhi is to create a tool, the sampo, which involves all of these essential elements. The word "sampo" means "'pillar,' leading some commentators to think it was a wooden idol; others interpret it as a magical mill bringing forth an endless supply of

salt, grain and money. Whatever the truth may have been it guaranteed prosperity for its possessors" (Allan & Phillips, *World*, 94). Väinämöinin must
concede, though, that he cannot alone provide these tools; instead, it is his
brother Ilmarinen, a blacksmith as well as a sorcerer, who is able to create
the sampo and win the right to marry Louhi's daughter. This marriage,
though, is short lived, as Louhi's daughter soon dies, and Louhi destroys the
brothers' boat as they try to make it back to Finland. Though the skills of
Ilmarinen are needed to harness nature, in the end of the epic, nature wins,
as Louhi destroys the mission. Having endured this lesson of the power of
nature, Väinämöinin is now portrayed as finally able to save the Finnish people by bestowing to them the items needed for survival—the elements of the
sampo.

   Often nature divinities serve as guides to mankind in myth; "The ani-
mistic deity ... is everywhere; its mysterious presence—what the Japanese
call *kami*, the Melanesian *mana*, or the Sioux Indians *wakan*—is felt primarily
in the natural world, and the natural world belongs to all" (Hamel 34). The
American Indian Lakota legend of the White Buffalo Calf Woman[6] portrays
nature coming in divine form to the people who need guidance in order to
survive. The Lakota people are depicted in this legend as near starvation
when two young men who are searching for food come across a divine appari-
tion; "at first they thought that it was an animal, but as the shape grew closer,
they saw that it was a woman. She was dressed in white buffalo skin and carried something in her hands. She walked so lightly that it seemed as if she
was not walking at all, but floating with her feet barely touching the earth"
(Bruchac 127). The first youth recognizes that she is sacred, but the second
man views her with lust; his impurity mythically destroys him, as lightning
immediately strikes and kills him.

   The White Buffalo Calf Woman then tells the first young man to leave
and tell his people to build a sacred lodge for her, so that she may come and
instruct them on the means to survive. He does so, and as promised, she
comes to the people holding the Sacred Pipe; she states:

> The bowl of the Pipe ... is made of the red stone. It represents the flesh and
> blood of the Buffalo People and all other Peoples. The wooden stem of the Pipe
> represents all the trees and plants, all the things green and growing on this
> Earth. The smoke that passes through the Pipe represents the sacred wind, the
> breath that carries prayers up to Wakan Tanka, the Creator [Bruchac 129].

The White Buffalo Calf Woman then shows the people how to respectfully
worship the earth; she tells them that if they remember her message that they
will receive back plentiful resources from nature. The people watch as she
leaves them; she is said to walk back towards the setting sun, stop, and then

roll upon the earth. The myth states that when she stands again, she is a black buffalo. Then when she continues to walk further, she rolls again, and stands up as a brown buffalo. She repeats this process a third time, standing as a red buffalo. And then finally, she becomes a white buffalo and disappears. Once she is gone, the people are provided for, as her promise of plenty comes to them in the form of innumerable buffalo.

The White Buffalo Calf Woman is nature. She reminds the people who witness her that they must not only respect the natural environment, but understand that like her, they are intertwined with it. The only way they can survive is to understand that the buffalo is a gift to the people, and the taking of its life is a sacred act, one in which they too will have to repay to assure the earth's continuous processes.

The American Indian Blackfoot also have a legend about their Buffalo Dance.[7] Long ago, the myth states, that the people were starving because no buffalo would fall to their deaths when the people drove them to the edge of the killing cliffs. The Blackfoot people entered a desperate state when a young girl, who was drinking water at a stream below the cliff looked up and saw a herd of buffalo grazing right along the cliff's edge. In partial jest, she called out that if they would only fall, she would marry one of them, and to her delight, and horror, they began to fall. A bull then approached her and instructed her to follow him, so that she may keep her promise; having no choice, she succumbed to her fate, knowing that she at least provided her people with meat.

After the people cut up the corpses of the buffalo, they began to starve again, and also missed the beautiful young girl. Her father resolved to find her and kill her buffalo husband. He went to their home and hid nearby; the woman found him, but fearing for both of their lives, she instructed him to return home. Her father refused. When she returned to her husband, he smelled a human stranger's scent upon his wife, so he set out with the other members of the buffalo herd and spotted her father. The buffalo proceeded to trample the man to death. All of the pieces of his body were so trampled by the buffalo that no one could see any recognizable piece.

The girl began to weep in mourning. Her husband then said to her, "'you are mourning for your father. And so, perhaps, you can now see how it is with us, we have seen our mothers, fathers, many of our relatives, hurled over the rock walls and slaughtered by your people. But I shall pity you; I shall give you just one chance. If you can bring your father to life again, you and he may go back to your people'" (Campbell, *Primitive Mythology,* 285). This mythic connection to the sorrow felt by the buffalo for their families to the mourning of the maiden for her father helps audiences see the cost that comes with providing sustenance; it explains the workings of nature, and its laws of survival of the fittest, but it also connects compassion in portraying a link between humans and animals.

The woman then turns to nature for assistance with the impossible task of resurrecting her father. She calls to the magpie to track down just one piece of her deceased father, and soon enough the magpie spots a piece of backbone in the soil. The magpie gives the bone to the woman. She sits over it and chants a magic song; again, the mythic archetype of a female raising life from a dismembered piece of a deceased person is evident. The woman is able to first form her whole father's back from only this one piece of backbone that emerged from the soil, and then continuing her magic chant, she is able to breathe life back into his full form.

The buffalo see her success and gain a respect for the people; they now concede that the people know the cost of death, and so they are ready to give their lives over for the people's survival once again. This myth twists the expected archetypal mythic format a bit; usually, it is the animals who teach humans that death is only a momentary experience when viewed in terms of the cycles found in nature, but this myth, first presents this lesson to the buffalo from the humans. From this lesson, an arrangement is made that allows for the survival of the humans; they have, through the magic of the daughter, shown that death is simply a part of the cycle of nature. After this, the buffalo teach the people a dance, which must be done adorned in buffalo costumes that will serve as a reminder to future generations of Blackfoot American Indians. This is similar to, as Esther Harding puts it, the "'belief that the bear dance will inevitably bring the bear to the hunt ... for the bear and man are felt to be in a continuum. And it must be admitted that sometimes the bear seems to feel it too, since reliable observers have stated that the bear does come when so called'" (qtd. in Swan 97).

The Navajo American Indians tell of a myth where First Hunter goes out into the mountains to hunt.[8] First Hunter soon spied an enormous buck with many antlers, but just as he got ready to shoot the buck with his bow and arrow, it transformed into a mountain mahogany bush, and then transformed into a man. The man told the hunter, "'do not shoot! We are your neighbors. These are things that will be in the future when human beings come into existence. This is the way you will kill us. And this is the way you will eat us'" (Swan 37). First Hunter then let the deer-man go, since he provided sacred knowledge for his people. Next, First Hunter saw a doe, but it also transformed just before he shot it into first a cliff rose bush and then into a woman, and she told him not to kill her, as she had information that would also sustain his people. She told him that her skins would protect the people, so First Hunter also let her live. Next, First Hunter found a two-pointed young buck, and the same pattern continued; it transformed into a dead tree and then a young man and told the man that if his people mistreated the animals, they would cause illness and hardship for mankind. Finally, First Hunter saw a fawn; the fawn turned into a lichen-spotted rock and then a young girl, who told the hunter that if people disrespected nature, she was the one who would respond by killing First Hunter:

> I will kill you with what I am.... If you do not make use of us properly, even in times when we are numerous, you will not see us anymore. We are the four deer who have transformed themselves into different kinds of things.... Moreover, we can assume the form of all the different kinds of plants. Then, when you look you will not see us.... If, when you hunt, you come across four deer, you will not kill all of them. You may kill three and leave one. But if you kill us all, it is not good [Swan 37].

It is significant within the myth that the final deer is a young girl who speaks for all of the deer and animals of the forest, as she represents the younger generation that is in jeopardy if nature's laws are broken. It is also significant that the myth enables the deer to transform from animals into plants, and then into human beings, because this shows a belief that all things are inextricably united.

The fawn girl continued on to tell First Hunter how to ensure the survival of his people. She told him how to properly hunt, respect the prey by offering thanks and using every part of it, and how to properly dispose of the prey's bones, so that "'they will live on; their bones can live again and live a lasting life'" (Swan 38). The myth reveals to audiences a message that life and death are part of a continuous natural cycle.

The Diminishment of Natural Divinity

As with many nature-based religions, the arrival of new faiths often modified or eradicated existing belief systems. However, many remnants of the older beliefs remained, though often they existed in altered form. For instance in Celtic mythology, many divine figures lost divine stature with the introduction of Christianity. The Tuatha De Danann became demoted, even by physically diminishing their size, to a belief in small fairies and sprites who given their diminutive stature became a thing of "fairy" tales, and thus held less importance. The once revered god Lleu of the Longbow is believed to also have been reduced in importance, and physical stature, becoming a leprechaun. Through this diminishment of importance and power, these once divine figures of nature became mere figures of trickery, or even demonic activity.

As has been discussed mythology often is produced with the intent on restructuring the belief systems of the people, as when male heroic figures overpowered female dominant representations. In Slavic mythology divine nature-based figures became demoted to an identification of evil, demonic beings who existed as dwarves or spirits of the forest, and who should be feared and shunned for their malicious intent. Though Christianity, in the case of the Celts and the Slavs, did "not diminish the anxieties of a life lived at the mercy of nature. The new scripture may have had no place for the old gods of water, wind, thunder, and fire, but there was still room in the hearts of the ordinary people" (Phillips & Kerrigan 60) for a continuation of their reverence for nature as divine. Many rituals and festivals were still practiced long after the coming of Christianity, and many Christian celebrations and holidays were merged with their pagan counterparts to make them more appealing to parishioners. Therefore, myriad mythological and religious components continue throughout many cultures, even into contemporary times, to present the earth as both sacred and divine.

4

Untamed Nature and the Unfettered Human

"Whosoever is delighted in solitude is either a wild beast or a god."
—Aristotle

"I went to the woods because I wished to live deliberately, to front only the essential facts of life, and see if I could not learn what it had to teach, and not, when I came to die, discover that I had not lived."
—Henry David Thoreau

Anthropologists point to Paleolithic caves as indicators of early mythology. The cave paintings of Lascaux in France and Altamira in Spain depict what many believe are portrayals of shamans dressed in the costumes of animals (Armstrong, *Great Transformation*, 24–5). These early cave paintings suggest a close tie to the elements of the natural world, specifically, to animals in order to obtain spiritual knowledge. Armstrong contends that

> shamans operate only in hunting societies, and animals play an important role in their spirituality. During his training, a modern shaman sometimes lives with animals in the world.... This is not regarded as a regression. In hunting societies, animals are not seen as inferior beings, but have superior wisdom. They know the secrets of longevity and immortality, and communicating with them, the shaman gains an enhanced life [*Short History,* 27].

Hunting societies, in ancient and modern times, often portray an understanding of the essential connection of human beings to animals. Mythology that portrays people seeking wild places, living like an animal, or even embodying an animal self are not providing negative or demoted representations. Oftentimes, contemporary culture views animal behavior or "wild" behavior as out of control, even as attributes of the mentally unfit, but myth shows us that a return to nature is most often a healing or spiritual process. In addition works from more modern times, such as Ralph Waldo Emerson's

Nature (1836), Henry David Thoreau's *Walden* (1854), and Jack Kerouac's *Dharma Bums* (1958) became famed works because they precisely offered a message of the spiritual benefit of "returning to nature." Yet, as also portrayed in modern literature, when things are perceived as animalistic or "too wild," questions arise on the toll unharnessed nature takes on the human who has been long civilized, take for example Joseph Conrad's *Heart of Darkness* (1899) or William Golding's *Lord of the Flies* (1954).

Myths, though, help audiences see what early societies embraced for their own survival—that the wild, even in its harshest and unsavory elements, is natural and essential to survival, and it is a firmly embedded part of all human beings. The wilderness has often been associated with mythology. Within the embrace of the wilderness, the mythic characters portrayed embody aspects of the wild. Nature at its core is displayed prominently for audiences to realize their own wild connections.

Animal Teachers

Animals have always held an important place within world mythology as they have been needed for survival since the beginning of human existence. Often animals act as guides to mankind within myth. When a culture reveres nature as divine, the animals that inhabit nature are often thought to hold intimate knowledge of natural law.

Many cultures believed that their first people were descended directly from animals. For instance, the members of the Turtle Clan of the Iroquois believe they descended from a large primal turtle who one day found that he was not able to hold the weight of the people any more upon his massive back, so he regretfully cast them off to start their own independent lives. The people of the Crayfish Clan of the Choctaw American Indians believe that their first people were indeed Crayfish that lived underground, only occasionally coming above the surface of the mud. The creation myth states that other Choctaws found these Crayfish and took them into their care, until they transformed into humans. The Navajo American Indians have a myth of creation that involves their cultural hero Spider Woman.[1] It was Spider Woman who protected human beings as they emerged from the womb of the earth. After the people emerged, Spider Woman watched over the Navajo, teaching them the means of survival. Some members of the Masai in Uganda believe that when a person dies, he or she is transformed into a serpent (Hamel 18). Also, in Tibet, one creation myth maintains that human beings were ancestors of a monkey and a rock ogress, and similarly the Mongols believed that they were descended from a "blue-grey forest wolf and a doe that ranged the steppes" (Allan & Phillips, *World*, 28).

Many American Indian ceremonies also include animal representations as a form of reverence for their animal brethren. The Plains Indians, for example, often wore the skins or masks of animals to honor the animal represented as sacred. American Indians respected animals as obtaining vital wisdom. People all around the world consider animals as wise beings. Pawnee Chief Letakots-Lesa stated his tribe's respect for their animal ancestors: "'in the beginning of all things, wisdom and knowledge were with the animals: for Tirawa, the One Above, did not speak directly to man. He sent certain animals to tell men that he showed himself though the beasts, and that from them … man should learn. Tirawa spoke to man through his works'" (qtd. in Swan 32). And Zimmerman states that the American Indian Crow people revere the elk because they believe that the elk holds "amorous powers, which is why in courting rituals men woo women by imitating elk sounds played on a long flute—a gift from Elk Man" (67). The American Indian Koyukons of Alaska, believe that the "natural and supernatural worlds are inseparable…. [They] see each person as having an animal symbol that best expresses their identity" (Swan 41). And many of the American Indians of the Pacific Northwest build towering totem poles to revere the animals that hold familial ties with the people.

The African Masai people of Kenya rely on the herding of cattle for their survival; therefore, cattle have become central to their mythology. The Masai explain the coming of the first cattle to the people by a myth that starts with a Dorobo man, a man who is from one of the nearby tribes of people who do not herd cattle.[2] The Dorobo man lived at the start of creation with an elephant and a snake. The elephant gave birth, and the Dorobo man disrespectfully approached the elephant and her offspring, so, as is an elephant's nature, the mother elephant attacked the Dorobo man in order to try to save her offspring. The Dorobo man again acted foolishly and killed the mother elephant, leaving the baby elephant unprotected. The Dorobo man then saw that a snake was close by, and again, disrespectfully, he decided to kill the snake as well. Seeing this destruction, the baby elephant feared for its life and ran away to a Masai tribesman named Le-eyo.

The baby elephant told Le-eyo what happened, so Le-eyo traveled to the home of the Dorobo and saw the man talking with the messenger of the gods, Naiteru-kop. Le-eyo heard Naiteru-kop tell the Dorobo man to meet him the next morning, so that he could be bestowed with a great gift, but Le-eyo decided to get there before the Dorobo man. Therefore, it was Le-eyo who heard the great gift given by the divine Naiteru-kop. Naiteru-kop told Le-eyo to go and build a fence around his home, slay a wild animal, and then go inside and wait (Wilkinson 168). Le-eyo did as instructed, but soon he heard outside of his hut a massive noise that initially frightened him. After some time had passed and Le-eyo built up his courage, he went outside and saw the sky god Enkai lowering down a giant herd of cattle. It is with this tale that the Masai explain why they were entrusted by the gods to become cattle herders, thus ensuring an easier means of survival than the Dorobo who were forced to remain hunter-gatherers. The myth makes it clear that Le-eyo's contrasting care and respect for the baby elephant, instead of the disrespectful hunting method of the Dorobo man, allowed him and his people to be the recipients of the precious gift from the gods that ensured their continued vitality.

As discussed at the beginning of this chapter, hunting from the beginning of human existence helped to define a people's perception of the animal kingdom. Paleolithic hunters knew that the large prey that they killed resembled themselves; their feelings of fear, shame, and jubilation at killing an animal is thought to have enticed some of the world's first rituals and myths. For instance, among the indigenous people of Scandinavia, the Saami, once they "killed a bear, they would carefully bury its bones in a grave, placing each bone in the same pattern it occupied when alive. They treated these burial sites just as they treated human graves; the Saami also showed respect for spirits of other animals killed by leaving their antlers and bones at the place where the animals died" (Swan 120).

In African myth hunters are often described in myth as "the adventurers who leave the safe human world and bring back the wealth of nature; they are also intermediaries between the spirits of the wild and other humans.... Hunters serve thus as cultural heroes—figures who helped to establish the people's way of life" (Belcher 38). The Fon people of Africa describe a myth where a hunter who is deep in the wilderness hears the beating of a drum. He peers into an opening in the bush where he sees what no man has seen: the agbui, spirits shaped like rats, dancing. Astonished,

> he watched the dance and he listened to their songs, and so he learned something of the history of the world: how first there were the trees, and among them the tree whose seeds are used in *fa* divination, and then humans and then the animals. And of all the animals, the bush rats said they were the oldest. After them came the lion and the leopard and the other great beasts of the earth, and then came the birds ... and then the beasts of the water.... All these creatures were sent by Mawu, who is the great goddess of the sky [Belcher 39].

Having glimpsed this knowledge of the workings of nature, how all natural beings are interconnected, the hunter was said to possess wisdom that allowed him to go back to his people and aid in curing the ill. This myth precisely portrays the hunter in the role of mythic hero or cultural shaman, as the hunter here, through his lone hunt in the woods is able to glimpse the secrets of nature because he is deeply immersed in it. As a solitary hunter, he has leveled the playing field with the prey he seeks; he is in jeopardy of possibly becoming prey, as he also must rely on his own instinctual animalistic abilities to successfully kill for the nourishment of his people. He is mythically permitted to see nature then as a greater process, and in glimpsing this, he also must concede that he is only one part of this natural process, not superior to it.

The African Mande people tell a myth of a hunter and his animal bride that also connects the human to the animal realm.[3] The myth states that a hunter found himself in a secluded spot in the bush when he spotted a beautiful woman bathing. He watched her, and when she left the pool of water, he saw that she didn't put clothes on, but instead put on the skin of an animal, and to his amazement, he saw that she transformed into an antelope. Awed he returned to the same spot day after day hoping to see her again, and one day he got what he wished for.

The hunter snuck up to the place where the mystical woman had left the animal skin while she bathed, and he put the skin into his bag. He then went up to the woman and expressed his undying love for her and asked her to come home with him and marry him. The antelope woman agreed, but she told the man that if he ever threatened her with fire, she would immediately leave him. He assured the woman he would never do such a thing, and so they left together and started a new life as man and wife. They had many children, but after they spent many years living together, they had an argument, and the man foolishly waved a torch in front of his wife as a half-hearted threat. Without uttering a word, she left her human life behind and returned to the bush again as an antelope. Distraught, the hunter sought his wife throughout the land, but he was unable to ever find her. In an attempt to drown out his sorrow, he began to become a fierce hunter. The man's people initially welcomed this as their cooking pots were always filled, but the man was spiritually hollow inside, as he longed for his antelope wife. One day, in sheer grief and anger, the hunter "saw and shot an antelope. He brought it home and set it to cook. But his children refused to eat the meal. He ate it by himself, and that night he died" (Belcher 41).

This myth relates mankind's connection to the animals, as it shows the man succeeding within the myth to win the trust of the antelope woman because he truly loves and respects her split human and animalistic nature. However, when the man breaks her trust, by waving around fire, an act that no animal, only a human can do, the hunter is viewed as a failure within the myth because he has lost touch with his connection to his animalistic bride. The hunter becomes removed from the natural world when he threatens his wife, and so he commits an act that shows his willingness to cease to exist, as he shoots and kills the one thing he loves. The fact that he kills and consumes the antelope, causing his own death, shows again a connection to himself and the world of the animals because as a hunter, he allows himself to die as the animals do again and again for the hunter.

The important belief in shamanism is also often deeply connected to myth. Shamans with the aid of nature, often particularly from animals, provide spiritual meaning for their people. Swan states that in shamanistic hunting cultures

> the animals were fellow-beings, in some ways equal to humans, and in some ways actually stronger and more powerful.... Through meditation, the shaman could enter the animal stratum of his own soul. In this way the dreamtime was recreated, the time before time when men and other animals were not yet sundered. The relation to the animals of power—such as the bear, the moose, the reindeer, or the loon—was both cosmic and initiatory. These animals were both the ancestors of man and the teachers and initiators of the shamans [102].

Oftentimes, shamans dress in animal skins or perform the ritualized movements of animals. The shaman is said to act as an "intermediary between the world of men and the gods, and has the power to descend into the realms of the dead. His spirit is believed to journey forth from his body, which remains in a state of a trance" (Davidson 118). Northern European communities, such as the Norse, were said to practice shamanism; in the Norse account of *Erík's Saga,* there is a depiction of a *vǫlva,* a female shamaness, who divines prophetic answers to an audience wearing animal skins.

The Buryat shamans of Siberia believed that they took on the form of animals or birds when conducting séances; "The early Russian missionaries and voyagers in Siberia in the first part of the eighteenth century noted that the shamans spoke to their spirits in a strange, squeaky voice.... The shamans of Siberia wear bird costumes to this day, and many are believed to have been conceived by their mothers from the descent of birds" (Campbell, *Primitive Mythology,* 257–8). In both India and China, spiritual advisers are often referred to in animal reference; the Indian title for a master yogi is Paramahamsa, "paramount ... wild gander" and in China the "mountain men or immortals" are pictured as birds soaring on wild beasts (Campbell, *Primitive Mythology,* 258).

The Aboriginal Australians also believe that their shamans can transform into animal form, like that of an eagle or snake to receive wisdom, and by doing this, they can also bridge the gap between the living and the dead

(Allan, Fleming, & Kerrigan 75). The Aboriginal Australians discuss myths that explain how their ancestors are portrayed often as animal spirit beings who in Dreamtime made journeys across the land, "bringing the land and all its geographical features into being, bringing to life all the plants, animals, and other living things that inhabit it, and giving life to all spirits of the place and beings who will be born in the future" (Wilkinson 205). In addition, the Aboriginals believed that "some mythic beings were shape-changing. They might appear in human form, or in the form of a natural species or element" (Berndt & Berndt 18). What is important is that when these mythic beings transformed during Dreamtime, they were not portrayed as changing away from the human selves into a completely different self; they always maintained a connection to their former self as well as the form they metamorphosed into; therefore, "what is implied is a common life-stream for all living things" (Berndt & Berndt 18).

Many cultures also portrayed their divine beings in animal form, the most well-known of which are found in ancient Egypt. In Egypt, "the Egyptians did not revere animals because they were sacred in themselves but rather because certain creatures were believed to contain the divine essence or physical manifestation (the ba) of certain gods. In worshipping the animal, they worshipped the power of the deity contained within or represented by that animal" (Fleming & Lothian 66). Egyptian gods and goddesses are often depicted in animal form, such as Hathor embodying the body of a cow, and Bastet, the goddess of sexuality often taking the form of a cat. Sobek, who embodied the power of the pharaohs, was often portrayed as a crocodile; Thoth, god of wisdom, was represented as an ibis, and Anubis often took the form of a jackal (Wilkinson 143). The bull was also considered sacred in Egypt; "sacred bulls were kept in the greatest splendor, paraded at religious festivals, consulted for their oracular powers and, on their death, accorded a mummification fit for a pharaoh" (Fleming & Lothian 68). The most celebrated of sacred bulls was the Apis held in Memphis; it was thought to be the embodiment of the god Ptah (Fleming & Lothian 68). Wilkinson states that "these animal forms gave the deities a strong sense of identity.... Certain animal forms—such as Sobek's crocodile, or the hippopotamus form taken by the birth goddess Taweret—were especially relevant to the daily lives of a great many Egyptians who frequently came face to face with them ... when working on the banks of the Nile" (143).

The Greek Herodotus wrote that all animals "'wild or tame, are without exception held to be sacred'" (qtd. in Fleming & Lothian 66), and this view is understood when paired with the portrayal of many Greek divinities mythically transforming into animal figures at whim. The Greek gods and goddesses often disguise themselves in animal form. Apollo once was said to transform into a crow; Zeus became a ram, bull, swan, eagle, etc., and Artemis was said to change into a cat. Poseidon was often connected to animals as well, most often the bull and the horse. Many of the myths focusing on Poseidon show him as deeply connected to the natural world, not only through his obvious connection as god of the sea, but also by his connection to plant life. As the god associated with water, he was also sometimes connected with Demeter, goddess of the harvest; their sexual union, which mythically occurred while both were transformed into horses, connects the two crucial natural elements, of earth with water, while in animal form. In addition, many Greek myths relate gods, most often Zeus, having sex with mortal women in the form of an animal; in fact, most of Zeus' animal guises within myth are adopted in order to trick a woman into having intercourse. This mythic element may appear strange, but it seems to represent a symbolic reference to a spiritual experience on the part of the woman. Sexual union with a god is a common mythic archetype, and it most often suggests an inner state of enlightenment, for the merging together, as symbolically portrayed in sexual terms, of human with the divine is a transformative experience. The tenet of Zeus appearing as an animal to myriad women, such as a swan for Leda and a bull for Europa, suggests a clear tie with human, animal, and the divine.

The Indian *Bhagavad Gita* states that "wise people see the same soul (Atman) in the Brahman, in worms and in insects, in the dog and the elephant, in beasts, cows, gadflies, and gnats" (qtd. in Hamel 15). In India, the god Vishnu, the preserver, often took the form of animals. As a fish he once was said to come to earth to save Manu Vaivasvata, the father of the human race, from a destructible flood that would have surely killed him and would then have prevented the birth of mankind. Vishnu also was mythically said to come to earth in the form of a tortoise in order to recover sacred objects needed to restore order to the universe. Phillips, Kerrigan, and Gould state that "scholars believe that pre–Aryan Indians worshipped the tortoise. They are thought to have seen the animal as an embodiment of the universe—with the upper shell standing for the sky above and the lower shell standing for the earth below, while the soft body of the tortoise in between represented the atmosphere" (59). Vishnu also was said to have appeared on earth as a boar who brought up the earth from the bottom of the vast and primordial sea.

Ancient myth also often shows mythic characters either being nursed by animals or raised under the guidance of animalistic teachers. In Roman mythology the legendary founders of Rome, Romulus and Remus, were nursed by a wolf after their mother, a vestal virgin, was forced to give them up for breaking her sacred vow of chastity. Again the Greek Zeus was suckled by the goat Amalthea on the island of Crete, while he hid from his gluttonous father Cronus. The Persian Cyrus I was said to have been nursed by a dog before growing to achieve fame in his later life. In addition, the Greek mythic characters of Jason, Heracles, Asclepius, Ajax, Theseus, Achilles, and Perseus all have myths that declare that the centaur, half man and half horse, Chiron raised them in a natural environment away from the confines of civilization. This mythic portrayal of an animalistic teacher as being necessary for the education of many of the world's most famous heroes reveals the value of human beings embracing their animalistic nature.

In Celtic mythology the role of animals is also crucial, as the Celts again venerated every aspect of the natural world. Many Celtic myths include animals as teachers or guides. For instance, the Irish Fionn Mac Cumhaill[4] spent his childhood living and learning from his home in the deep forest. Fionn was portrayed at the age of seven as obtaining great wisdom because he tasted the flesh of a mystical salmon that swam in the Boyne River where nine sacred hazel trees grew from which "nuts that held great wisdom" grew (Fleming & Husain 63). The bard Finnegas was said to have captured the salmon and gave it to Fionn. Fionn, then was instructed to cook the fish, but under no circumstance was he to eat the salmon. Fionn obeyed the rules, but as he was cooking the mystical fish he burned his thumb and put it in his mouth to cool the burning sensation, which was all that was needed to impart the wisdom of the salmon into the being of Fionn. This partaking of the flesh is symbolic of Fionn becoming a part of the salmon. It shows a connectivity to nature. It also is an aspect of many mythic rituals where the flesh of a being must be consumed in order for the one who is consuming it to become connected to the consumed, take for instance the Lakota practice of eating the heart of the buffalo after a kill, the Greek priestesses drinking the blood of the sacrificial bull in Achaea before prophesizing (Frazer 34), or the Aztecs consuming the dough representative of their god Vitzilipuztli (Frazer 79). In close association with nature, druids "were intermediaries between the natural and the divine worlds" (Wood 108). For instance, "when a new kin was to be chosen, a druid would consume the flesh and blood of a sacrificed bull and then wrap himself in the beast's flayed skin. He then fell into a profound sleep during which he would learn the identity of the next High King" (Wood 108).

Myth repeatedly shows that if one fails to embrace the animal or wild aspects of him or herself then self-affirmation is unattainable; "The belief that men can change into animals and animals into men is as old as life itself. It originates in the theory that all things are created from one substance"

(Hamel 1). Myths remind us of the fact that we are indeed animals ourselves. Just as with myths that remind audiences of the interconnectivity of all life with the portrayals of humans in natural terms, so too do myths that tie humans to their animal brethren remind listeners of myth that they must not forget or shun their own animalistic nature.

Untamed Nature and the Wild Human

The Roman Ovid in his *Metamorphosis* presents myriad myths where humans are transformed into elements within nature, most often animals or plants. The mythic transformations within *Metamorphosis* often serve to show a truer portrayal of the mythic character's inner state; for example, in the myth of Lycaon, he is portrayed as a wicked human for mocking the superiority of the gods, so his transformation into a wolf upon completion of the myth seems natural. This mythic transformation of human to animal as representing the true components of one's character is a common archetype. In Homer's *Odyssey*, Circe turns Odysseus' scouts into swine, and from their behavior thus far in the text, this transformation is portrayed as suitable. The famed Persian text *One Thousand and One Nights* also recounts many tales where humans are transformed into animals as suitable punishments for improper behavior. Metamorphosis thus reveals the characters' true inner character.

Still, in world mythology, there are many myths that recount the transformation from human into animal as a positive metamorphosis, not a means to reveal the animalistic inner character of a person as a negative quality. For instance, again in Ovid's *Metamorphosis* the myth of Cadmus and Harmonia shows the elderly, married couple transform into gentle serpents who maintain their love for one another after their metamorphosis. In Ovid's myth of Callisto, a handmaid to the goddess Diana, Jupiter tricks Callisto into having sex with him by appearing to be the goddess Diana herself. Callisto later finds that she is pregnant by Jupiter, and to save her from the wrath of the virginal Diana, Jupiter turns Callisto into a bear. Callisto before her transformation was presented as preferring the solitude of the unfettered wilderness, and with her transformation into a bear, she can live in peace within the deep woods.

Apuleius' *Metamorphosis* or *Golden Ass* also recounts its protagonist Lucius being transformed into a donkey. Throughout most of the text Lucius must concede to the difficulty of living life as a beast of burden, as he is often starved, beaten, and even repeatedly threatened with death. He sees through this experience what it is to live as an animal that is often reviled by humanity, and the text suggests that he experiences a psychological, even spiritual, transformation because of his physical metamorphosis into a donkey. At the end of the text he has a vision that he meets the Egyptian Goddess Isis, whom he remarks is the purest form of the Mother Goddess of myriad civilizations, and her connection to nature is clear, as she states, "'I come, Lucius, moved by your entreaties: I, mother of the universe, mistress of all the elements … representing in one shape all gods and goddesses. My will controls the shining heights of heaven, the health-giving sea-winds, and the mournful silences of hell; the entire world worships my single godhead in a thousand shapes'" (Apuleius 197). After meeting Isis, Lucius is finally able to be transformed back into his human form, through Isis' aid, and because of this, he concedes that now, after his experience as an animal, he feels he must devote his life to worshipping Isis as one of her devotees. The final scene of the *Golden Ass* then suggests that Lucius has experienced a heightened spiritual transformation directly because of his time spent living as a lowly donkey, as often the Mother Goddess representative within myth appears to signal that the mythic character has attained an intimate understanding of nature, thus often attaining wisdom.

Many American Indian myths also present mythic characters turning into animals, and these transformations are again most often viewed as positive, and moreover, their metamorphoses are portrayed as quite natural. In many American Indian tribes animals were believed to aid human beings in self-transformation. Animals were thought to possess spiritual importance; "the souls of animals could … be enlisted by people as their guardian spirits. In many communities, animal souls were sought out by apprentice shamans and young men and women undergoing initiation rites at puberty" (Lowenstein & Vitebsky 69). To connect with the spirit of an animal acknowledged the bond between all living creatures; it symbolically accounted for the mythic metamorphosis from human into animal form. This is why shamans often dressed in animal guise, and people often sought intuitive messages from animal guides.

The American Indian Passamaquoddy tell a myth about the origin of the black snake.[5] Long ago a husband and wife lived deep in the wilderness next to a large lake. One winter day the wife, a young, beautiful woman, went to the frozen lake and cut away a hole in the ice; when she looked in the water, she saw two shining eyes looking up at her. Immediately entranced she felt that she couldn't move; suddenly when she could focus again, she saw a slender and elegant man standing before her, his skin dazzling in the sunlight. The woman learned that his name was At-o-sis, the serpent, but she didn't care. She embraced him, and they became lovers. The woman left her home, and husband, each day to seek out At-o-sis.

One afternoon, her husband noticing how often his wife was leaving to go into the forest, followed her on her daily excursion. He witnessed the strange man rise out of the water and kiss his wife again and again. Dazed, he returned home, and when his wife returned, he begged her to leave this strange man and remain with him, and thus remain with her people. But the wife refused, so the husband left her forever.

The woman's mother and father visited her to see how she was doing now that she was living alone in the wilderness, and they found that she was doing quite well, as her home was full of food and furs; she told them, "'I have another husband … one who suits me. The one I had was bad and did not use me well. This one brings all the animals to me'" (Leland 279). This indication within the myth that the wife is choosing her own path is central; though her path is dangerous, and breaks away from confines of societal acceptance, she remains steadfast and solitary, so as to pursue this path of breaking down the boundaries between human and animal.

The woman sent her parents away and told them not to return until next spring; this seasonal aspect is again central to the myth's message. In the spring, her parents returned, but they found that their daughter had turned completely white and was heavily pregnant. The parents stayed with her until she gave birth. She eventually gave birth, but the parents were shocked and filled with fear when they found that their daughter gave birth to hundreds of snakes. As the parents were about to leave, their daughter told them, "'When you come again, you may see me, but you will not know me'" (Leland 280). The parents never returned, fearing the magic that must be involved in their daughter's transformation, but the myth closes with a group of hunters coming many years later, and finding the daughter's home abandoned in the woods. Close to her home, they also find that the wilderness if full of black snakes; miraculously the black snakes band together, forming one cohesive shape that looks like a human being. This mass of snakes stands before them, looking them in their eyes; then the snakes disband and separately slither away. The hunters are left with the distinct feeling that the snakes meant them no harm.

The transformation of the woman into myriad snakes recounts the common theme of animal transformation as a mythic symbol of connection with the natural world. Here the woman's transformation, as well as her role in the assurance of the prosperous future generation of black snakes, speaks towards the woman's willingness to lose herself in an acceptance that she, like all earthly inhabitants, are inextricably connected to the natural world.

This loss of selfhood becomes a central component in mythic characters obtaining spiritual enlightenment.

In Korea there is a myth[6] that tells of a young maiden being betrothed to a man who unexpectedly dies before she can meet him. The maiden is so distraught that she makes a daily trip to the grave and only sits and weeps; one day as she is weeping, the earth at the gravesite opens up for her, and without hesitation she emerges into the ground. This myth again explicitly connects a mythic character being quite willing to lose her life in order to unite with nature. The maiden waits to be returned into the earth, and it clearly welcomes her. The myth continues to show that her choice induces a transformation, which is not at all viewed as fatalistic. A piece of the maiden's clothing that ripped off when a servant, who accompanied the maiden to the fiancé's grave, tried to grab the maiden before she leapt into the hole, suddenly transformed into a beautiful butterfly. The remnant of fabric metamorphosing into a butterfly sends a mythic message that life is inextricably connected to the natural world and its cycles, as a butterfly undergoes a clear pattern of birth, death, and rebirth—first it appears as a caterpillar, then enters into a stage that appears similar to death within its chrysalis, and finally seems to undergo a mystical rebirth as a butterfly. It is this same pattern that is followed in this Korean legend, showing that from the death of the maiden, new life must emerge.

Metamorphosis from humans to animals is a common theme in Celtic mythology as well; in a poem "attributed to the semi-mythical Welsh poet Taliesin, the bard declares 'I have been in many shapes before'" (qtd. in Wood 94). The Fenian cycle in Irish mythology recounts many accounts where humans take on the forms of animals. Fionn's divine wife first appears to him as a fawn. Fionn's aunt was turned into a dog and gave birth to a son who was also a dog (Wood 96). The Irish myth of the "Children of Lir" recounts King Lir's children being transformed by their step mother into swans that must endure nine hundred years of living on three different lakes that become increasingly harsh habitats in which to live. Their mythic transformations teach first their distraught father, who discovers the fate of his kids, and finally a solitary priest, who also finds out that the swans possess human souls, that their metamorphosis offered a message of the necessity of endurance even among harsh natural conditions.

The Welsh *Mabinogi* also presents mythic portrayals of humans being transformed into animals. In the fourth branch of the *Mabinogi,* the king of Gwynedd, Math, must keep his feet in the lap of a virgin at all times, unless he is going to war. His nephew, Gilfaethwy, though it will undoubtedly cause his own downfall, falls irretrievably in love with the virgin, and so he becomes an adversary of Math. Gilfaethwy discloses to his brother, Gwydion, his love for the maiden, and Gwydion schemes a plot to help unite Gilfaethwy with the maiden. The brothers trick Math into starting war with a neighboring kingdom, and Gilfaethwy ends up raping the virgin because she refuses to be disloyal to Math. As a result of Gilfaethwy's action, Math, upon learning of the crime, transforms both Gilfaethwy and Gwydion into three sets of animals. The brothers first become a stag and a hind, then a boar and a sow, and finally a male and female wolf, and what is more, each time they transform into these animals, they must mate with each other to produce offspring. Math states upon delivering this punishment that becomes a lesson to the brothers, "since you are in league with each other, I will make you live together and mate with each other, and take on the nature of the wild" (*Mabinogion* 52). In continually mating in animal form to produce offspring, the brothers partake in a clear connection to the natural process, and it is this process that serves as their lesson.

The mythic maiden often represents a tie to nature; as portrayed with the Greek Persephone, maidens frequently serve as representations of springtime. To take away, by force, the virginity of a mythic maiden disrupts the natural order; once the symbolic representation of spring is forcefully stopped within myth, a transition occurs like that witnessed in the change of seasons; these myths often portray a period of drought and decay once the spring-like maiden is sundered. The maiden who protects Math possesses, for him, mystical powers that keep him alive and at peace, qualities often mythically associated with spring. The myth states that the only time he can take his feet away from the lap of this maiden is when he goes to war, which connects again the maiden serving as a life-giving role for the king and his people; her virginity, like other mythic maidens, promises everlasting fertility, but once it is taken away, like Persephone's abduction by Hades, a period of death follows, portrayed here with Math going to fight a war. Gilfaethwy must learn through his metamorphic experience how to correct the natural order. In his and his brother's animal forms, they finally learn, first-hand, the necessity of the regenerative aspects of nature, as instead of aborting the symbolic spring with its abundance, they learn the necessity of creating new life. After their third animal pairing that again produces new life, Math allows the brothers to return to their original human forms, thus mythically signaling that the processes of nature have been restored.

Math continues to look for another virginal maiden to rest his feet upon her lap, so he invites Aranrhod to hold this important position, but upon testing if she is a virgin by having her step over his magic wand, she instantaneously gives birth to a baby boy, who proceeds to go live in the sea; "as soon as he came to the sea, he took on the sea's nature and swam as well as the best fish in the sea" (*Mabinogion* 54). Again, this connection to maidenhood and nature, as depicted in the animalistic portrayal of her son, still points towards this new maiden serving as a mythic representation of a harbinger of the life cycle. Next, Aranrhod is also depicted as giving birth to a "small something" (*Mabinogion* 54) that becomes another son. To further the myth's message of understanding the role of nature and the maiden, Gwydion finds this "something," wraps it up in a piece of cloth, and hides it by his bed, until it has becomes a boy; Gwydion's care of even the smallest, and yet unformed living being suggests his psychological transformation from having experienced life as an animal. Gwydion presents the child to his mother Aranrhod, who upon being surprised of his birth, does not wish to name or care for the child. Aranrhod's resistance to embrace her own child, "'it is because of him you are angry, since you are no longer called a virgin. Never again will you be called a virgin'" (*Mabinogion* 55), shows her resistance to leave the powerful role of mythic maiden to step into the role of mythic mother. She misinterprets, though, the power of the mythical mother role and its connection to the maiden. She assumed she would gain renown holding the sacred duty of allowing Math to rest his feet upon her lap, but upon immediately giving birth, with the text portraying it as a surprise to her, it carries the role of maiden to its next necessary, and just as valuable, role— that of mythic mother.

The text continues to show Aranrhod refusing to name her son, arm him with weapons, or allow him to marry; in her attempt to keep these things from her son, she is stunting his ability to attain manhood. Aranrhod is tricked into granting all of these things however to her son, who she names Lleu. The fact that she is responsible, socially and mythically, for granting her son the means towards manhood reveals the power of her role as mother.

Lleu, through the help of Math's magic, obtains a wife who is clearly associated with nature. Math creates Blodeuedd from the flowers of the oak, broom, and meadowsweet; she is described as the "most beautiful maiden that anyone had ever seen" (*Mabinogion* 58). Lleu and Blodeuedd marry, and though she does not remain a virgin long, her role within the myth still points towards her power as maiden. She represents another aspect of the mythic maiden before she moves into the mythic mother role—lust and sexual energy. Blodeuedd soon tires of Lleu and falls in love with another man; she tricks Lleu into telling the intricate details required for someone to kill him. She convinces him to stage the process required for his murder, until her lover finds him in such a state and murders him. This scene reveals, again, the connection of the mythic maiden to the cycles of life. Lleu is almost invincible, since it is so hard for anyone to ever kill him, but as is the case in the renowned Irish myth *The Táin,* the hero Cúchulainn at his height of strength and vigor, must face the Morrígan, tripartite goddess often associated with nature, who appears to him to show him the flaw of only believing that this one vigorous stage of life will continue. The Morrígan shows Cúchulainn old age and death as a natural occurrence, and so too does Blodeuedd show this to Lleu. Lleu, as are all mortals, is vulnerable to death, and it is Blodeuedd's role within his life to reveal this to him.

The myth shifts to again tie it to the cycles of nature through another transformation from human to animal form. Lleu transforms into an eagle just before Blodeuedd's lover successfully kills him, though he is now severely injured. Because of Lleu's wounds, pieces of rotting flesh begin to fall from his body, as he sits perched in a tree. The myth still portrays a continuation of the natural cycle because a farmer's sow is directly gaining nourishment from the body of Lleu, as it goes to the woods each day to sit beneath Lleu's tree and consumes the pieces of Lleu's flesh that fall to the ground. Gwydion is eventually able to find Lleu by following this sow, and thus he proceeds to convince Lleu to come down from the tree, so that he can be healed. Lleu recovers, but as a punishment fitting this text, Gwydion transforms Blodeuedd into an owl, so that she will forever clearly reside in the natural cycle she embodies, as a bird associated with death, just as the Irish Morrígan is often connected to the crow.

Animal metamorphosis as a representation to the lessons of nature's seasonal laws is clearly evidenced in the events of this myth, from Gilfaethwy and Gwydion being forced to experience life as mating animals, Lleu transforming into an eagle upon being almost fatally wounded, and Blodeuedd being creating out of flowers and being transformed finally into the form of an owl. This aspect of mythically identifying tales where humans must experience life as their animal brethren shows a cultural value of the lessons that can be learned from tapping into one's animalistic nature. When a character mythically embodies an animal, often the character embraces the most basic law of nature—that of life, death, and rebirth. In the animal kingdom, death is abundant; it must constantly occur in order to provide subsistence for larger predators. It is also soon realized that the cycle of death to feed others is a recurring and never-ending process. As discussed, many hunting communities identify myths where the hunted animal understands that it serves a purpose of keeping others alive, so many myths portray animals as conceding that they are part of a natural law that promises upon their death, that life will continue. The mythic portrayal of humans into animal form then teaches the characters of myth that they too must accept that they, as all humans, too are part of the same natural process. Life as an animal instructs the mythic human to forego his or her societal ties and revel in a more animalistic, freer self, but more importantly, it teaches the human about the natural, unceasing cycle of life. Also, the widespread belief in the concept of reincarnation, that humans after death can be born again into or born from the life of an animal connects this same idea that humans and animals are irrevocably connected by nature's laws. Death, with this natural view, then mythically becomes something not to be feared but embraced for its promise of natural regeneration.

Mythic Creatures

Mythic creatures have also always been an imperative part of myth. Oftentimes these mythic creatures are portrayed as part human and part animal, such as centaurs, harpies, sirens, satyrs, gorgons, sphinxes, etc. The mythological representation of creatures that are part human and part animal often instantaneously ties them to possessing both animal and human abilities; therefore, their appearance in myth often signals important lessons. Satyrs and centaurs are often portrayed, for instance, as overcome by attributes described as animalistic, like insatiable sexual appetites. Some, hybrid mythical creatures, though, are described as possessing mystical powers, which are sometimes portrayed as destructive, like harpies, sirens, and gorgons; this mythical portrayal of distrustful animalistic and human creatures presents a timeless unease by mankind for the natural world. Quite often mythical creatures, whether they are part human and part animal, or part animal and part monster, serve to capture the mysterious and terrifying aspects of nature in relation to human lives.

Celtic mythology is full of mythic creatures that possess animalistic qualities; "winged beasts and hybrid creatures" appear throughout Celtic art and myth, such as Cernunnos, the antlered deity, who holds a snake with the head of the ram (Wood 49). Temples in southern Gaul showcase menacing animalistic monsters that devour human heads and limbs (Wood 49). In addition, to account for the phenomenon of lightning, the Serbians believed in a giant named Vii, who would seldom open his fierce eyes, but once he did, the gaze would burn anyone near to ashes. And Bohemians and Slovaks also believed in a similar explanation of a mythic, animalistic creature causing thunder and lightning, as "amid the vast Eastern European plains, thunder and lightning were a constant, angry presence and the source of several myths" (Phillips & Kerrigan 31).

The Sphinx, one of the most well-known of mythological creatures in Egypt, was part human and part lion. It was believed to protect the areas it guarded; "an inscription on the base of one late-first-millennium BC[E] Sphinx states proudly: 'I protect the chapel of thy tomb, I guard the gate. I ward off the intruding stranger. I hurl thy foes to the ground and their weapons with them. I drive away the wicked.... I destroy thine adversaries in their lurking place'" (qtd. in Fleming & Lothian 71). The Greeks also revered the Sphinx, though their artistic representations sometimes incorporated features of birds. The Sphinx was highly regarded at Delphi, and perhaps the most famous Greek encounter with the Sphinx was presented at Thebes with the myth of Oedipus. The Sphinx of Thebes was said to be presented to the city by Hera from Egypt. Oedipus having partially fulfilled the prophecy from Delphi in killing, unbeknownst to him, his father Laius, arrives at the city of Thebes where he encounters a Sphinx who tells him that he will be king if he can solve its riddle. Oedipus does, and the Sphinx is said to have either thrown itself off of a cliff and died or consumed itself before Oedipus' eyes.

The ancient Greeks undoubtedly had many mythic representations of mythical creatures that depict aspects of the natural world. Scylla and Charybdis, for instance, portrayed the indeterminate savagery the sea often presented to sailors, with Scylla represented as a six-headed monster that would indiscriminately eat six men aboard any ship, and Charybdis, opposite Scylla, described as a massive whirlpool that would swallow whole ships into the unknown depths of the sea. The Titans and the Hundred-Handers were often portrayed as forces of the earth's elements. Cyclopes, harpies, sirens, dryads, nymphs, and satyrs were all thought to haunt the deep recesses of the remote wilderness, and because of this they were often viewed as distrustful. Also there are many depictions in Greek mythology of unruly and larger-than-life animals that cause havoc to the communities they encounter, such as the Nemean Lion, Calydonion Boar, the Horses of Diomedes, etc. These unruly mythic animals reveal a human terror of unfettered nature. Finally the part human, part animal representations of creatures like the Minotaur or Medusa identify again a fear of the natural world when it infringes too closely upon civilization, yet these mythic creatures also often serve to propel a message of the necessity, and even benefit of facing these fears, as the Medusa's skin and head gives power to Perseus and also the Goddess Athena.

The American Indian tribes of the Eastern Woodlands and Great Lakes believe that nature possesses powerful forces, called Manitous, which live everywhere around them. Some Manitous were benevolent, but some were also thought to be malevolent, like Windigo, "the cannibal monster who lay in hiding to await the unwary traveler" (Zimmerman 84). The Kwakiutl tribe believed in Yagim, a shark-like spirit that would follow people as they canoed, capsizing their boat and eating anyone who fell into the water (Zimmerman 77). The Ojibwe believed in Mishipeshu, an underwater panther, which had the head and paws of a panther but was covered in serpent-like scales. The Ojibwe believed that this powerful creature could be dangerous to anyone attempting to travel the treacherous waters of the Great Lakes by canoe, but also they believed that Mishipeshu held mystical ties to the underworld. The Thunderbird was also a mythological creature in many American Indian tribes; its mythic portrayal serving as a direct representation of the earth's elements. The Thunderbird, a giant eagle-like bird, "whose wings make thunder and whose eyes and beak generate lightning, was primarily associated with the rain that brings fertility" (Lowenstein & Vitebsky 65). The American Indian people believed that they must learn methods to appease these powerful spirits that were representations of the elements of nature.

In addition, many African myths recount tales of mythological creatures to explain seemingly mysterious aspects of nature. The Mongo-Nkundo of the Congo have myths where sharp-toothed dwarves, known as biloko, haunt the deep recesses of the forests; "they sprout grass on their bodies where hair should grow and live in the hollow trunks of dead trees…. Their mouths, which form a snout like a wild beast's, can open wide enough to swallow a human body whole" (Allan, Fleming, & Phillips 110). One myth of the biloko[7] tells of a wife accompanying her husband on a hunting trip in the dark forest. Her husband left her alone to check on his traps, when a biloko came to her "giving off a smell of rotten vegetation" (Allan, Fleming, & Phillips 110). The biloko appeared to her with a haunting cry, stating that it was hungry; in a daze from the incessant piercing cry, the wife agreed to let the biloko taste her arm. The husband retuned the next day with his own bounty from the forest, but found that his wife had been reduced to flesh and bone.

Chinese mythology is also replete with mythological creatures that function to explain natural phenomenon. For instance, dragons feature prominently in myths from China:

> In Chinese myth, dragons seem to have their origins as rain deities, and the connection with water always remained strong. They were usually thought of as living in lakes and rivers. They were regularly invoked in time of drought … dragons were generally portrayed as protectors … keeping watch over waterways and the clouds and winds. Their image of beneficent power was appreciated by Chinese rulers, who appropriated the dragon as an imperial symbol [Allan & Phillips, Chinese, 93].

The Incas of western South America believed that lunar eclipses were in fact a monster that would take a bite out of their moon goddess Mama

Kilya. Thus they considered lunar eclipses to be omens that would spell impending disaster, so they would wave weapons at the sky to try to scare the malicious being away (Wilkinson 201). The Incas also thought that rainbows were a two-headed dragon deity named Chuichu; whenever they saw a rainbow, they felt that it was a good sign because Chuichu was thought to connect the sky with the earth, bringing both sun and rain, elements needed for the growing of crops (Wilkinson 201).

These mythical creatures serve as representations of humanity's perception of the natural world; they remind audiences that nature can also be indiscriminate and destructive. However, mythical creatures also reveal again the message that wild places, and their inhabitants, even if they are portrayed as terrifying or mysterious, can be spiritually transformative for the characters who journey into the remote wilderness. Sometimes mythic characters are visited by these mythic beings to remind them of the necessity of recognizing one's connection to the wild within.

The Wild Is a Harsh Teacher—The Trickster

As discussed, nature has been depicted as a place that can instruct and heal human beings psychologically, physically, and spiritually, but myth must portray nature as realistic, so mythology often takes into account the apparent ferocity and indifference of the natural environment. Mythology, as stated in the introduction of this book, focuses on the timeless human dilemmas of why we are here and why we die. Myths that portray humans as tied to nature must present what may appear to humans as the harsh aspects of the natural world in order to fulfill lasting messages to humanity's oldest and most enduring of quandaries.

Nature as viewed by human perspective can appear incredibly fierce; seemingly without warning hurricanes, volcanoes, blizzards, tornados, etc., can strike and even decimate entire communities. In nature, it is soon evident that the law of survival of the fittest dominates; death is a necessary and unceasing part of nature, and mythology does not shy away from these facts. Myth fully embraces the harsh aspects of nature alongside the beneficial features of the environment. Myth incorporates a realistic portrayal of nature to decisively persuade audiences of their inescapable connection to nature as it is.

The trickster is an important aspect of world myth, and often the role the trickster serves is central to the myth's message of the harsh aspects of nature. Tricksters often display uncontrollable aspects, similar to those found in the Greek satyrs; they often have insatiable appetites for sex, food, wine, and contrariness. They act in accordance to an independent code of what they alone feel is justifiable. They are portrayed in myth to represent all that cannot be explained; they also appear in myth to remind audiences that curiosity, revelry, and mischief are essential aspects of life. For instance, the Norse Loki is responsible for the destruction of the earth in Ragnarok, but this event causes a new and better world to be created. The Hindu god Hanuman similarly acted as a trickster in his youth, once trying to swallow the sun, but later he becomes a cultural hero because he possesses archetypal trickster qualities, such as curiosity and perseverance. And the West African myths of Anansi, their mythic trickster Spider, show him as delivering fire to the people out of such trickster archetypes.

Many tricksters within myth are portrayed as animals, such as Coyote in various American Indian myths. The Nez Percé have a creation story that involves the trickster Coyote.[8] In this myth, first Coyote slayed a massive monster, getting earth ready for inhabitants. As seen in many creation stories discussed in chapter 1, Coyote used the pieces of the primordial monster to create life. He scattered the pieces of flesh throughout the land, and everywhere a piece landed, a different tribe of American Indians emerged. Fox comes to Coyote and points out that Coyote did not create a tribe at the location that he killed the monster, and this filled Coyote with great sadness. Thinking of some way to commemorate the death of the ferocious monster, he then wiped the left-over blood from his own paws and said "'Here make the Nez Percé; their numbers will be few, but they will be strong and pure'" (Zimmerman 90).

In one myth from the Jicarilla Apache,[9] Coyote wishes to marry, so he takes his own heart from his body, cuts it in two, and places half on his nose and half on his tail. He then finds a suitable girl he wants to marry; she agrees only if he will allow her to kill him four separate times. If he is able to be resurrected all four times, she will agree to be his wife. The maiden kills Coyote with an axe the first three times, breaking all of his bones, but seeing him come to her each morning renewed, she decides to use a knife for her final attempt to ultimately kill Coyote, but again, Coyote only arrives to her the next morning as if nothing happened to him. Here Coyote, as mythic trickster, embodies what many mythic tricksters portray—the characteristics most in tune with the laws of nature. Coyote, fully embraces the fact that he is a natural part of the wilderness, and in his willingness to show how one, in nature, moves so seamlessly from death into life instructs audiences of myth on the harsh, but necessary lessons nature myths portray.

Mythic tricksters often teach audiences to see that nature indeed is indiscriminate and harsh, but in this undifferentiating aspect of nature, rewards of renewal are always promised. For instance, Raven, in the mythology of Northwest Coast, simply chooses reincarnation to accomplish his goal of finding the source of the light of the sun. As a mythic trickster, he is curious about the immense glow the sun provides, so he resolves to identify the source. The way he proceeds to achieve his mission is connected again to nature references in a way that shows the cyclicality of nature's processes. After becoming a pine needle and being swallowed by a maiden as she drinks water from a stream, he is born again, not as a raven, but as a child who looks like a raven. He lives with the Sky Chief, the father of the maiden, and his mother. The Sky Chief sees the interest of his grandson for the box that holds the sun, so the Sky Chief simply tells his daughter to give the box to the child. Raven child then opens the box and instantaneously transforms once more back to his former form, the raven, and flies away, carrying the sun with him and then freeing it to provide light and warmth to the people. This myth shows the role that the trickster provides in continuing the existence of life on earth, as the mythic trickster is simply a representation of the unfettered quality of the natural world. Similar to this myth of Raven, through his trickster characteristics, finding and securing the needed element of the sun for the people, so too does Zimmerman point out other examples of American Indian tricksters serving an essential role for the people: "The Kiowa trickster-hero Saynday brought the sun from the other side of the world. Sweet Medicine gave the Cheyenne sacred arrows and the buffalo hat. Lone Man saved the Mandan from a great flood" (75). Not all trickster myths are portrayed as positive, though, but they are explained as all essential to the continuation of life in its natural element.

In African mythology, the trickster is often a central component. The Fon people believe in Legba, a divine trickster who often creates mischief just for its own sake. Aboriginal Australian mythology is also replete with mythological tricksters that explain the unpredictability of nature. Aboriginal tricksters, like Ngandjala-Ngandjala of western Kimberley steals a reliable food source for the people just for the fun of it (Allan, Fleming, & Kerrigan 72). Whenever there is a natural disaster such as a fire or flood, myths often recount explanations of tricksters.

One of the most well-known trickster character in myth is that of Loki in Norse mythology. Loki is complex; he is part of the Norse pantheon of the Aesir, but as a trickster, he is also viewed as often outside of the confines of the Aesir. He was born from natural elements; his father, Farbauti "struck stone against flint and a spark leapt into the undergrowth of a wooded island said to be Loki's mother, Laufey" (Auerbach & Simpson 51). Loki was thus conceived in the form of fire. Like other trickster characters, the Egyptian Sêth for instance, the role of Loki is not one that can be overcome; Loki's presence within the realms of the Aesir must be tolerated. Loki, again like other mythic tricksters shows a side of nature that is realistic, as nature can not only provide a sanctuary, but it is also harsh and spontaneous. Loki, thus, has a voracious sexual appetite, as again, he represents nature unchecked. He, also, similar to other mythic tricksters was sometimes presented as being able to transform into either sex, as "he was the mother of Odin's marvelous eight-legged horse Sleipnir," and "once became pregnant by eating the half-burnt heart of a woman, and from this gestation came all female monsters" (Auerbach & Simpson 51). Loki, and other tricksters, often bring this element into myth. Loki shows the Aesir that death is not something that can be avoided, as he brings forth the downfall of the Aesir and the entire world, a myth that will be discussed in chapter 6 of this book, through his offspring: Hel, the goddess of the underworld, the wolf Fenrir, and the giant serpent Jormungand. In other Norse myths, Loki is a character that explains the destruction of nature's cycles, as his myth with Sif the corn goddess portrays. When Loki cuts off Sif's golden hair, apparently for no reason, which is common for most tricksters, the result is that the crops will not grow, and the people begin to starve.

The Indian incarnate Krishna, from the god Vishnu, is portrayed in the *Bhagavata Purana* as a young boy, who is fond of playing the trickster role. In this portrayal of him,[10] he is a child who has been accused of eating dirt. When he opens his mouth to offer evidence that he did not eat the dirt, his mother sees "mountains, islands, seas. She saw the winds, lightning, the moon, the stars. She saw the elements, the strands of matter, and life, time, action, hope—the entire universe appeared before her in the boy's gaping mouth, and she was stunned.... Is my little son a god in whom the unfathomable universe is present? Through this god, am I given the illusion that I exist" (Leeming & Page, *God,* 28).

When Krishna is accused of eating dirt, this is a symbolic reference to the futility of such an accusation because Krishna is the earth, as evidenced when his mother looks within his mouth. Furthermore, his mother, through this experience, understands that she now has witnessed the natural fact of existence, that even her existence is an illusion. She sees in her son's mouth, Krishna as a young trickster, the entire universe, and she also sees that her role within the universe is the same as her son's, for in Hindu belief all people are a part of the universal Brahman. Seeing nature within her son's mouth allows her to see her role within a cyclical and broad reality. Krishna, as a child playing the role of trickster, revels in making light of life, and as such immediately reveals to his mother, and the audience of the myth, the Hindu principle that all life is really an illusion, and thus should not be taken too seriously. This light-hearted embrace of life is central to understanding the mythic trickster.

Untamed Nature and the Unfettered Human

Often in world myth there is a tendency to display humans within the wilderness as undergoing a transformation into wildness. In Greek mythology the maenads, followers of the god Dionysus, often dwelled within the deep recesses of uncharted nature, and the myths associated with them portray them as wild women who become so intoxicated with wildness that they commit acts abhorrent to members of a "civilized" and "tamed" society. Similarly, as discussed in chapter 2, the initiates of the rituals performed for the Phrygian Mother Goddess Cybele also often resided in remote areas of wilderness and reached again such a frenzied state that priests, the Galli, were renowned for periodically castrating themselves to honor Cybele's connection with Attis. Again, the castration of the Galli served to tie them to an acceptance of the power of nature, presented by Cybele, in her promise of renewal for all that was sacrificed. The critical component when looking at myths that present characters as becoming "wild" is that often because of their immersion in the deep wilderness, a spiritual awakening within the characters often occurs.

For instance, in the Celtic myth of Suibhne, a prince of the Dal nAraide, he "was said to have gone mad during a battle in the year 637 CE. After the conflict, he went off to live by himself in the wilderness" (MacLeod 78). And similarly, in Celtic mythology, the well-known character of Myrddin, later Merlin, also was depicted as going insane due to the mental strain of battle, so he fled human society to live in the wilderness (MacLeod 79). After his embrace of the wild, the mythic character of Suibhne held the ability to directly speak to the animals of the forest; as cited in MacLeod:

> Little antlered one, little bellowing one, melodious roaring one
> Sweet to us the call you make in the glen....
> Beautiful blessed birch, a shrine of music
> Lovely is every joining branch on the top of your head...
> Little fawn, of the slender shanks, forbearance for your power
> I am riding upon you from peak to peak.

MacLeod continues by saying that "Suibhne describes his journey as lonely, but also says that if he were to search all the mountains of the earth, he would rather have for his dwelling a single hut in the beautiful valley of Glen Bolcáin. He praises the waters of the glen and ... the songs of the birds are music to his soul" (79). Suibhne is also defined as madly running throughout the countryside, evading all people, and sleeping in the tops of trees. In his myth he is given animalistic attributes as he becomes one with his environment. One Celtic text in which he appears shows him declaring that he "has endured many hardships 'since feathers grew on my body' (possibly reflecting a change in spiritual state). Suibhne also announces that his name is not a fit one for him. Potentially indicating that he has taken on a new incarnation. He suggests the name 'Horn-Head' would be better" (MacLeod 79).

In Celtic myth there is also a character named Sliabh Mis who is said to have gone insane after her husband was murdered, and due to her mental state she takes on the attributes of animals and nature. For instance, Mis is said to be able to "run and fly like the wind"; she also "was described as having grown *clúmh* all over her body—a word that means either feather or fur" (MacLeod 79). Soon, the people of the neighboring village view her as a threat, and the local king offers to pay a ransom to anyone who can catch her. The king's harpist, known as "Dark Knowledge," eventually entices her with his music and the riches that he places before her. The harpist asks for food from her, and she proceeds to catch and kill a deer. As she consumes the raw flesh, he encourages her to first cook the meat; when she does, she gains part of her memory back. They then have sex, and this act further humanizes her. MacLeod states that this myth portrays a common theme in Celtic mythology involving shamanistic practices, where "wild" men and women leave the community to go into the unknown wilderness to become what is known as the "geilt":

> The *geilt* is often said to be able to run swiftly, make great leaps, fly or levitate; they are also known to perch in trees (an activity credited to Hungarian shamans as well).... The geilt is often naked, and ... has grown fur or feathers on their body. The geilt appears to be in deep connection (and communication) with the natural world.... These experiences mirror many aspects of the initiatory ordeals of the shaman, after which they formally return to society and utilize their newfound knowledge for the benefit of the community [80].

In the Sumerian *Epic of Gilgamesh*, the king of Uruk, Gilgamesh, is portrayed as an insufficient king as he abuses his power at the expense of his subjects. The people beg the gods to deliver them a means to remedy Gilgamesh's behavior, and the gods grant this wish by sending Gilgamesh his equal, the clearly wild Enkidu. The character of Enkidu is represented in the text as living in the wilderness among the animals and drinking from their same watering source; his body is even covered entirely in fur. It is by merging with Enkidu, through friendship, that Gilgamesh is finally able to become a righteous king, because in embracing Enkidu, Gilgamesh has acknowledged the more natural components of himself.

The Greek myths of the goddess Artemis, or the Roman Diana, also show her often as a representation of nature, sometimes in its harsher aspects. Some myths portray Artemis, the virginal goddess of the wilderness, as kind, as portrayed when Agamemnon attempts to sacrifice his daughter Iphigenia to gain her approval and secure success in the Trojan War, but Artemis, unbeknownst to Agamemnon, sweeps in and mystically replaces Iphigenia with a lamb. Artemis is believed to also be one of the best representations we have in the Greek Olympian pantheon of the Neolithic Mother Earth Goddess. After the culture transformed in Greece away from primarily goddess worship to a male-dominated pantheon, discussed in chapter 2 of this book, Artemis is one of the best examples of the earlier Neolithic Goddess preserved in later belief systems. Artemis, twin sister of the god Apollo, was born into full adulthood and served an essential role in assisting her mother Leto in delivering Apollo. She then remains an elusive goddess as a later edition to the original six members of the Olympian pantheon, as she mythically is portrayed as preferring a solitary, virginal existence within the deep recesses of the wilderness. When encountered within this environment, mythic characters must tread lightly when interacting with Artemis. The hero Heracles had to secure Artemis' Ceryneian Hind as his third labor; this of course insulted Artemis as Heracles attempted to carry the animal away with him, but Heracles was successful in accomplishing his task because he had the fortitude to understand that he must respect both Artemis and the Hind, so he deferentially asked permission from Artemis to take her Hind if he promised to return it. Similar to his treatment of Cerberus, the three-headed dog that guards the gate of Hades, Heracles knew that he could not overcome the unharnessed aspects of Artemis' power as a nature divinity, so he simply borrowed the Hind and returned it to her unharmed.

Quite often Artemis is mythically described as representing the harsh aspects of the natural environment, but in these myths that often appear severe, one must see Artemis as not vengeful but realistic. The myth of Artemis and Actaeon portrays Artemis as stern. As briefly discussed in chapter 3, the character of Actaeon was hunting with his dogs in the woods when he spied Artemis bathing in a secluded stream. Actaeon upon seeing the full splendor of the nude and virginal goddess, only stood stunned and watched her. Artemis discovered this transgressor, and as a representation of the aspects of nature that cannot be polluted by mankind, she demanded that he remain silent. But, Actaeon, not mythically understanding the magnitude of what he chanced upon, attempted to speak with the goddess. In order to prove to Actaeon the laws of nature, Artemis transformed him into a stag. Instantly, Actaeon, now as a stag, became the prey of his own hunting dogs. They fell upon him, one by one, and devoured his flesh. Though this tale is gruesome, it projects a theme of the natural cycle of life. Actaeon, by chance, happened to witness a secret of the natural world; if he remained devoutly awed by the majesty of the nude and virginal Artemis, he seemingly would have been permitted to live. But, Actaeon could not display the necessary reverence for the sacred sight he witnessed, so by speaking he proved he had more to learn about the laws of nature. Artemis, reverent of the Goddess and male consort myths of chapter 2, teaches Actaeon his proper place within the larger cycles of the environment. She, as a representation of unfettered nature is not symbolic prey to be overcome by the mortal male; she is eternal, so she makes this point clear to Actaeon by having him experience the same fate as many of his previous prey suffered, as he becomes the hunted. Stange states of the Greek Goddess Artemis:

> Artemis's connection ... is to the violence—the life-death-life process—of the wild world. Indeed, she "is herself the wilderness, the wild and untamed...." It is therefore not surprising that the Mistress of Beasts is a goddess of sacrifice and transformation, death and renewal.... As remote as the moon or the mountain-top, as intimate as the first cry or last breath, she commands recognition that in our beginnings are our ends [143–4].

The myths surrounding the Greek god Dionysus or Roman Bacchus also portray consistent messages of untamed nature touching upon the characters who encounter or revere him. When Dionysus appears in myth, he is often represented in "wild" associations. As the god of the grape harvest, and so also the god of wine, he is connected to the altered state of intoxication. It is a disservice to his myths, though, to only see them as expressing messages of alcoholic revelry, because the state of drunkenness Dionysus inspires in people is also spiritually transformative when viewed with the backdrop of the unfettered natural world he embodies. In his myths, the wine that Dionysus brings to humans enables them not to become mere drunken fools, but to become more "wild," which signals that they are becoming more in touch with their natural selves, and this is critical to understanding the mythology of Dionysus.

Dionysus was late to come to the Olympian pantheon; he is believed to have more ancient origins and to come from the Near East. In Thrace and Anatolia, along with the mountain goddess Cybele, Dionysus was highly revered. In later Greek religion, Dionysus, like the Norse Loki, remains a figure who is part of the Olympian pantheon, but he is also in many ways contrary to the values of the high gods.

In terms of classical Greek mythology, Dionysus was said to be born from a mortal woman named Semele and Zeus, who disguised himself as a mortal to have sex with her. After getting Zeus to promise her anything she desired, Semele, pregnant with Dionysus, asked Zeus to reveal his true self to her. Zeus, incapable of breaking his promise, sadly complied. When Zeus appeared in all his divine splendor, Semele instantly died in a flash of lightning. The unborn Dionysus within Semele's womb was placed within the thigh of Zeus until he was able to be born, which finally resulted in a divine birth directly from the body of Zeus, similar to Athena. When Hera found this illegitimate baby born from yet another affair on the part of Zeus, she had the Titans tear the body of Dionysus apart. Rhea, Dionysus' grandmother, felt pity for him, found the pieces of his body, and put them back together, resurrecting him. Rhea then gave Dionysus back to Zeus, disguising him as a ram to protect him. The symbolism of this myth surrounding nature is quite telling.

From the story of Dionysus' birth, he is immediately recognized as a harvest god, the god of the grape harvest. The cutting up of his body by the forces of the earth, a common representation of the Titans, is a popular theme in agricultural myths, as discussed in previous chapters. This part of the myth also provides some indication of Dionysus indeed coming from Eastern sources. In Dionysus' myth he is resurrected by Rhea, a figure recognized as an Earth Goddess, as stated in chapter 2. What is interesting is that Dionysus' myth starts at this point that usually in more ancient agricultural myths would be the myth in its entirety. But instead, the myths of Dionysus continue on to show profound lessons of the reality of the wilderness and the promise of cyclical nature. The preservation of Dionysus also allows him at a young age to experience life in animal form, as Rhea changed him into a ram to further save his life; this animalistic experience in his youth also points to the messages he imparts in his later myths. As an adult Dionysus was often described as transforming into animal form, such as a leopard, and many of his myths show him transforming others into animals, like when he transformed a group of unruly pirates into dolphins. The followers of Dionysus were also said to wear animal skins within their wilderness revelry. Dionysus, and the myths of his frenzied followers, teach audiences to remember their animalistic and wild selves.

In one myth Dionysus was said to travel to the underworld to save his mother Semele from the cruel fate she suffered upon seeing Zeus' true form. Myths of descent to the underworld are filled with terror, as the underworld is a place of death, but myths where a living being travels to the underworld, particularly to save a loved one who has died, often signal a message about mortality as it is related to nature. As stated in chapter 1 and 2, the underworld can also be portrayed as womb-like, so myths that portray a living being going to the underworld is, and has been since the most ancient of civilizations, indicative of the seasonal cycles of nature. Death is of course a crucial element of the underworld, but it can also be a place of regeneration. The myth of Dionysus' descent to the underworld portrays the cyclical aspect of human mortality as being tied to seasonal change. Like the myths of the Earth Goddess and her male consort, Dionysus experiences symbolic death in his descent and facing of the underworld elements, but, like many myths of the male consort, he is resurrected, his second resurrection, to show the audience of the myth that mortal death can also be attached to the same cycles present in nature. Dionysus, in this myth, dies for a time, trying to save his mother Semele, and then is symbolically resurrected to show that human beings fit into the same processes of nature as all other living beings. Frazer states "the local Argive tradition was that he descended through the Alcyonian Lake; and his resurrection, was annually celebrated on the spot by the Argives, who summoned him by the water by trumpet blasts, while they threw a lamb into the lake as an offering to the warder of the dead" (325).

Again, Dionysus is often portrayed as associated with wildness and unfettered nature, as are his followers, the maenads, who are usually depicted as women who broke the confines of their societal position to roam the wilderness dancing in ecstatic frenzy; "In the midst of these revels, Dionysus asked the local women to join in, and the ground shook with their insane release from the shackles of decorum" (Leeming & Page, *God*, 101). The maenads were portrayed as fully embracing the wild aspects of themselves, as their connection to the wilderness and the animals that reside within it were central to their myths. The maenads "drew their strength from Dionysus, so that nothing—neither fire nor the sword—could stop their dance or bring them to harm" (Wilkinson 29). The portrayal of the maenads was often harsh, as true mythic representations of nature often are. They were said to tear apart any creature that came across their ecstatic path, like the myth of Pentheus, where his own mother having joined the maenads unknowingly dismembers her own son. This appears horrific, but when viewed in terms of natural symbolism, Dionysus, and many other mythic figures such as Osiris, Orpheus, and Dionysus himself, were also torn into many pieces and spread throughout the land. And again these mythic figures are often reassembled, usually by Mother Goddess figures, and resurrected in order to show that in nature, death is merely a necessary stage that is always overcome by new life. The maenads, as a representation of women freed from the confines of their suppressed role in classical Greek society, are represented as being free precisely because they have tapped into their wild and more authentic selves. They, in terms of myth, have accepted the reality of nature, and therefore, the reality of life for all living beings. In their embrace of cyclical nature, they have become immune to harm because they have become part of a greater cycle that is constantly renewed. Downing states that "Dionysus represents the sacredness and fearfulness of all boundary-dissolving experience: intoxication, sexual ecstasy, madness.... [He] exposes *us* to a kind of dismemberment and death" (182).

With the myths of Dionysus, one often sees the realization that life is as fleeting as the vicious cycle of nature, but it is also secure in its promise of continual resurrection. The merriment and revelry that is connected with Dionysus, therefore, must be associated with his extensive mythic background—Dionysus, despite a harsh upbringing, and having survived dismemberment and the underworld, is still depicted as merry. His myths associate the need to let go of struggle in life, eradicate the fear of wild abandon, and even overcome the fear of death, so that one may finally embrace life as it is. The merriment that accompanies Dionysus is experienced by a band of initiates who have resolved to live life fully while they stand in the sun. They forego their connections to society and simply live wild and free in the wilderness, because most myths that educate audiences on the importance of embracing death as natural do so to reveal that the stage of life within nature's cycle must be embraced as fleeting but also as vibrantly wondrous.

Trees of Knowledge and Botanical Metamorphosis

"Those who contemplate the beauty of the earth find reserves of strength that will endure as long as life lasts. There is something infinitely healing in the repeated refrains of nature—the assurance that dawn comes after night, and spring after winter."

—Rachel Carson

"Give me the storm and tempest of thought and action, rather than the dead calm of ignorance and faith! Banish me from Eden when you will; but first let me eat of the fruit of the tree of knowledge!"

—Robert G. Ingersoll

"'Come, Boy, sit down. Sit down and rest.' And the boy did. And the tree was happy."

—Shel Silverstein

One can imagine that since the beginning of human existence, man has marveled at the botanical elements of nature; the same is evidenced today, and throughout recorded history, as innumerable texts recount reverence for the silent, botanical partners in our existence. As discussed in the previous chapter, the animal inhabitants of the wilderness offer myriad lessons that help human beings realize their own animalistic selves, but it is the botanical aspects of the environment that arguably give human beings the most quandaries. Plants have often been regarded as holding mystical powers throughout world mythology. Plants live consecutively both above and below ground. Sometimes, they hold medicinal or hallucinogenic powers and can enable one to heal or be healed. Plants also sustain and protect mankind. Sometimes they mythically serve as representations of divinities, as has been discussed with the Neolithic Goddesses of the harvest. Innumerable plants needed for human survival silently go endlessly through the cycles of life, death, and rebirth, making humans marvel at what this process means within their own lives. Trees have always provided shelter to human beings; they often live on as generations of humans come and go; their leaves can change color, fall to the ground, and then sprout anew each spring. In botanical nature, one can see a pattern that is never-ending; in looking at one majestic pine tree that has stood for centuries, one can often see below it rotting portions of once-taller trees beside seedlings of new growth.

In Viktor Frankl's modern book *Man's Search for Meaning* (1946), he recounts a story of a woman near death in a Nazi concentration camp in World War II who finds a lesson similar to the message presented in myths from around the world in relation to human beings and botanical nature:

> This young woman knew that she would die in the next few days. But when I talked to her she was cheerful in spite of this knowledge. "I am grateful that fate has hit me so hard," she told me. "In my former life I was spoiled and did not take spiritual accomplishments seriously." Pointing through the window of the hut, she said, "This tree here is the only friend I have in my loneliness." Through that window she could see just one branch of a chestnut tree, and on the branch were two blossoms. "I often talk to this tree," she said to me. I was startled and didn't quite know how to take her words. Was she delirious? Did she have occasional hallucinations? Anxiously I asked her if the tree replied. "Yes." What did it say to her? She answered, "It said to me, 'I am here—I am here—I am life, eternal life'" [69].

The lives of humans can be seen to follow the same patterns of botanical nature; mythology repeatedly captures this message. Plants, like humans, emerge, grow if nourished, thrive, and then decay. Plants possess numerous other qualities that inspired storytellers to connect human beings to vegetative characteristics. Even today, botanical phrases like "taking root" and "branching out" are applied to human actions. Therefore, mythology too has made use of the natural example surrounding human beings from the beginning of recorded existence. Embracing one's connection to nature allows mythic audiences a harsh, but also comforting, assurance in the everlasting continuality of the botanical.

Nature as Refuge

Nature provides human beings with a refuge away from their busy lives. Texts from around the world throughout the eras discuss the natural world as severe, as discussed in the previous chapter, but also as a place of respite where one can be alone and tap into a deep reservoir of spiritual meaning.

In India, "toward the end of the late Vedic period (roughly between 900–500 BCE), the ritualistic religion of the Aryan conquerors turned increasingly toward meditation and ascetic withdrawal, as Brahmins became not only sacrificial officiants but also forest-dwelling hermits whose philosophical speculations on the relation of the human soul to the universal spirit culminated in the early *Upanishads*" (Torrance 120). At a particular age, after a Brahmin has met his obligation towards family and the community, he can choose to live the life of a hermit within the isolation of the forest. If he chooses this life, he may only eat the food the forest provides, only wear clothes found in nature, and never enter a city. This ascetic life in nature was highly revered and recommended as aiding one towards finding enlightenment.

In the sanctuaries and other sacred sites of Greece, there always remained a natural marker; "at the centre [sic] of the Eleusinian sanctuary stood an unhewn rock that was always left open to view ... in Delphi the stone worked in the characteristic of the navel was regarded not only as the centre [sic] of the sanctuary, but of the world. The tree, however, is even more important than the stone in marking the sanctuary, and this corresponds not only in Minoan-Mycenaean but also Near Eastern tradition.... The shade giving tree epitomizes both beauty and continuity across the generations. Most sanctuaries have their special tree" (Burkert 85). In Athens, Athena's olive tree guards the Erechtheion and the Pandroseion at the Acropolis, as on the island of Delos, Apollo's palm tree guards the site, and "particularly old and sacred was the oak ... of Dodona which imparted the oracle with the rustling of its branches" (Burkert 86). The sacred grove for Zeus at Dodona was believed to be so consecrated that the priests would walk barefoot upon the ground, so as to receive prophecies directly from contact with the earth. Greek sanctuaries often had to be cut off from the societal world; they remained in natural settings to connect them to their sacred purpose.

The Pomo American Indians have a myth that tells of Wintun,[1] a primordial being who fills his time at the top of vast mountain ranges, or in deep ravines, listening to the sound of the wind, trying to find its meaning. Wintun's father is said to have grown concerned for his son who chose this path of reflection in nature over learning the traditions of his people. Wintun's father eventually dies, and still Wintun prefers to sit among the sacred mountain Konocti, until he grows into an old man. Starving, he emerges from a cave and finds an injured bird; the bird fears Wintun will eat him, but Wintun only tells him, "I could hardly eat you, for you're in even worse shape than me" (Ferguson 150). Instead, he chooses to nurture the bird back to health. Many years pass, and Wintun, quite old now and near death, is scavenging for food, when the bird returns to him and reveals that since Wintun healed it, instead of consuming it, the bird will sing the song of the wind—the same song Wintun pursued all his life—and this song will heal Wintun back to renewed youth and health. With restored vigor, Wintun returns to the remaining Pomo people and teaches them the sacred song he learned after a lifetime of searching for it.

This myth shows the importance of not only seeking the wisdom the earth possesses, as Wintun even breaks away from his community to pursue this knowledge, but it also shows an embrace of valuing nature. Wintun could have easily killed the bird and gained some nourishment, but instead, he values that the bird is connected to him in its ill health, so he takes it upon himself to help the bird heal. The myth solidifies a cycle that if humans care for nature, then nature too can aid humankind.

Gardens have also long been used as mythic devices; they have been repeatedly described as places of idyllic natural beauty where people can mythically find spiritual wisdom. Gardens, or teien, are considered sacred in Japan, "offering the practitioner the means to create a visual, spiritual and psychological impression of the harmony and totality evident in nature through its five elements of river, sea, mountain, forest and field" (Allan & Kerrigan 132). The Aztecs believed that their rain god, Tlatoc, lived in four places, each on top of a separate mountain where he kept a tub of water. One mountain tub provided the light rains of morning, the other the afternoon showers, and the other the drizzle of the night. The fourth provided the water that produced violent storms. Tlatoc also possessed an idyllic garden that held verdant nature different than the most beautiful imaginings of the Aztecs. It was just this idyllic garden that the Aztecs believed would provide solace to the people who died at too young an age due to illness. Also, this garden of the afterlife was said to be the resting place of those who had died due to one of Tlatoc's violent storms; if someone was struck by lightning, then he or she was permitted to enjoy eternity in this ethereal realm. As Humphrey states, it is "in the garden that we observe constant reminders that death follows life follows death in endless cycles" (5).

Sacred Trees

Trees have appeared in the earliest of mythologies. They have always provided human beings with the components needed for survival, such as food and the means to make fire, shelter, canoes, weapons, etc. Trees, to the perception of humans, seem to stand stoically by while generations of humans go through their lives, and so trees became mythic representations of providers and even spiritual guides. The worship of trees and groves has long been a part of world mythology:

It is understandable why trees were the first plants to be worshipped by man. They were not only the largest living things around him, but they were always there, when he was a boy, a youth, a man, and elder. He learned that the trees were already standing in the same groves when his father, and even his grandfather were boys themselves.... He grasped the idea that the same trees would still be standing, long after he himself would be gone, when his children would be no more, and his grandchildren would be growing old. No wonder that ... trees became the very symbol of strength, fecundity and everlasting life. They are Nature's perfect example of reproduction and eternity [Lehner & Lehner 15].

In addition, trees reveal the cycles of nature explicitly each year; therefore, trees are often portrayed as a "potent symbol for immortality" (Bierlein 88). Seeing a tree lose its leaves in a grand display of gold, orange, and red, and then watching the leaves fall to the ground, only to see them bud again in a state of rebirth, left ancient people assigning trees with "a supernatural intelligence" (Porteous 149). The Ancient Persians "considered the tree to be the emblem of human existence owing to the changes which it undergoes during the various seasons, and it was also regarded as a type of immortality owing to its lengthened period of life" (Porteous 151). The Persians also were said to have connected seasonal change with a belief in immortality of the soul (Folkard 21).

The symbol of the sacred tree is seen in many ancient civilizations, such as Assyria, Babylonia, Arabia, Egypt, Asia, Europe, and the Americas (E. Lehner & J. Lehner 16; Bierlein 88). In Europe it is evident that tree worship extends back to ancient times, and even today this reverence has been preserved in the customs held in times of festivals; for instance, the European maypole festivals at the solstice commemorates a more ancient practice. In ancient Phrygia, "an Almond tree was considered as the father of all things" (Porteous 156), and similarly many Semitic and Aryan people believed in "trees that brought forth human beings, and of trees that were themselves partly human" (Folkard 117). In addition, The Kabyles of North Africa believed "that the men who led the tribes are formed from the Ash tree," and the aboriginal people from Encounter Bay in Australia "say that the first man was formed from the gum of a Wattle tree" (Folkard 159).

In Egypt there also was a belief in a sacred sycamore tree; "the sycamore fig along with the date palm, being the two great food producers of ancient times" (Porteous 220) are depicted throughout Egyptian art; in one such example "a goddess is shown issuing from the top of the tree, holding out a tray of figs with one hand and pouring out a stream of water from a vase held in the other" (Porteous 220). In addition, the oak tree "was in antiquity sacred to the Hebrews, because Abraham received the angel of Jehovah under its branches; the Greeks dedicated it to Zeus because his oracle in Dodona ...

was located in a grove of oaks…. It was the celestial tree of the Celtic Druids, and no druidic ceremony or rite took place without the aid of the oak…. The oak tree was also the sacred tree of the…. Dagda … the Creator of the ancient Irish" (E. Lehner & J. Lehner 42). In addition, "the oak and the ash have both been great progenitors of mankind" (Porteous 157); the Greeks believed that the oak produced the first men and called oak tress "the first mothers" (Porteous 157).

Sacred groves are also prominent throughout world mythology. In Africa, "almost every village has its sacred grove…. They were looked upon as gods, and when calamity threatened the country they were consulted" (Porteous 57). Similarly in New Zealand, Greece, Italy, Germany, and Prussia sacred groves resound.

As stated earlier in the text often the Celts did not worship their divinities in permanent structures, as they chose to hold their sacred rituals in natural environments, such as near springs, lakes, or groves. The Celts felt that "forest groves were especially hallowed as natural spaces where people could gather to venerate gods and spirits. The word for 'sacred grove' was *nemeton,* and it occurs widely throughout the Celtic world. The Greek writer Strabo … claimed that the Celts of Galatia met annually at the 'Drunemeton' ('Oak Sanctuary') to decide important religious and political issues" (Wood 32). The Roman Tacitus in his *The History* (109 CE) discusses what scholars believe to be the Isle of Rugen in the Baltic where worshippers believed in a Mother Earth Goddess by the name of Hertha. In her sacred grove, it was believed that she arrived in her chariot drawn by consecrated cows to initiate the beginning of spring; "every place the goddess visited became a scene of festivity; no wars were undertaken; arms were untouched; and peace reigned supreme" (Porteous 79). Hertha during the festivities would fulfill her sexual appetite and then retreat back into the sea. It is said that those who witnessed these festivities, though, were close to death (Porteous 80). A clear connection is made here with fertility being tied to the natural aspects of the earth, and death is a natural part of this linkage. The Celts also showed their veneration for nature in the artifacts they left behind in their many rituals in celebration of the sanctity of the sacred grove; for instance, the Celts gave small offerings to the soil to ensure its fertility, as well as to water for its continued benevolence.

The Grove of Uppsala in Sweden was held as highly sacred to the Norse people; "Every tree in the grove surrounding the temple was regarded as divine…. Every ninth year, at the Vernal Equinox, a great festival was held in the grove in honour [sic] of [Thor, Odin, and Freyr]…. Each day six victims, one being a man, the others dogs and horses, were sacrificed, and their bodies were hung from the sacred trees" (Porteous 80).

The American Indian Iroquois present another version of creation[2] where the first people lived high in the sky because no earth yet existed. In the myth the chief's daughter becomes very ill, so a village elder tells the people to find the root of a sacred tree so that it may heal her. The community comes together to partake in this endeavor to save the girl; they find the tree and dig a giant hole around its base, but unexpectedly, the entire tree and the girl fall through the hole into the abyss below. Within the earth, like discussed in many creation myths in chapter 1, there was only a primordial ocean, yet this sea had two swans continuously swimming in it. The swans alarmed by this event sought the Great Turtle, who advised them to find the tree and "bring up the magic soil that was attached to its roots" in order to make an island for the girl to rest upon (Bierlein 63). All of the animals who lived in the sea helped with this task, but finally the toad, and in some versions the muskrat, succeeded in carrying a bit of soil within its mouth, coming up above the endless water, and spitting out the dirt to create land. This effort on the part of the toad cost it its life. Yet, the earth remained dark until the girl told the Great Turtle about her world full of light, so the Great Turtle told the animals to burrow holes in the sky until the celestial light reached their realm.

The myth states that "the girl is the mother of all things" (Bierlein 63). Her connection to the tree and the soil that its roots clutch to is crucial in identifying her in her role as creator. Her illness connects her to the tree, and like the natural cycles of life witnessed in the seasonal changes trees best portray, she dies a mythic death moving into an underworld below her divine home. But the myth presents the tree and the girl only in a dormant state. Together, as they fall into the underworld, here presented as a primordial ocean, they ensure the renewal of the cycle of life. In this new realm, their seed-like plummet into fertile waters produces the assurance of new life; just as a small seed produces bountiful harvests, the small bit of soil the tree's roots hold onto is enough to create a habitat for all living things.

The Polynesian myth of Pare and Hutu[3] tells of a beautiful maiden, Pare, who came from such noble parentage that she was considered sacred among her people; therefore, she was kept secluded from the rest of the tribe in a solitary home where no youths were permitted to visit. One day, in conducting games to see which eligible male could earn the noble hand of Pare, she came out of her house and saw the handsome and skilled Hutu masterfully winning all of the games. She went to him and invited him to enter her home, but knowing that he was a stranger among her people, and thinking of what they would think if he was caught alone with her in her house, he refused. She begged him, but still he adamantly refused and left her alone. Dejected for the first time in her life, she committed suicide. Her people, upon finding her body, screamed in mourning; they hunted down Hutu and demanded that he give himself over to them, so they could murder him as payment for the death of their sacred maiden. Hutu, himself distraught at her death, agreed that this was just, but he requested that the people first give him three days, after which he promised to return to them and face his death.

In a myth similar to the Greek myth of Orpheus, Hutu is determined to retrieve Pare, and thus save his own life. Hutu "sat down and chanted the *karakia* which *tohunga* chant over themselves when they think of death and of Te Reinga, the abode of spirits" (Andersen 300). Hine-nui-te-po is the female guardian of Te Reinga, the "world below," and she instructed Hutu to bring a basket of food from the land of the living and eat it sparingly upon his journey, for if he ate the food of the dead, he would never return. Hine-nui-te-po also told Hutu that in Te Reinga everything is upside down from the world he was used to. Hutu descended and saw what no mortal should witness; Te Reinga was filled with spirits of the dead. He inquired after Pare and found that she indeed resided there but had no desire to see Hutu who once shunned her. Hutu then decided to hold games in the land of the dead to try to win Pare's heart. Initially, his plan did not work, but soon he asked for a long tree to be brought to him. He had the spirits help him fasten ropes to the top of the tree until it bent low to the ground, and then he climbed on top of it with another dead man. Hutu instructed the spirits to let go of the ropes, and the tree catapulted Hutu and the dead shade high into the air, to the delight of the onlookers. Seeing the commotion, Pare came to watch, and soon Hutu convinced her to sit with him on the tree. They both sat together, and the tree flung them so high into the air that they were both flung back into the upper world in the roots of the same tree, as again in the underworld, the tree grew upside down. Pare and Hutu returned to her people, and after much rejoicing, they become husband and wife.

This myth holds many natural elements that provide important meaning. The component of not eating the food of the dead is a common mythic archetype. Food, as essential to survival, is often connected to nature myths. As discussed often throughout this book, the harvesting of food, especially to early agriculturally-dependent communities, was a process that was deeply connected with death and sacrifice. Death often was connected to the assurance of continued crop production. Mythically eating the food of the underworld throws off the balance of nature. If it is consumed, then whoever partakes of it must remain dead, becoming symbolic fertilization themselves, or else the natural cycle needed to keep mankind alive is disrupted.

In addition, the portrayal of the upside down tree growing strong in the underworld reveals a belief that again nature fully needs its inner realms, the underworld, to sustain life on earth. The upside down tree still is viewed as alive and strong in its underworld dormancy; it also is mythically depicted as the only thing capable of bringing back to life both Pare and Hutu. The tree, like a birthing episode, pushes the two protagonists out of the womb-like chamber and back into the upper world, only by their ability to cling to its roots.

Many Polynesian people held a belief that after a person dies, he or she must return to the underworld by the aid of a sacred tree. The Maoris believed that a person descended to the underworld by a long root of a sacred tree (Poignant 62). In the Hawaiian Islands of the South Pacific, the native inhabitants recount a belief that when they die, they believe that the soul of the person leaps over a cliff, but as soon as they take the leap, a massive tree, the Bua tree, emerges from the Spirit World to catch the soul; "the branches of the tree are covered with fragrant blossoms, and each tribe has a special branch reserved for it. The branch reserved for the soul's particular tribe is put forward nearest to him. By some miraculous force, he is compelled to climb this branch…. As soon as he is on the branch the Bua tree descends to the lower world bearing the soul with it" (Porteous 214). In addition a common Polynesian belief was that the tree often held "misleading branches," where a person's soul might be tempted to grasp hold of the deceiving green and lush branches, but in doing so would fall to Po, a place of bleak nothingness (Poignant 63). But, if the person, apparently accepting his or her death, rightly grasped the dry, brittle branches, then he or she could return to the safety of the womb-like underworld awaiting regrowth.

World Trees

The concept of a World Tree also exists in many mythologies. In Slavic mythology, there is a belief in a World Tree where the world is portrayed as an oak tree, with the underworld as part of its roots (Wilkinson 88). The Slavic god of thunder, Perun, sits in the top branches in the form of an eagle. Also the ancient Assyrians believed in a World Tree; "part of the Izdubar Epic, begins by saying that in Eridhu a stalk grew, its roots were of white crystal which stretched towards the deep. Its seat was the centre [sic] of the earth, while in its foliage was the home of Zikum, i.e., the heavens, the great primeval mother" (Porteous 207). Assur, the prominent deity of the Assyrians "was the Sacred Tree, regarded by the Assyrian race as the personification of life and generation" (Folkard 6).

In India "the World Tree of Hindostan is the symbol of vegetation, of generation, and of universal life, and consequently of immortality. It bears various appellations, and is, in itself, considered to be the god Brahma.... All of the other gods of the Hindu religious system were considered to be branches from this divine tree, which branches overshadowed the universe" (Folkard 3). In Hymn 81 of the Tenth Book of the *Rig Veda* the question is asked: "'what was the Forest, what was the Tree from which the sky and earth issued?'—the answer being that the Forest, the Cosmic Tree, was the god Brahma himself" (Porteous 196). The Indian *Vedas* state that when the Cosmogonic Tree is threatened then all life is threatened. This Tree is said to have produced the fruit that provided sustenance to the first men. It also provided "knowledge, wisdom, and inconceivable bliss" (Porteous 197). The connection of this Cosmogonic Tree, as realized for its power to provide for the inhabitants of earth, is a vital realization; it is made clear that if humanity loses sight of their connection with the natural world, then all of humanity is doomed.

The ancient Celts also held a belief in a World Tree as the sacred center of the earth; "Sacred assemblies were held beneath ... hallowed trees, and it was forbidden to damage them in any way" (MacLeod 66). The Celts often captured the symbol of a World Tree in their art work, as the Tree's "seasonal cycles linked it with death, rebirth, and growth" (Wood 55). An eighth century Irish manuscript presents the character Fionn mac Cumhaill encountering what appears to be a Celtic description of a World Tree.[4] Fionn finds a man sitting in the top of a tree with a blackbird on his shoulder, holding a container with a living trout in it. At the bottom of the tree is a deer; "the mysterious figure in the tree was cracking open hazelnuts, symbolic of divine wisdom. He gave half of the nut to the blackbird and ate the other half himself. From inside the bronze vessel he took an apple, symbolizing passages between the worlds, again giving half to the stag and eating the other half himself. He then drank a sip from the vessel so that he, the trout, the stag and the blackbird all drank together" (MacLeod 67). The interconnectivity of the natural world to the world of man is undeniable in this portrayal of the World Tree, as all are depicted as equal. MacLeod states that the Tree represents a connection to the upper, middle, and lower worlds as being depicted within the myth, as she states the blackbird symbolizes the upper world, the stag the middle, and the trout the lower world.

The Norse also held trees as sacred in their mythology. They believed that the first man was created from the ash tree, and the first woman was created from the elm tree. In addition, the concept of a World Tree, Yggdrasil, was an important part of Norse myth. Yggdrasil was an ash tree; "Its branches spread themselves all over the world, and it stands over the sky. Three roots support the tree and they are spread very far apart. One is among the Aesir. A second is among the frost giants where Ginnungagap once was. The third reaches down to Nifheim, and under this root is the well Hvergelmir; but Nidhogg ... gnaws at this root from below" (Sturulson 24). The portrayal of Yggdrasil is vital to an understanding of Norse mythological thinking and reveals the connection of nature to their myths. As stated Yggdrasil resides in all the Norse worlds, the upper, middle, and lower realms, so it alone stands for the cycles of life. Like nature itself, the tree holds within it all life; without it, all living beings would perish, as it literally holds the earth together. Its branches hold eagles, hawks, squirrels, and deer that are said to constantly feed off of its branches and foliage, and serpents surround and consume its roots; this is central to the portrayal of Yggdrasil:

> "The ash Yggdrasil
> endures hardship,
> more than men know.
> A stag bites from above
> and its sides rot;
> From below Nidhogg gnaws.
> More snakes
> Lie under the ash Yggdrasil...
> [and] will always, I believe,
> eat away the tree's shoots" [Sturulson 27].

Yggdrasil is a natural representation of life itself. It both provides and endures constant suffering; like nature it both bestows life and then must take it away.

Trees of Knowledge

Trees have also been associated with holding the ability to provide mythic characters with knowledge. This may seem an odd connection to attach the botanical to human thought, but its mythic inclusion in myriad texts around the world points to a significant attempt to identify nature as possessing spiritual wisdom. Again, as has been discussed in this chapter, human beings have long been connecting one's seclusion in nature to the attainment of wisdom, but the specificity of a single tree imparting knowledge to a solitary individual is integral in showing a culture's value of nature as connected to humankind. In Hinduism there is a belief in a Tree of Life and Knowledge that also "symbolizes the human nervous system, which itself holds the key to life's secrets ... for life-energy is said to be expressed through the five senses" (Allan & Phillips, *World,* 21). In addition the Persians believed that the first humans were interconnected to a tree that imparted knowledge to mankind. One Persian myth states that the first humans "grew up as a double tree with the fingers of each folded over the ears of the other" (Allan & Phillips, *World,* 157). When the tree finally reached maturity and parted, it was said to have created a male and a female, each with a soul and each with the gift of knowledge. Similarly, as has been discussed, the Greeks provided documentation of revering trees, like Zeus' sacred grove in Dodona, as priests and priestesses residing over the site were believed to interpret the rustling of the leaves or the chiming of bronze objects hung in the trees to arrive at their prophetic revelations. The myth of Jason and the Argonauts makes it clear that the trees from Dodona possessed wisdom, as Athena designed the figurehead of the Argo using a trunk of a tree from Dodona, and thus the prow of the ship could reveal prophecies to the Argonauts.

The Bodhi tree is also considered a tree of knowledge and is highly significant to Buddhism, as the Buddha was believed to sit under this tree while he attained enlightenment. After having attempted many different methods to find the wisdom he sought, such as personal deprivation, he found that simply sitting under the Bodhi tree allowed him to attain nirvana. The Buddha was said to encounter all fearful and desirable aspects of life while under this single tree, and once he was able to face them all, he placed his hand upon the earth, signaling his newfound wisdom. The Bodhi tree here seems connected to the enlightenment of the Buddha, as he came to recognize that his life, and all life, follows the same natural patterns as the tree he sat under. According to Buddhism, all living beings will live, die, and be reincarnated into a new being, much like the seasonal life cycle of a tree. To break the cycle of samsara is to recognize that the self is unessential, as it is only one part of an endless, natural cycle. The Buddha can be said to realize that he is essentially nature.

In one of the most important of Norse myths, Odin goes to the well of Hvergelmir at the base of Yggdrasil to obtain wisdom, as Mimir, the well's owner who resides in Nifhelm "is full of wisdom because he drinks of the well from the Gjallarhorn" (Sturulson 24). Odin embarks on his own quest by descending into the underworld to ask for one drink from this well, so that he might attain the boon of all heroic journeys—spiritual knowledge. But, to be allowed to receive this spiritual wisdom, Odin must sacrifice one of his eyes. The sacrifice of sight to obtain wisdom is a common theme in world mythology; for instance Tiresias in Greek mythology is blinded after seeing the divine form of Athena, but he is then able to foresee the future. Oedipus Rex grows into a mythic character who was believed to hold wisdom after his initial and defining tragedy, as once he found the truth of his identity, he blinded himself, but as his representation in Sophocles' theatrical trilogy continued, the loss of his physical sight enabled him to gain internal wisdom to truly meet the Delphic proclamation of knowing thyself. In the Norse myth Odin, similarly, loses part of his physical sight but gains spiritual knowledge from his sacrifice, and again, this wisdom comes from the natural source of Yggdrasil, the World Tree. Odin is said to have first had to hang from Yggdrasil for nine days and nights, "without food or water, slashed with a spear and sacrificed ... until screaming he was able by virtue of his suffering to reach down and seize the magical runes" (Aurbach & Simpson 31). From the poem "The Sayings of Hár: Hávamál" in the *Poetic Edda,* Odin states of his self-sacrifice for wisdom:

> "I wot that I hung on the wind-tossed tree;
> All of nights nine,
> wounded by spear, bespoken to Óthin,
> bespoken myself to myself;
> [upon that tree of which none telleth
> from what roots it doth rise]....
> I looked below me—
> aloud I cried—
> caught up the runes, caught them up wailing,
> thence to the ground fell again....
> Then began I to grow and gain in insight,
> to wax eke in wisdom" [36].

Yggdrasil stands as a symbol to Odin of the cycles of nature, and this myth of his quest to obtain wisdom is connected to his knowledge that one day even he, the all-powerful member of the Norse Aesir, must also succumb to death, as he learns that he and all of the other members of the Aesir, as well as the earth itself, will be destroyed in Ragnarok. Again, Yggdrasil is a symbol of this; "The gallows tree was an emotionally significant site for the passage between life and death, and is a fitting symbol for the World Tree as the cause-way connecting the heavens and the underworld" (Byock 120). Through the aid of the World Tree, Odin learns, similar to the Buddha, that he is part of the same cycle of the Tree; even as a god, he must concede that his fate is the same as all beings in nature before he can receive wisdom.

Also among the Tungus-speaking people of Siberia there is a belief that their shamans' souls are reared in the tallest of trees, called Tuuru, and it is this rearing that enables them to become spiritual guides for their people. The shaman's drum comes from a part of the tree in which his soul was raised. In addition, as Tungus shaman Semyonov Semyon states, "'in memory of the great tree Tuuru, at each séance the shaman plants a tree with one or more cross-sticks in the tent where the ceremony takes place, and this tree too is called Tuuru'" (qtd. in Campbell, *Primitive Mythology*, 256). The belief is that the shaman climbs his Tuuru to speak with the divine during his séance, and in planting a new tree each séance, he is giving homage back to the tree's process of perpetual growth. This also signals that like the Buddha and Odin, the Tungus shaman concedes that his own life is no different than the seasonal cycle of the tree; wisdom comes from knowing the natural process, which is the same for all living beings.

Similarly, the Christian story of Eve also showcases a Tree of Knowledge of Good and Evil. Adam and Eve, the first man and woman in Christian ideology, are said to exist in a terrestrial paradise called Eden that was created for them by a monotheistic God. Adam and Eve live in Eden at one with their environment, signaled within the story by their lack of shame at their nudity and their life of ease with the endless natural resources of Paradise. Eve is described as being tempted by Satan who appears to her in the form of a serpent, as discussed briefly in chapter 2, to step forward towards the Tree of Knowledge in order to admire its beautiful fruit, though Eve knows that the tree has been ordained by God to be off limits for her and her counterpart Adam. Eve, though, sees the apple, and is unable to resist it, so she plucks it and bites into it, which for Christian doctrine signals that she committed the first sin. Because of her sin, Eve is said to have caused humankind to become cognizant of their own shame in living naturally, so she and Adam, and the rest of mankind, must forevermore cover their nakedness. In addition, because Eve ate the fruit of the Tree of Knowledge, women must suffer in childbirth, and men must toil at work. It is significant that the natural symbol of a tree, and its fruit, is used to describe Eve's first sin; especially significant is that the Tree provides knowledge to Eve, and subsequently to all mankind. This use of symbolism suggests again a connection with nature that must be remembered by human beings.

The Tree itself is not evil, and the knowledge obtained by Eve is not portrayed as entirely sinful as well, since under the watch of an omniscient God, it seems this act was ordained, so that humans possessed the knowledge that would enable them to know what acts were good and which were evil. The knowledge the apple gives to Eve seemingly provides mankind with free will, as without knowledge between right and wrong acts, no one holds the ability of choice. Once Eve bites into the fruit of the Tree of Knowledge, her and the rest of mankind, must also concede to experience suffering as a part of life; this element is also crucial to this story, as within Christian doctrine suffering is often viewed as the vehicle that enables humans to achieve spiritual wisdom. Similar to Odin choosing to experience physical suffering by hanging himself from Yggdrasil, the suffering caused by Eve biting the apple from the Tree of Knowledge gives to mankind the ability to also taste spiritual knowledge. In addition, with Eve tasting the fruit of the Tree of Knowledge, the story states that mankind must now contend with death. Again, similar to the other myths that present Trees of Knowledge, the aspect of death is an integral component to the work. Death is mythically linked to knowledge because wisdom can only be obtained from accepting the demise of all living creatures as natural. And again, the portrayal of the Tree and its fruit as providing death shows a message within the story that human beings must concede that they are tied to the same seasonal cycles as the Tree itself.

Benefits of the Forbidden Fruit

Just as the Christian Eve consumed the apple from the Tree of Knowledge and provided humanity with knowledge, so too do many world myths connect the symbol of fruit with spirituality, and again spiritual wisdom is mythically linked with the necessity of accepting death as natural. Often myths from around the world connect the eating of fruit with aspects of the mythic underworld, which links botanical elements with death. The consumption of fruit within the underworld holds an important role as "stories involving a taboo against eating underworld food goes back to the very beginnings of recorded myth" (Allan & Phillips, *World,* 117). Many myths recount the portrayal of fruit as a representation of both life and death. The Greek Persephone eats the seeds of the pomegranate within the underworld and is condemned therefore to stay within its domain for part of each year. Also, within Celtic legend there is a tale of a man named Conle, who was forced to remain in the Otherworld after eating an apple given to him by a maiden of the Otherworld (Allan & Phillips, *World,* 117). Like the myths that portray one being consuming another to obtain the essence and power of the consumed, like Mot does to Baal, or the Lakota do to the heart of the hunted buffalo, eating fruit suggests that if one consumes a botanical component, then he or she gains a knowledge of the botanical processes of seasonal change.

The underworld, like a piece of fruit, serves to show audiences of myths the cycles of nature—just like a piece of fruit starts out as a seed, emerges as a plant from the soil, grows into ripeness upon its stem, and then is eventually plucked and consumed for the continuation of the life of another species, myths portraying the consumption of fruit in association with the underworld make this connection to the cycles of the fruit-providing plant with the cycles of a human life. Therefore, the mythic characters who journey to the underworld and coincidently eat fruit, shows their own connection to the same cycles each natural element must succumb to.

As stated in chapter 1, the Japanese myth of Izanagi and Izanami shows fruit playing a nebulous but prominent role within the creation legend. When Izanagi travels to the underworld to retrieve his deceased wife, Izanami, and finds to his misguided horror that she has already begun to decay, he flees in terror, which subsequently causes Izanami to react in anger, attempting to bring death to her husband. Here already within the myth, a lesson of the cycles of life is apparent. With fruit, and all living matter, there is a necessary stage of decay; to the living mortal, this stage may be horrific, as it is for Izanagi, but it is also a part of reality and must be accepted. The myth shows Izanagi as undergoing a process towards accepting this harsh fact of existence. Izanagi throws fully ripe peaches, or sometimes grapes or bamboo shoots, at the spirits of the dead that Izanami unleashes to try to drag her living husband back into the underworld. The botanical items instantaneously work to deter the spirits, as they eventually retreat back to their underworld realm. Fruit within myth, as in this myth, perfectly showcases the cycles of nature. The only thing that can combat death is renewed life. Fruit must decay to provide nourishment for the growth of more fruit. Even the maintenance of fruit-producing plants can sometimes be considered a violent process, as the fruit must be picked to help the plant continue its production; also acts like burning fruit-producing plants, such as raspberry plants, can invigorate new growth. Therefore, when Izanagi throws ripe produce at the dead, their power fades, but the myth closes with the reminder of the necessary processes of life: Izanami will always kill one thousand people a day, and equally Izanagi will cause one thousand five hundred people a day to be born, as the propagation of fruit, and all living beings, requires death and decay for continuation.

The pomegranate in the Greek myth of Demeter and Persephone, which will be discussed in more detail in the next chapter, also is the agent that forces both Demeter and Persephone to personally accept the fact of death. In this myth Demeter, the goddess of the harvest, unexpectedly loses her daughter Persephone to Hades when Hades decides to marry her. Hades is portrayed as mythically dragging Persephone into the underworld in symbolic death. Demeter, as a Mother Earth Goddess, in grief causes all crop production to cease, and humanity begins to starve. The myth ends with Demeter retrieving Persephone back into the land of the living, but finds that Persephone has consumed the seeds of the pomegranate. This act of consuming the fruit of the underworld is mythically the one thing that causes her to remain bound to the cycles that will forever be found in nature—summer and autumn inevitably will always lead to the dormancy of winter, but also will always produce a renewed state of growth in spring. Persephone's consumption of the seeds of the pomegranate connect her, and subsequently all humankind, to the fruit itself. Like the fruit, all living beings must decay, but her intake of the seeds shows the everlasting promise that comes with death, for the seeds beneath the earth will become nourished there, and will assuredly rise, just like Persephone each spring.

Fruit also plays an important role in Celtic myth. Often fruit is associated with knowledge in Celtic sources, as MacLeod states, "'The Fruits of the Tree of Wisdom' [represent] the sacred skills and divine wisdom of the Otherworld so frequently mentioned in Celtic wisdom texts" (102). The Scottish tale of Thomas of Erceldoune recounts his trip to the Celtic Otherworld where he came upon the Queen of Elfland and then ventured into her domain.[5] Thomas, as is common for myths where the protagonist enters into the Otherworld, does so by accident; he simply stumbles upon the otherworldly Queen. She invites him into her realm, but he finds that he must stay there for seven years. Within the seven years, he embraced his experience, but also longed to go home. After seven years were up, the Queen gave him an apple with a skin that enabled him to foresee the future; with this boon of his experience in Elfland, Thomas returned home. He returned to his people as a prophet, but many years later, he saw an omen he knew was sent to him from the Otherworld of Elfland—a white doe, so he immediately knew that he was being called back to the realm of the Otherworld. The myth describes the Otherworld, the apple, and the doe as a lesson of mortality, as the myth shows Thomas as accepting his call to return to the Otherworld, though it spells death for him from the viewpoint of the people of the village as they never seen him again.

The Norse myth of Idun shows the gods and goddesses of the Aesir aging when Loki succeeds in luring Idun away from her golden apples. Loki got into this predicament when he, Odin, and Hoenir were traveling. They killed an ox but found that they could not cook the meat, as every time they tried to eat the meat, they found that it was still raw. An enormous Frost Giant, in the guise of an eagle, tells the gods that if they share the meat, then the Frost Giant will ensure that they are able to cook and consume the flesh. The myth continues to show the eagle eating too much of the meat, which angers Loki, who tries to kill the eagle, but instead he ends up getting carried away in the giant eagle's talons. The only thing that will ensure Loki's survival is to help the eagle capture Idun and her magical apples. To save his life, Loki achieves this task. But the Norse pantheon immediately begins to age without Idun bringing them her mystical apples. Loki is then sent to now save Idun, which he does by turning her and her remaining apples into a single nut. Loki carries the nut to Asgard, and the gods light a fire that causes the eagle, in pursuit of Loki, to die as he flies into the flames.

This myth presents the cycles of life through the symbolic use of nature as well. First, the inability to cook the flesh of the hunted animal for the gods' consumption suggests the failing of the gods to grasp the reality of death. To come to terms with the life they took, they must undergo the lesson of mortality. Idun's apples serve as a natural representation of the cycles found within nature. Her apples indefinitely give the Aesir what they need to exist and remain youthful; once the fruit is taken away, they taste mortality, which immediately terrifies them. Loki then retrieves Idun and her needed apples by changing them into the form of a nut, and this representation shows again the cycles of nature, as from one nut, all bounty will be returned. Inherent in Norse mythology is the accepted belief that even the gods and goddesses know that they will one day die in Ragnarok; this myth again reveals the importance of recognizing this inevitable fact. It reminds the Aesir of the importance of understanding the laws of nature.

Natural Otherworlds

The elements within the natural world have long been linked with providing mythic characters with spiritual wisdom, whether it be a grove, a tree, a piece of fruit, or as discussed in the proceeding chapters, the cycles of the harvest, the sun and moon in the sky, or the animals that inhabit the forest. World myth interestingly portrays places that often teem with natural elements but are described as mystical environments known in myth as Otherworlds. The mythic Otherworld is often accidently transgressed by an unsuspecting character. When in the Otherworld, the mythic character is often overcome by the natural beauty of the place; this is usually one of the first devices mentioned when the Otherworld is found, as the environment seems often untouched by civilization and is often botanically plush and verdant. Often the resources within the Otherworld are never-ending, as food and drink never need replenishing. The beings within the Otherworld also are often presented as ageless and immortal. The Otherworld is a place in myth that is most often identified as idyllic, much like the natural refuges people find away from civilization, but the Otherworld is also more. The lesson learned by the mythic voyager into the Otherworld is again often connected to the wisdom one learns from embracing nature's cycles as tied to the lives of human beings. The fact that Otherworld resources and beings never perish represents the everlasting regenerative aspect of the natural world. Viewed in natural terms, nothing truly dies or is wholly depleted, and the Otherworld mythically presents audiences this lesson.

In Tibetan mythology the belief in Shambhala connects the wondrous beauty of the natural world with the concept of a spiritual paradise; "Shambhala is a paradise of Earth, a land of *bodhisattvas,* where the enlightened live free from conflict and pain" (Kerrigan, Bishop, & Chambers 89). Hidden away in the sacred Himalayas, the kingdom of Shambhala is the home of the dynasty of spirit kings, who teach the "Kalachakra (Wheel of Time) Tantra—a collection of mystical writings used as a guide to help adepts attain enlightenment" (Kerrigan, Bishop, & Chambers 88). The exact location of Shambhala always must be kept mythically secret, as it suggests a psychological realization of inner peace rather than an actual place, though many western authors and explorers attempted to find the sacred city. The placement of the hidden, mythical city also is central, as the immense beauty of the peaks of the Himalayas where the legendary city is located inspired the myth itself, and this realization also seems part of the myth's message. Shambhala provides transgressors with inner peace because it represents, in its perpetual tie to unfettered nature, the constant and renewing cycles of the natural world.

In addition, the Chinese tale of "The Peach Blossom Spring" by Tao Yanming[6] shows a utopian community that is accidently discovered by a fisherman as he is alone fishing on a river. First he sees a forest filled entirely with blossoming peach trees where thousands of petals cover the ground and dance through the air. This abundantly beautiful natural element signals instantly to the fisherman that he is in an Otherworld. The fisherman then sees a community living there that is described as idyllic for the concepts the people live in adherence to. This Otherworld had been overlooked by civilization's ever-increasing desire to expand and improve for centuries, so that it was left completely natural, which also enabled its inhabitants to retain a timeless morality and wisdom because of their close tie with their abundantly beautiful environment. The fisherman finds that in this mystical Otherworld he is happy, but after some time he longs to return to his former life. After leaving the place, he tells others about what he found, but when he tries to show them where to find the Otherworld, he discovers that he can no longer find it. When the fisherman leaves the Otherworld, he cannot go back because he is mortal. The Otherworld experience serves to allow him to glimpse the timeless lesson of nature. Like the Fon myth of Africa discussed in the last chapter showed the hunter stumbling upon an opening in the bush and briefly being permitted to see the dance of the agbui, the spirits, that showed him the inner workings of nature and its necessary cycles, so too does the fisherman here witness a glimpse of an ever-renewing environment that promises him individual peace. The fisherman, though, must leave this Otherworld, as most mythic characters must, because again if the Otherworld signals the renewing promise of nature, it only represents one stage. Broadly speaking, nature itself in its constant cycles then becomes the mythic Otherworld, but the characters within the myth, who most often leave the Otherworld, serve to reveal a message to audiences that mankind only plays a small fleeting part of this broader cycle.

Celtic mythology also recounts myriad legends that showcase an Otherworld as a place teeming with verdant, benevolent nature that often holds never-ending resources, such as found in the myth of Pwyll's journey to Annwn in the *Mabinogi*. The inhabitants of the Otherworld are sometimes titled fairies, or the "*Síoga* (Modern Irish), ... the *Sítheachain* [(Scottish)], or the *Daoine Síth* (Scottish Gaelic). The fairies are the recent ministrations of the *Áes Síde*.... In Wales ... they are known as the *Plant Annwn* ('The Children of Annwn') or *Tylwyth Teg* ('The Fair Family').... Many people refer to them as the *Sidhe*, a word popularized in the poetry of William Butler Yeats" (MacLeod 148). The beings of the Celtic Otherworld are inextricably part of nature; "the Otherworld could be reached in many ways: through a hill, a lake or a mist" (Fleming & Husain 71). Their representation in myth shows them as fully connected with their natural realms. The Celts believed that the people of the Goddess Danu, the Tuatha De Danann, continued to dwell in an Otherworld far away in the deep recesses of nature, "where they dwell to this day ... without touch of age.... Deep underground they built themselves timeless abodes" (Campbell, *Primitive Mythology*, 431), and sometimes, they permit humans to enter their mystical realms.

As with voyagers into Shambhala and the fisherman in "The Peach Blossom Spring," those who chance upon an encounter with the inhabitants of the Celtic Otherworld often do so accidently. But ancient Celts also believed that on its four most important holidays: "Imbolc, Beltaine, Lugnasad, and Samain" (MacLeod 148) access to the Otherworld and the world of mortals often became intermingled. The residents of the Otherworld frequently teach mortals a message of the interconnectivity of mankind to nature. Their otherworldly lessons are sometimes harsh, but as representations of nature, they teach the lessons of a cyclical and natural existence. Thus, the Celtic Otherworld is viewed as an essential component in aiding mythic characters towards finding spiritual knowledge.

One Irish myth involving Tadg[7] shows him accidently discovering the Otherworld as he sets forth upon a journey to rescue his stolen wife and sons from neighboring invaders. After an intensely severe storm, the men find that the seas have suddenly grown calm. They look into the distance and spot a beautiful island of abundant natural splendor. The men, though they were not traveling far, are amazed to see that it is summer on this island, as it was winter in Ireland; "moreover, despite the hardships they had been through, they felt not the slightest hunger" (Fleming & Husain 71). On the island, Tadg finds that a beautiful woman instructs him that the island holds the seats of the rulers of Ireland, and she foretells that Tadg will one day come to rule Ireland. She then sends Tadg home, and with the newfound wisdom he has gained on his journey, he finds that he easily is able to catch up to his family's captors and save his wife and sons. The Otherworld as a place of exquisite natural beauty shows Tadg the means to take control of his life seemingly because Tadg has glimpsed a reality that is broader than the immediate dilemma that dominated his life. Through his experience in the Otherworld, Tadg glimpses the timeless quality of nature's cycles, so that he leaves psychologically renewed to thrive in his own life.

Again the Celtic Otherworld often serves to teach nature's laws to mortals, as with the Irish tale of the "Voyage of Bran." Bran is said to have heard beautiful music one day that lulls him into a state of sleep. Upon awakening he sees that a silver branch was set before him. An Otherworld woman comes to his compound and tells Bran about the Otherworld. Again, it is described as filled with overt natural beauty and resources that never run out. Bran determinedly calls forth Ireland's finest warriors and sets off to seek the Otherworld. Along the way, Bran and his men see a chariot coming near them upon the sea. They find that it is the god of the sea, Manannán mac Lir, who tells them that they indeed are not at all on the sea, but on a flowery plain. Immediately, this aspect of the myth identifies that Bran and his crew accidently happened upon the Otherworld. The Otherworld as a mystical place is often presented with confounding psychological components working within the protagonist; it is a place where the mythic characters must often resolve to set aside their preconceived conceptions of reality. Manannán mac Lir tells Bran that in his divine reality many chariots are striving to overtake Bran and his men, but that they are safe because they stumbled into the mystical realm of the Otherworld. They eventually make their way to the Isle of Women where they each are perfectly paired with a woman, suggesting a state of everlasting fertility. Bran and his men revel in their time here, eating, drinking and enjoying themselves for many years, though to them it seems like only one year has passed. This element of time appearing slow to Otherworld voyagers, as it speeds by in their former realities, points to the Otherworld again as being a representation of the broad cycles of nature. The Isle of Women is presented as always being in a state of summer; this mythic representation of a land in the seasonal state of perpetual abundance shows the promise of the ever-renewing components of nature's cycles.

And again archetypally, one of Bran's men wishes to leave the Otherworld because he has grown homesick and longs to see his family and Ireland. Though Bran resists leaving the Otherworld, they all sail home to only glimpse their former lives, as the Greek Orpheus can only glimpse his wife Eurydice on his attempt to free her from the underworld, but like Orpheus, Bran's men are instructed to the limitation that they are not allowed to step foot on the soil of Ireland. However, also like Orpheus, one man is so overcome with his longing to go home, that he does not heed the warning and jumps off the ship, and as he does so, he turns into a pile of ashes.

If the mythic Otherworld is a place where natural lessons of renewal are presented, some mythic characters are portrayed as not being ready to embrace the lessons of the Otherworld. Often in myth the travelers who accompany a central mythic protagonist, like the crewmen with Odysseus on Circe's island in Homer's *Odyssey,* fear or grow bored of the Otherworld and simply want to return back to their former lives. The central mythic characters who reluctantly leave the Otherworld are presented as hesitant to leave because they grasp the larger spiritual meaning the Otherworld reveals. This myth shows that the Otherworld, like the underworld, represents aspects of the cycles of nature; therefore, it prepares audiences for the concept of inevitable death. Bran and his men have undergone a death of their past selves, since they clearly are not permitted to return to their former lives. When Bran and his crew come near Ireland, the people do not know him but only recognize his name from legends of long ago, thus signaling the death of Bran and his men, but it is interesting that death is not at all discussed in the myth, as the men are described as living in a state of perpetual life in the Otherworld, just as nature remains in perpetual summer. Instead of presenting Bran and his men as dead, they are mythically portrayed as living in one everlasting seasonal state showing mythically that death is never an end when viewed in nature's terms.

In yet another myth involving the Celtic Otherworld, "The Voyage of Mael Duin,"[8] shows Mael Duin sailing away with a crew of men to avenge the death of his father. Before Mael Duin sets sail, however, a druid instructed him to take no more than seventeen men, but upon setting sail, Mael Duin's three foster brothers leapt into the sea and begged to accompany the sailors. Mael Duin knew that he would forsake the wisdom of the druid if he took his foster brothers, as the number of men would exceed seventeen, but looking at the thrashing of his foster brothers in the deep waters, he knew they would surely drown if he did not agree, so he consented to take them along.

Soon enough, not to Mael Duin's surprise, as he expected something bad to happen for breaking the druid's instruction, a strong storm raged, taking the men far from their desired goal of the home of the killers of Mael Duin's father.

The winds of the storm finally subsided, and the men found that they were among strange and mystical islands. Soon, they realized the islands were inhabited by magical creatures, such as an island of giant ants, and another of giant horses. Again, it is clear here that the Otherworld is a mythical representation of unharnessed nature at a pure and unrestricted state. On one island, Mael Duin found three apples "each of which fed the whole crew for forty days," and on another island the men gathered "fruit in orchards tended by red, fiery pigs whose underground sites heated the whole island. When all the fruit had gone, they found another island … full of food and treasures … guarded only by a cat. They ate their fill under its watchful gaze, but as they were leaving, one of Mael Duin's foster-brothers snatched a necklace from the wall. The cat at once leapt right through him and reduced him to cinders" (Fleming & Husain 73). The men continued to voyage among the islands of the Otherworld, encountering mystical abundance, but eventually the journey took the life of another foster brother, as the tale foreshadowed.

The men finally came again to the Isle of Women where each man married a beautiful wife who promised them eternal youth, but the men eventually wanted to leave the Otherworld to return to their former lives in Ireland, but Mael Duin and his beautiful Otherworld queen, found ways to keep the men from leaving. The men found out about Mael Duin's desire to stay, so they came up with a plan to escape and tricked Mael Duin into leaving with them. The men, with an angered Mael Duin at having been deceived into leaving his desired home, finally come to an island called the Isle of the Laughing Folk where the inhabitants live in "perpetual joy." The third foster brother was left behind as he could not be convinced to leave this eerily happy place. With all of the foster brothers gone, the men were able to sail home to Ireland, as a falcon came and led them home. On the way home, Mael Duin encountered the murderers of his father, but they were confounded that Mael Duin survived the Otherworld, so they "greeted him like a hero," and "with no heart left for vengeance, Mael Duin recounted his extraordinary adventures" (Fleming & Husain 73). When Mael Duin encountered the Otherworld, he experienced archetypal qualities that psychologically transformed him and taught him to embrace a broader view of reality because of having witnessed nature's laws. The myriad islands he and his men encountered represented alternative realities than the ones in which they were aware of before leaving upon their journey.

It is crucial that Mael Duin disregarded the warning of the druid; it suggests Mael Duin's early disregard for the cycles of nature. Druids in Celtic myth were educated on the cyclical laws of the natural world, and in connection to this, death is presented as a central theme of the myth. In order to avenge his father's death, Mael Duin must first learn to accept the death of his three foster brothers, either by heeding the warning of the druid and letting them immediately drown as they pleaded to accompany him, or by watching them succumb one by one while on the journey. It is only after Mael Duin concedes that each foster brother will be lost, can he fulfill his mission, which is decidedly a different goal than the one he believed he would accomplish. What is also important to note is that Mael Duin comes to place where he seems to concede his own will to live; this is a central component of many myths that speak towards a message of embracing the laws of nature. Even by initially allowing the three foster brothers to accompany them, there is an indication that Mael Duin lets go of some of his own desire to live, as their presence jeopardizes his own life. In addition, while Mael Duin lives on the Isle of Women, he alone does not wish to leave to return to his former life; this suggests a willingness to let go of his former identity to embrace the natural timelessness of the Otherworld, signaling that he has attained spiritual wisdom as a result of his voyage.

The Otherworld for Mael Duin, and for many other Celtic transgressors, teaches him the lesson that the druid apparently was trying to impart—that death must be accepted as natural, and with this acknowledgement comes wisdom of nature's ceaseless patterns to renew all that has been taken. Mael Duin and his men happen upon islands where nature is unfettered; the creatures are of enormous size, and the food supply never runs out. They also see an Otherworld where they are both forever young and fertile; if they stay here, as Mael Duin wants, they remain in one stage of nature's seasonal cycles, the representation of which shows a portrayal of mythic enlightenment. Nature to the perception of living beings appears sped up, moving always in and out of its seasonal patterns, yet portrayals of the Celtic Otherworld, like this one for Mael Duin, shows the cycle as a symbolic sphere, not changing, not running out of resources, but always in a state of natural renewal. This Celtic Otherworld is then similar to the nirvana of the Buddhists. Samsara, or the perception that individual lives come and go, as Mael Duin and his men believed the world to operate before embarking on their mythic quest, can be overcome when the wisdom of knowing that the individual is merely a part of a broader, never-ending natural cycle is embraced. Mael Duin in wishing to stay on the Isle of Women acknowledges that his former life, with his previous ambition to avenge the death of his father, was illusory. This is why when he finally does leave behind the Otherworld, as mythic characters most often have to do since mortals cannot remain in this halted state of nature, his former goal for revenge is easily resolved, as he meets and forgives the murderers, signaling his spiritual transformation as a result of his Otherworld experience.

In the Celtic myth *Echtrae Chormaic i d'Tir Tairngire*, "Cormac's Adventure in the Land of Promise,"[9] a sacred event appears to the protagonist Cormac mac Airt, the High King of Ireland. On a consecrated day for the Irish, the first of May, Cormac found a stranger walking towards his kingdom. Immediately Cormac knew that the stranger was from the Otherworld, as he was dressed impeccably and carried with him a silver branch that held golden apples. Cormac instantaneously invited the mystical being into his kingdom, and holding the customs of the time which stated that a visitor must give a gift to his host, Cormac asked for the branch and the apples. The Otherworld man agreed to hand the branch and apples to Cormac upon the condition that in return he would ask for three wishes. After receiving the branch, Cormac found that it held magical powers because when he shook it at any one in his kingdom, he or she immediately fell into a deep sleep. The Otherworld man told Cormac that he would return in a few months to collect his first wish, and indeed after three months passed, the man returned and asked for Cormac's daughter in marriage. Cormac happily handed over his daughter to so fine a suitor as a man from the respected Otherworld. Again the man requested to fetch his second wish in another few months, which he did, this time asking for Cormac's young son, so that he may raise him, a common practice in Celtic culture, and again Cormac knew that his son would be well cared for in the abundant Otherworld, so he again readily agreed. The process repeated itself, and the Otherworld man reappeared after three more months, and this time asked for Cormac's own wife. But, this time Cormac paused; he did reluctantly hand her over, but found that he was alone and lonely, so he sought out the Otherworld in an attempt to retrieve her.

The cycles of the seasons are directly connected to the man from the Otherworld and the ages of the gifts requested. First, in apparently a spring-like state, the man asks for Cormac's young daughter to marry; this can be connected to the starting of a human adult life. The second wish of Cormac's young son can reflect a state of summer, where humans often reap the benefits of their marriage/harvest, with children. The final wish reflects an autumn-like state, when the man from the Otherworld requests Cormac's own mature wife. This is the point, reflective of death, that Cormac finally feels loss. It is this time that Cormac ventures to find the Otherworld, seemingly because he is ready to learn the lessons it imbues.

In seeking his destination, Cormac found that he fell into a state of sleep, which is a common theme in Celtic myth when a hero enters the Otherworld; to all onlookers, the person is asleep in his or her normal life, but his other self or spirit self truly resides in the realm of the Otherworld. Cormac awakened and found that the man from the Otherworld who repeatedly visited his kingdom was actually the god Manannán mac Lir, "king of the Land of Promise." MacLeod states that Manannán mac Lir imparted an important lesson to Cormac that is reflective again of a wisdom that is connected to nature:

> He tells Cormac that he has brought him to the Otherworld to show him the wonders of this sacred realm. Cormac is given a vision of the Well of Wisdom, where nine purple hazel trees grow and drop their nuts into the fountain. The five salmon that live in the fountain crack open the nuts and send their shells floating down the streams. Manannán mac Lir explains to Cormac that the five streams represent the five senses through which knowledge is obtained [101].

The Well of Wisdom in Celtic mythology is significant because of its connection to the natural elements it contains. Celtic myth often reveals the interconnectivity of nature and its elements, as it does in this myth; the Well of Wisdom, and the knowledge Manannán mac Lir bestows to Cormac, is a wisdom that reveals that all nature, even humanity, is interconnected. The hazel trees that have branches that reach towards the sky provide the food that falls to the earth. The nuts, the sustenance of the earth that assures the continuation of the whole system, flow downstream into presumably the sea, which marks for Cormac a greater life source, the embodiment of which is Manannán mac Lir himself, as god of the sea. The five streams that are inextricably connected with all the elements of the natural world symbolically represent all five senses within Cormac because it is through experiencing all aspects of nature, seeing, tasting, smelling, hearing, and touching all that exists, that reveals to Cormac his place in the universe. Therefore, his Otherworld experience serves to teach him that he is only one part of a greater system, but he is an essential part, as essential as any other part.

In another Irish myth found in the *Metrical Dindshenchas* about Sinann,[10] a woman from the sacred race of the Túatha Dé Danann who was said to possess mystical powers, like many other members of the Túatha Dé Danann, makes an attempt to gain more wisdom by going to the "edge of a river where she saw some 'beautiful bubbles of wisdom' (bolca áilli immaiss)" (MacLeod 100). Interestingly, though, the myth relates that Sinann goes too close and is drowned. In most stories this would be a tragedy and would suggest a cautionary tale, teaching readers to avoid seeking a knowledge that should remain beyond their grasp, similar to how some may interpret the

Biblical Eve's enticement of the fruit of knowledge, but in Celtic myth, as presented in this myth, there is no knowledge that an omniscient god holds as forbidden. In this myth Sinann dies to only her former self but is transformed as the river itself, as it is said she becomes the spirit of the river Shannon. As stated the Celtic Otherworld often presents a glimpse for the transgressor into the interconnectivity of all life, as it does in this myth. Sinann becomes nature, and instead of a tragic event, it releases her, so that she may be provided with what she sought—spiritual knowledge. As presented, the Celtic Otherworld is often described as infinitely benevolent; its resources never cease, and there is no death. The transformation, not death, of Sinann, shows that the mythic Otherworld is often a psychological experience within the protagonist where he or she embraces the wisdom of nature's processes and reaches a stage of mythic apotheosis where death is viewed as only a temporary stage in the broad cycle of the seasons.

Botanical Metamorphosis and Spiritual Wisdom

As discussed in the previous chapter, when mythical characters metamorphose into animals, they often experience a spiritual transformation; the same is also true when mythic characters transform into botanical elements such as plants and flowers. Characters are repeatedly transformed into plants within world mythology, and when this mythic metamorphosis happens, the spiritual wisdom obtained is elevated because in the transformation from human to plant, as opposed to human to animal, the self seems completely dispelled. The lesson of botanical metamorphosis rather than animal metamorphosis then becomes more closely aligned with the procurement of spiritual wisdom that comes in relinquishing the autonomy of self, as seen in the Otherworld myths of Mael Duin and Sinann.

Death is often a central component in myths of botanical metamorphosis, as mythic characters often are portrayed as dying an actual or symbolic death before they are transformed into a botanical element. For instance, there is a Chinese myth that tells how "Yaoji, a daughter of Yandi, died at a young age before she could be married" and in rebellion for being forced to descend to the "underworld, she became transformed into a tree" (Humphrey 20). Many American Indian myths also recount mythic characters being transformed into botanical components upon their deaths. An American Indian Ojibwe myth portrays a woman being transformed into the flower, the lady slipper, after having died trying to save her people. The myth surrounding the "night-blooming tree of sorrow" tells of a young South American Indian maiden, Parizataco, "who fell in love with the sun. But when the sun rejected her love and scorned her she withdrew from all human companionship into the deep wilderness. In her grief she slew herself" (Lehner & Lehner 92). When the people of her tribe found her body, they cremated her, and from her body the tree of sorrow emerged, only opening its blossoms at night. This mythic portrayal of death as simply transformation from one element, that of human form, into another element, botanical form, reveals a reincarnating concept of nature's consistent process of life, death, and rebirth. The message of such myths promotes audiences to view their own inevitable deaths in similar terms in order to obtain spiritual wisdom.

One myth of Celtic creation involves the Tuatha De Danann coming in to Ireland to conquer the existing forces of the Fir Bolgs. This myth captures death with clear botanical references. The myth shows the king of the Tuatha De Danann, Nuada, losing his arm in battle, and gaining a prosthetic arm made of silver, but after his prosthetic begins to malfunction, the myth shows a young doctor finding Nuada's decomposing arm, reattaching it to Nuada's body, and then reanimating it so that it functions good as new. The tale continues to show the young doctor's father becoming infuriated at his son's miraculous medical abilities, so he repeatedly attempts to wound his son by hitting him on his head with a sword, but the son only repeatedly proceeds to heal himself. After the father grows increasingly angry, he finally cuts the young doctor's brain in two, which successfully kills him. The father then buries the head in the ground, but from the decapitated head of his son grows "365 stalks of grass. Each blade could cure an illness in one of the 365 nerves in a person's body" (Rosenberg 281). However, this natural cure for life's maladies is not to be realized because the father sees this new development from the corpse of his son and irrevocably mixes the plants up, so that no one will ever know what plants will cure each illness. This myth explicitly shows death as a process that is the same for humans, animals, and plants alike. Here the doctor, in being wounded, acts as a plant would by growing a new shoot once an old one has been damaged. And upon his death, the doctor simply, in terms that evoke the conception of reincarnation, comes back as myriad plants that hold the ability to heal mankind.

The myth of Kaguya Himé[11] displays an old couple who lived contentedly in the remote mountains of Japan; the only thing they longed for was a child. The husband was named Taketori or Bamboo Cutter, and one afternoon he left to cut bamboo when he "noticed that a soft ethereal radiance streamed out from the lower section of the bamboo" (Faurot 89). The man bent closer and carefully cut the bamboo, and from out of the stalk he saw a tiny baby staring up at him. He took the child back home to his wife, who was overjoyed. They raised the child, naming her Kaguya Himé; as she grew, she resembled the natural product that birthed her. She was described as budding into maidenhood with such beauty that suitors came from far away to seek marriage with her, but Kaguya Himé refused them all. She was portrayed as not quite human; "on every moonlight, from the beginning of spring, she would look up into the boundless heavens with a faraway look, and then would fall to sobbing" (Faurot 90). Kaguya Himé finally revealed to her parents that she was from a celestial place called Moon Land, and that soon she must leave them behind and return to her home. The parents tried every possible solution to keep their daughter with them, but to no avail; though they even cried "blood-like tears" (Faurot 94), Kaguya Himé still left them forever.

This myth showcases that the element that allows the husband and wife to survive, bamboo, meets not only their financial needs, but offers them spiritual sustenance as well. The bamboo provides them with the one thing they long for, mythically binding the old couple together with the botanical world, as the bamboo directly produces their daughter, Kaguya Himé. But, the myth explains more in its lesson about the cycles of nature. Like the bamboo plant, Kaguya Himé buds forth, then blooms into full radiance, but also like the bamboo plant, she must symbolically die and return to "Moon Land." This allegory connects the cycles of plants to the lives of the old couple; they receive what they want most in life from the plants they harvest, but they also must concede this precious gift back from where it came. The connection of the moon is associated with darkness and dormancy, so as a botanical daughter, Kaguya Himé naturally must return to her dormant state.

There is another Asian myth of a woman being created from a tree by four travelers as told by W. R. S. Ralston in "Forest and Field Myths" (1878),[12] and her series of transformations also shows a mythic message of the interconnectivity of humans with botanical nature. The myth states that the first traveler carved the woman from the trunk of a tree; the second made her clothes; the third gave her jewels, and the fourth, a holy man, brought her to life. The four men fought for the right to marry her, but the gods deemed that "to its origin shall every created thing return" (Porteous 158), and the maiden while leaning against a tree was suddenly swallowed inside. This myth shows a belief that humans, here portrayed by the woman, will always be inextricably tied to the botanical world. The mandate of the gods that all things must return to their source serves as a reminder to audiences that they too must concede to the same fate as all vegetative elements.

Ralston in "Forest and Field Myths"[13] also discusses a Czech myth where a nymph can be seen on earth among humanity during the day, but at night she returns to live in a willow tree. She marries a mortal man and has children with him, but the myth states that the husband, unbeknownst of the severity of his action, cuts down the wife's willow tree, causing the wife to immediately die. The myth continues with the cut down willow tree being made into a cradle, which was able to immediately calm the wife's baby, and later in life, the remnants of the tree was said to be able to converse with her children. This myth decidedly points to the connection of humanity with the arboreal environment.

Many Greek and Roman myths additionally portray tales where humans transform into botanical elements following their human death. For instance, in the Roman text of Virgil's *Aeneid,* Aeneas travels to Thrace on his mission to found Rome after the fall of Troy, and wanting to make a sacrifice to the goddess Venus, he enters a grove of young trees and tries to pull one up by its roots, but he finds that blood pours out of the tree; the tree commands him to stop. Polydorus' spirit, the Trojan King Priam's youngest son who had been murdered by the King of Thrace, resides within the tree; "the spears that had been used to kill him had become stuck deep in the earth and had grown up through and around his body, so that he was transformed into one of the trees" (Humphrey 58). Accepting this explanation, Aeneas then performs a proper funeral for him in hopes that his spirit will be set free. In addition, the

> Greek mathematician and philosopher Pythagoras ... shunned the eating of beans, because he believed that the souls of some dead humans resided in beans before being reincarnated. He was said to have cited the resemblance between a bean in its early sprouting stages and a human fetus.... Some versions of the story of his death describe Pythagoras as being chased by enemies into a bean field. Rather than trample on the bean plants and kill what he believed were fellow humans, he allowed himself to be taken by the murderous mobs [Humphrey 59].

Ovid's *Metamorphosis* relates many myths of botanical metamorphosis upon death. The myth of Myrrha, as discussed earlier in this text, shows her being transformed into a tree to avoid death by her royal father for having tricked him into having sex with her, which impregnated her with her son Adonis. Adonis upon dying also was said to metamorphose into the flower that holds his name. A kind elderly couple, Philemon and Baucis, are described as being transformed into intertwining trees so that one would not have to live on after the death of his or her spouse. And Apollo's lover Hyacinthus, who accidently was killed when Apollo threw a discus, was also transformed upon his death into a hyacinth flower. Each of these myths of botanical metamorphosis shows a belief in natural rebirth.

In India, the legend of the mango tree[14] states that the daughter of the Sun, and wife of a king, was attempting to escape the anger of an enchantress, so she leapt into a pond and immediately was transformed into a yellow lotus. The king of the land wanted to possess this otherworldly flower, but the enchantress burned it to ashes. It is said that from the ashes, the mango tree emerged. The king brought the tree to his kingdom, and when the fruit was ripe, it fell to the ground, transforming once again back to the shape of the king's wife.

The Australian Aborigines tell of a myth where out of blood, flowers were created; in this telling of the myth, the flowers spoke towards justice from a horrendous massacre.[15] Long ago, there was a beautiful maiden, Purlimil, who fell in love with a young man; they made plans to marry, but her tribe deemed that she should marry a man, Turlta, who was detestable to her for his brutality. Knowing her sad fate ordained by her people, she fled to a pristine lake with her young lover, where they happily remained for many years. But, eventually Turlta, who was never able to forget his slight by Purlimil, vowed to find her and kill anyone with her. Turlta found her living near the lake with her lover and a new community of people who loved her, and in a rage he killed everyone, even accidently killing Purlimil. Turlta left the place with the fallen corpses looking up to him with black eyes, as their blood soaked into the earth. A year passed, and in spring, Turlta returned to the place of the massacre to gloat over the bones of those he killed, but to his astonishment, he found that there were no bones left; in their place was a field of magnificent red flowers with black centers. Seeing the blood-red flowers with the black centers, like the eyes of those he killed, he immediately knew that this place held firm the spirits of the dead who he slayed. He attempted to run away from this place, but mystically a spear fell from the clouds and killed him instantly. The beautiful lake eventually turned to salt to commemorate the sad events of the environment, and the Aborigines know that the "Sturt's desert peas" are really the "Flowers of Blood" (Mountford 46). The natural ease with which this tale allows nature to respond to the plight of the people shows the close connection of the Aboriginal Australians with their environment; the flowers and the lake reflect the events in the lives of the human beings. The fact that the people's bodies are transformed into flowers that cyclically bloom reveals a belief that though they died, they are assured an annual resurrection. This mythic archetype of blood in connection with flowers is still carried over to modern works, such as John McRae's poem "In Flanders Fields" where the fallen of World War I live on in the poppies that annually remind viewers of the devastating events of the past.

In China there is a legend that tells of a mother who was widowed; she had two boys, one her own biological son and one a step-son.[16] The mother loved her biological son very much and treated him kindly, but she treated the step-son cruelly; she often withheld food from him, so that her own child would grow healthy and strong while leaving the step-son weak. The mother devised a plan to get rid of her step-son by handing the boys two bags of seeds; she instructed them each to plant their seeds, and if one did not eventually sprout and produce plants, then that boy should not come home. The woman's biological son often felt bad for his step-brother, and to compensate for their mother's ill treatment, he often handed over his food and possessions to his step-brother, and now too, he gave his bag of seeds to him. They found that the step-son's seeds began to grow, but that his brother's did not. The biological son of the woman decided of his own accord to never return. Seeing her son missing, she proceeded to beat her remaining step-son telling him he must search for his brother; "and should you fail, wretch, rest assured that this is the last spring that you will ever see" (Ferguson 39). The step-son, unsuccessful in his search for his brother, was pitied by the gods and transformed into a cuckoo bird whose sad cry continues to resound throughout the region. Finally the boy, as a cuckoo, perched on a branch and wept tears of blood and died. And again, from the blood, the glorious red azalea emerged, an important symbol in China.

As stated metamorphosing into a plant often mythically shows that such a transformation is a positive thing, as it is portrayed in this Chinese myth as a gift from compassionate divinities. Mythic metamorphosis suggests that the suffering of mankind is relieved in a concrete way by the natural world, as the azalea serves a purpose of beauty to mankind, but it also suggests a connection to a belief in reincarnation, since the protagonist is portrayed as moving from one life form into another. The mythic transformation into flower or plant is of special significance, as in plant form often the character is assured a more lasting life, since in plant form he or she clearly now abides by the cycle of nature that promises new life from each death. The step-brother becoming both a bird and then a flower sends a resounding message that the death of humans is only one fleeting stage of the natural life process that always will continue.

The lotus flower also is a symbol of rebirth used in myriad world myths. It served as a representation of "immortality and eternal youth" to the Egyptian Horus. It is said "to be a symbol of resurrection, because the lotus flower closed its petals at night, only to rise above the surface of the water and to open again in the morning" (Lehner & Lehner 35–7). In Buddhism the nature of the lotus growing out of the mud and blooming as a flower of spectacular beauty represents the concept of reincarnation and enlightenment, and it is this same element that can be seen in myths that capture the transformation of a mythic character into a botanical element.

The Greek and Roman myth of Echo and Narcissus tells of a young man, Narcissus, who is so infatuated with himself that he cannot pull himself away from his own image reflected in a pool of water thinking that he has found the perfect person to love. In the *Metamorphosis,* Ovid holds Nemesis as accountable for making Narcissus fall in love with himself. The myth is often interpreted as a warning of being too narcissistic, as the fate of Narcissus in the myth shows him pining for himself so much that he dies of starvation, but still the gods and goddesses take pity on him and transform him into the narcissus flower. But the mythic transformation of Narcissus into a flower suggests something more than a cautionary tale.

In the myth, Narcissus shuns the love of all women before being pierced by the arrow of Cupid. The myth suggests a contemplative nature to Narcissus, as he prefers to remain solitary. Narcissus is said to be loved by the nymph Echo so much that even after he falls only in love with his own image, she follows his every move, hiding in a nearby cave as he wastes away. Echo, herself then fades away, just as Narcissus does, and the gods transform her into just a voice. The portrayal of Echo as a voice that is only capable of repeating Narcissus heavily indicates that spiritual autonomy is an important theme within the work. Narcissus loves himself, but Echo loves Narcissus in a detrimental way; she only follows and repeats what he has to say; whereas Narcissus may have an over-abundance of self-awareness, Echo has no sense of self. The connection of these two mythic figures within the myth is essential to understanding Narcissus as more than just an egotistical representation.

Narcissus' transformation into a flower upon his death indicates the natural cycle. Instead of being transformed into a mere voice only able to copy the expressions of another, he is transformed into a tangible flower that will continue on forever. His metamorphosis is viewed as a gift, and this is indicative of his spiritual transformation. Staring day in and day out at only his image suggests contemplation of identity; it can be construed as identifying a separation between true identity and persona, as reflected by the separate image in the pool. In loving his own image in the water, and shunning all love offered by the outside world, he has entered an internal state. He gives up a life of societal normalcy, as an ascetic would, to seek self-knowledge; it can then be said that Narcissus achieves spiritual enlightenment. His transformation into the narcissus flower connects his newfound spirituality with a representation of nature. Narcissus instead of innocently not knowing his own reflection, perhaps knows all too well that he, like all living beings, is indeed only a fleeting reflection in a pool of water. Narcissus' enlightenment is signaled within the myth by the symbol of his transformation into a narcissus flower, making his story not a cautionary lesson, but one that is similar to the story of the Buddha; it is a spiritual tale of letting one's identity go to merge with the greater cycles of nature.

The Greek and Roman myth of Apollo and Daphne showcases the nymph Daphne also being transformed into a laurel tree as a positive metamorphosis. Wishing to repel the advances of the god Apollo, Daphne flees from him, until finally without any more energy, she falls to the ground and begs the gods and goddesses to transform her into something forever separated from Apollo, and Daphne gets her wish and becomes a laurel tree.

This myth precisely captures the message of botanical metamorphosis. Daphne, for elusive reasons, does not wish to couple with the divine Apollo. Instead, she chooses to remain firmly connected to the tangible earth. She uses all of her physical strength to evade the god and prays to be transformed into a natural element that will last longer than even the divine Apollo. Daphne, in becoming the laurel tree, chooses to fully relinquish her identity and become a clear part of the endless cycle of nature. By becoming a tree, she will never die, thus becoming truly immortal, like all of the mythic characters who metamorphose into botanical elements.

6

The Seasonal Life Cycle and Myths of Destruction

"Plants feel no thanks for their flowering in spring's wind,
Nor do trees hate losing their leaves
under autumn skies...
The rise and the ending of all things
is just the way things are."

—Li Bo

"Nature's first green is gold,
Her hardest hue to hold.
Her early leaf's a flower;
But only so an hour....
So dawn goes down to day.
Nothing gold can stay."

—Robert Frost

The mythic representation of the seasons has always been an important part of world mythology. As seen in the Mother Goddess and male consort myths discussed in chapter 2, seasonal change in the environment was a defining aspect of the lives of ancient peoples, and myths evolved to explain this cyclical change as connected to divine representations. In these mythic explanations of seasonal change, the patterns of nature were connected to the lives of human beings. If the earth came alive in spring and then aged in autumn and died in winter, it was not a far stretch to connect these same patterns of nature to the lives of human beings. Therefore, countless myths explain the life span of a human being in accordance to the seasonal change of the earth—all are born into the world, age, die, and like nature are represented as being mythically reborn.

174

The Myths of the Seasons

The American Indian Seneca tribe personify the seasons of spring and winter as divinities.[1] They tell of a myth where the earth was newly created, and a very old man produced the season of winter wherever he went. As he breathed, the air became ice, and where he stepped, the ground became frozen. The plants and animals were forced to flee when he came near. The man sat in his lodge with only his friend the North Wind, until one day they sensed that something was different in nature; the snow was beginning to melt. Nervous, the old man stayed within his lodge, until a knock came upon his door. A young man stood at the door, walked into the old man's abode, and holding a green stick, began to stir the old man's fire. The old man tried to force the young man to leave, but the young man stated, "'Surely you know who I am. Do you not feel how warm my breath is? Wherever I breathe the plants grow and the flowers bloom. Where I step the grasses sprout and snow melts away. The birds and animals come to me.... Wherever I travel I bring the sunshine and you cannot stay'" (Bruchac 92). The myth closes with the old man melting away and disappearing, but of course built within the myth is the cyclical promise of the inevitable return of the same seasonal battle year after year.

The Aboriginal Australians living at Groote Eylandt explained seasonal change with their god, Bara, being taken captive for seven months of each year.[2] Bara would mythically remain in a hollowed out tree during his imprisonment, and when he remained within the tree, the world would fall into a barren state of winter. In the springtime, the people would come, and through sacred rituals they would attempt to entice Bara from his imprisonment, and once he was mythically released, it was believed the spring rains would finally fall. This pattern of personifying the seasons is seen throughout the world, as with the Hittite myth of Telepinu, the Greek myth of Demeter and Persephone, the Egyptian myth of Isis and Osiris, etc.

In Hawaii, the seasonal myth of Lono also defined a similar pattern.[3] The myth explains how Lono, the god of rain and fertility, stopped initiating these essential elements when he learned that his beloved wife died. In emotional agony, he left the Hawaiian islands in a boat far into the sea to heal, but he promised the people that he would always annually return for their survival. It is believed that Lono returns once a year through the aid of the sacred rituals practiced by the people, providing them with the much needed springtime rain.

The Seasonal Life Cycle—Myths of the Maiden, Mother, Crone as Spring, Summer and Autumn

As discussed, myths often present tales that serve as representations of the natural seasons in connection to the lives of human beings. As the Roman Ovid portrays the Greek Pythagoras as stating in the *Metamorphosis*:

> Do you not see how the year moves through four seasons, imitating human life: in early Spring ... resembling infancy.... The year now waxing stronger, after Spring it passes into Summer, and its youth becomes robust.... Autumn then follows ... that ripe and mellow time succeeds between youth and old age.... Then aged Winter with his tremulous step follows.... Our bodies also, always change unceasingly: we are not now what we were yesterday or we shall be tomorrow. And there was a time when we were only seeds of man.... But Nature changed us with her skillful touch [362].

Myths of youth are usually tied to the season of spring. The connection of youth to the initial season of growth inextricably binds humanity again to nature. It is easy to see the relationship of youth to the nascent stage of seasonal growth. Myths of spring-like youth, often present characters as full of life and vigor, but just as in nature, this verdant stage cannot last. Quite often women are portrayed within myth as maidens, mothers, or crones, and sometimes all three simultaneously, to serve as examples that the cycles of human life are tied to the cycles of nature—the youthful maiden, representing spring, the mother as a state of mature summer, and the crone representing autumn. Mythic women, more specifically goddesses, are also often represented as triad characters who can either interchange forms between youth, maturity, and old age, like the Irish Morrígan, or they consistently appear in myth as tied to each other, like the Greek Persephone, Demeter, and Hecate.

The cultures of the Arabian Peninsula worshipped a triple goddess, Al-Lat, who was also an Earth Goddess, and as such she was believed to control fertility. Sometimes Al-Lat was connected to both the sun and moon as well. Al-Lat was often associated as a triple goddess with Manat and Al-Uzza, who together represent the daughters of Allah (Wilkinson 110). When represented as part of this sacred triad, Al-Lat was portrayed often with the symbol commonly associated with fertility and the harvest—a sheaf of wheat. Al-Uzza known as the Strong One, was the goddess of the stars, love, and war, and was often portrayed with big cats as her companions. Manat was the goddess of fate and death; she was often represented with her symbol the moon as an old woman "holding a cup of death" (Wilkinson 111). This example shows how often the triple goddess in myth serves to bridge the concept that a human life follows the same patterns of nature—birth, life, death, and rebirth—because the portrayal of a female goddess, as discussed in many chapters thus far, has long been associated as a representation of the earth. Therefore, world myths often use the triple goddess as a representation of nature's seasonal processes, teaching audiences the importance of conceding that one's life must follow the same patterns of nature.

The mythic maiden is a harbinger of life and vitality; she signals spring and the generative promise of fecundity and prosperity. She is often portrayed as full of youth and highly beautiful, sometimes identifying her as a worthwhile prize for the mythic hero in his prime. Virginity is often associated with her, and so too is her power to illicit lust in the men around her; her sexuality, or her promise of sexuality, links her to her mythic role.

Virginity is an attribute that is frequently connected to female divinities, such as the Greek Athena, Artemis, and Hestia, the Japanese Amaterasu, the Egyptian Anat, etc.; the virginal state of these authoritative goddesses suggests their complete autonomy. Maintaining their virginity therefore gives them authoritative rule. As discussed earlier in the text, Athena is a prime example; she is known for maintaining her virginity. It is Athena's permanent virginity that allows her to hold extreme influence in the Greek pantheon; "because she remains a virgin perpetually, Athena is free from the sexual drives associated with the bodies of mortal virgins.... Unfettered by the demands of marriage and reproduction, Athena is able to move outside the strictures assigned women.... It is Athena's virginal status that enables her to move in areas associated with both male and female productivity" (Fosket 65). This tenet of the powerful virgin needs to be remembered when analyzing maidens within myth.

The mythic maiden, as a representation of spring, is directly tied to the cycles of nature, but she is also a representation of death because her appearance in myth signals the whole seasonal life process. When she appears, audiences recognize the sweet vitality of youth, but also concede that her role within the myth will fade, as spring always fades into summer. The mythic maiden, as a representation of spring, is also the closest in some ways to death, as cyclically, she just emerged from a state of winter; this explains why many myths of the maiden shows her succumbing to an untimely death, like Persephone being abruptly abducted by Hades. The death of the mythic maiden, though, must serve more as a reminder of the continuality of the natural life cycle, as she and her other female counterparts, the mother and the crone, are themselves representations of a continuous natural cycle. The mythic maiden often teaches those around her, sometimes the mythic hero, that the youthful stage of abundance and prosperity must come to an end. Through the mythic maiden, one sees that life is full of vitality, but also that this time is fleeting, and so must be embraced, but she also reminds one to allow this stage to pass for the other stages of the natural cycle: propagation and death. Death, when perceived through the mythic maiden, becomes only one stage in a continuous cycle; she therefore reminds one of death but promises everlasting renewal.

The Hopi American Indian myth of the Blue Corn Maiden[4] discusses a seasonal tale that presents a mythic maiden with male personifications of the seasons. This myth also connects the mythic maiden to death, thus further ensuring a message of the seasons being directly connected to the lives of human beings. The Blue Corn Maiden is abducted by Winter Katsina, the spirit who brings winter to the earth. The Blue Corn Maiden is depicted in the myth as being forced to stay with him, though she is treated very kindly, as Winter Katsina loves her. This tenet of the myth presents the maiden as paired with the mythic, and male, representation of winter, which can be symbolic of death, this is a common mythic archetype, as seen with Persephone and Hades for example. As with these renditions of the mythic pairing of the maiden with a male death, Blue Corn Maiden is associated with needing to live with Winter Katsina for half of the year, and while she is captured by Winter Katsina, the earth is in a state of frozen dormancy. The myth tells of Winter Katsina leaving one afternoon, so Blue Corn Maiden leaves and searches for signs of summer underneath the snow. She finds parts of yucca plants, takes them back to Winter Katsina's lodge, and lights a fire, and suddenly Summer Katsina appears. Summer Katsina and Winter Katsina fight once Winter Katsina returns home, but finally Winter Katsina concedes the necessity of each of their roles, so Blue Corn Mother is allowed to live with each for half of the year. This myth portrays the maiden as required to embrace both life and death as represented in the natural seasons. The Blue Corn Maiden, in name, signals that she is tied to vegetative growth; in her acceptance of the necessity of her annual symbolic life, in summer, and death, in winter, she can enable the Hopi people to prosper with the harvest she can now provide.

The Greek myth of Persephone and Demeter[5] is probably the most renowned of the myths that tie the maiden to her role of both herald of life and death. Persephone is the daughter of the goddess of the harvest, Demeter, and as Demeter's offspring, it is clear that Persephone is connected to nature and its cycles. The myth starts with Persephone in nature picking the narcissus flower when she is abducted by Hades, god of the underworld. The motif of flowers is a common association with the mythic maiden; the Welsh Blodeuedd is also connected with this theme. Persephone is depicted as picking these flowers in the springtime as a reminder of her mythic connection to nature; there can be no flowers without death, and as it is spring, this fact of nature becomes actualized through her role in the myth. She too, as symbolic flower, must die, so that regrowth is possible.

Hades abducts Persephone and takes her to the underworld. Here, the theme of death is clear; the underworld is only a place for dead mortals, and though she has a divine mother and father, Zeus, Persephone is experiencing death. Demeter is devastated by the loss of her daughter and searches the land for her. The myth shows Demeter disguising herself as an old woman and serving as a nanny to king Celeus and his queen. She attempts to make the infant she is caring for, Demophon, immortal by holding him in sacred flames, but the mother spies her doing this and intervenes; Demeter, incensed, curses the mother and flees. This section of the myth only further solidifies the futility of immortality; her own daughter, having two divine parents, should not experience death, even a symbolic one, but Demeter was powerless to stop it. When Demeter is told of the abduction, she hides herself within a cave, refusing to allow the crops to grow.

Mankind begins to starve, as without the mythic maiden or mother, regeneration is impossible. The myth continues to show Persephone and Demeter as part of a tripartite symbol when the goddess Hecate, portrayed as an old woman who is able to travel to the underworld, assists Demeter in finding Persephone. As Campbell states, "there is a trinity of goddesses identified with the local food plants, the pig, the underworld, and the moon, whose rites ensure both a growth of the plants and a passage of the soul to the land of the dead.... The marriage of the maiden goddess ... is equivalent to her death, which is imaged as a descent into the earth and is followed, after a time, by her metamorphosis into food ... grain" (*Primitive Mythology,* 186). Campbell also connects this myth to ancient Greek rituals that connect sacrifice to the success of the harvest; "the women of the Greek Thesmophoria ... placed figures of flour and wheat, representing snakes and human beings, in the *Megara,* together with the pigs; the pigs being left until the flesh rotted, when their bones were brought up and revered as relics, while the figures of wheat were consumed by snakes" (*Primitive Mythology,* 186–7). Campbell contends that this ritual, and many like it in neighboring communities, served as a symbolic form of sacrifice that shows an understanding that propagation of nature requires death and sacrifice. Instead of human sacrifice, symbolic figurines and food could be left as a form of payment to entice the earth to produce sustenance, just as Demeter will be enticed to emerge from her cave.

Soon, the Olympians hearing the plight of the starving people coax Demeter out of her cave by assuring her that Persephone may return to the land of the living on the one condition that she has not eaten the food of the dead. But she did eat the seeds of the pomegranate while in Hades, so the myth concludes with its cyclical obligations—Persephone must remain in Hades part of the year, and can ascend to the realm of her mother and abounding life for the other portion. It becomes clear that Persephone, as the maiden offspring of the harvest goddess, represents the cycles of nature. Persephone is the seed, going into the underworld, so that she can annually be reborn and blossom.

The myth of Demeter and Persephone showcases a generational portrayal of the cycles of life, as tied fully to nature. The youth of Persephone, the maturity and motherhood of Demeter, and the role of elder Hecate portray a theme common to world myth—the tripartite goddess. As stated in chapter 2, the Earth Goddess became divided into lesser roles as patriarchal societies obtained domination. As was seen with early representations of the Greek Mother Goddess becoming divided into separate parts in the new Olympian pantheon, so too are tripartite goddesses often subparts of a central, and sometimes more ancient, goddess. Triple goddesses are portrayed as again embodying the stages of life for human beings: youth, adulthood, and old age. They serve as reminders to audiences that each stage of life is temporary, but also that each stage is intertwined, just as the maidenhood of spring leads to the adulthood of summer, so too will summer eventually lead into the old age of fall, which inevitably leads to winter or death. The goddess in being represented in three parts shows that these stages of human life are bound to the same cycles of the natural world, but in this connection, the tripartite goddess herself shows that like nature, humanity too will cyclically continue.

The Eleusinian Mysteries, which centered on the myth of Persephone and Demeter, were considered sacred because they taught initiates to connect the lesson of the myth to their mortal lives—that like the young maiden Persephone, the mother Demeter, and the old woman Hecate, so too will they follow the same seasonal pattern in their own lifetimes, and that in the acceptance of this, one can find solace in the regenerative aspect of the cycle, as Persephone never truly dies.

Persephone is later depicted as falling in love with Hades (O'Hare-Lavin 200), as she values both her time on earth with her mother, but also her time in the land of the dead. In Persephone losing her virginity, or mythic maidenhood, as wife to the god Hades, she has fulfilled her role as mythic maiden by embracing death. She is not portrayed in later myths as weak or lesser for losing her maidenhood, but stronger, as she fully now contains the cycles of nature, and so with this wisdom, she is depicted as ruling alongside Hades.

In Celtic mythology triple goddesses were also common. The Irish goddess, the Morrígan, for example, is usually associated as being a tripartite goddess; though her roles change, the persona of a maiden is certainly one of her important roles. The Morrígan is also associated with battle and death, as her portrayal on the battlefield often signals a warrior's impending demise, though "war *per se* is not a primary aspect of the role of [the Morrígan] ... her association with cattle suggests ... [she] was connected to the earth, fertility and sovereignty" (Herbert). The "'triple mother' seems to have been considered particularly powerful by the Celts. They represent both human fertility and the bounty of the earth and have dominion over human life and well-being. They also seem to symbolize the span of human life—many trios of goddesses take the form of women of different ages" (Wilkinson 73). As Wood states, "The complex symbolism of mother goddesses was reinforced by the fact that they were often grouped in threes. Several maternal images found in Rhineland depict two older goddesses flanking a younger one. In Burgundy, one goddess commonly holds a newborn baby" (42). Triple goddesses were believed to represent "the cycle of life, from birth to old age and death" (Wood 42). The representation of threes is a common theme in Celtic belief, and may "signify the continuity of time (past, present, and future)" (Wood 60).

The Welsh *Mabinogi*⁶ presents the mythic archetype of the maiden throughout the text. In the first branch, Rhiannon appears to Pwyll as an unattainable maiden, radiant upon her otherworldly horse. She rides at a slow, ambling speed, but Pwyll's fastest riders cannot catch up to her. After an exhausting attempt finally by Pwyll himself, he realizes that he simply must ask her to stop and converse with him, which she readily does, and proceeds to tell him that she was indeed waiting for him to make this realization, as she intends to escape an upcoming marriage to a man she does not love to marry Pwyll instead. Rhiannon, as maiden, in this first section of the *Mabinogi* signals a theme for the rest of the work. Rhiannon possesses aspects that Pwyll longed for; he is first depicted as being bored with his present state of luxury, longing for something that will fill an internal void, but it is not until he views Rhiannon that he realizes that the void needed to be filled with love of this otherworldly maiden. The two eventually marry, propelling Rhiannon from her mythic maiden role to that of the mythic mother, as she has a son with Pwyll.

One night, though, Rhiannon's and Pwyll's baby disappears, which only furthers the mythic portrayal of the seasonal role of Rhiannon. The nursemaids wake up to see the baby gone, and as to avoid being punished by death for losing the royal couple's child, they kill a dog and smear its blood all over Rhiannon's face and hands to make it appear that she has killed and eaten her own son. King Pwyll refuses to believe that his wife killed their child, though all the people of the kingdom are convinced that she has done this terrible deed. Rhiannon, overcome with grief and guilt takes to sitting outside the castle compound and telling all those who pass by what she is accused of and tells anyone that they may ride upon her back as she crawls on all fours.

The myth continues to show Rhiannon's connection to a more ancient representation of a triad nature goddess, when it is discovered that her son has indeed been abducted by a figure that lives in the deep wilderness, perhaps a representation of the demanding cycles of nature itself. A man named Teyrnon finds that each year his horse gives birth to a beautiful colt, but each year on the night of the horse's birth, it disappears. It is discovered that this happened on the same night as the birth of Rhiannon's and Pwyll's son. And in fact, Teyrnon finds that the night he finally tries to outsmart the annual thief by bringing his horse into his own home so as to guard his horse and her colt, he finds that a clawed hand comes in through the window to abduct the colt. He rushes outside to find the creature, but only finds that when he returns into his home that the colt is indeed missing, but in its place is a new-born baby. He and his wife view it as a gift in compensation for their lost colts and raise the child. Years later though, Teyrnon realizes that the boy looks like the king and brings him back to his royal parents. Rhiannon discovers that she has done no harm to her child and accepts her son, Pryderi, back into her care.

Rhiannon is often connected with the Celtic goddess Epona, goddess of horses, and this myth certainly evidences this connection. Rhiannon, by allowing people to ride upon her back, shows this connection to the goddess Epona. She is deeply connected to the birthing horse portrayed in the myth, as both Rhiannon and the mare experience the same loss of their young on the same night. The characterization of Rhiannon also suggests aspects of an older Mother Earth Goddess who both gives and takes life back within her, with the presentation of Rhiannon being accused of consuming her newborn child. The common mythic archetype of annual loss through death being returned with a symbolic resurrection also serves to identify her as an Earth Goddess. Rhiannon in being connected to the mare mythically shows the annual pattern of nature's seasons with the representation of the newly birthed colt disappearing with annual certainty. The monstrous hand belonging to an unidentified creature in the deep woods certainly can serve as a representation of death itself, and the promise of nature's resurrection is also made clear when Rhiannon has her child returned to her once more. Rhiannon then is portrayed in triple goddess form throughout the myth, as she first appears in her maidenhood full of vitality, then clearly is presented in the role of mother, and then symbolically is tied to the figures, like the tripartite Morrígan, who signals the necessary loss of life. With Rhiannon serving as a mythic portrayal of all the aspects of a single human life cycle, with also a nebulous annual abduction that takes place in the deep wilderness, the myth serves to remind audiences of nature's seasonal patterns being tied to the lives of human beings.

The American Indian Cherokee have a myth of Grandmother Sun and her daughter that also explains the human life cycle in terms of the seasons of nature.[7] In the myth Grandmother Sun and her daughter live together in a house high in the sky; Grandmother Sun is depicted as angry because the people of the earth do not worship her as she feels they should. She grows jealous of Moon, as she thinks the people adore him instead of her, so she plots to kill all of mankind. She sets herself firmly within the sky and refuses to budge; the people begin to suffer from the dirge of unrelenting heat, and the land becomes barren. Distraught, the people beg for help from spirits known as Little Men. The Little Men vow to help, so they transform themselves into snakes and try to kill Grandmother Sun. One Little Man, as a rattlesnake waits by the door of Grandmother Sun's home, and at last the door opens, but it is her daughter who is struck by the snake. She soon dies, and now Grandmother Sun, in her extreme sorrow, reverses the scourge upon mankind by shutting herself up in her house indefinitely. Soon, the people of earth realize that they need Grandmother Sun, as without her heat they will all die of cold, and nothing will grow to sustain them. They pray again, and the Little Men this time vow to get Grandmother Sun to shine once more upon the land.

In a myth that resembles the Greek myth of Demeter and Persephone and the Hittite myth of Telepinu, the Little Men do whatever they can to coax Grandmother Sun from her home. The Little Men go to the underworld to try and retrieve Grandmother Sun's daughter; they succeed in capturing her ghost, but accidently let her spirit out before they reach the house of Grandmother Sun. The myth describes this moment as the time when death came to the people as something irreversible, because it is this point that Grandmother Sun realizes that she will never get her beloved daughter back. With this realization, Grandmother Sun wept uncontrollably, so much so that a great flood threatened now to drown all the earth's inhabitants. This time the people sent up dancers to Grandmother Sun to distract her from her unrelenting sorrow, "and the sun looked up. The new music and the young people were so beautiful that the old sun gave up her grieving and once again smiled" (Leeming & Page, *The Mythology,* 27). The symbolism of the old Grandmother Sun losing her daughter, but smiling at the beautiful young dancers, again recounts the cyclical nature of life. In the myth of Demeter, she too is coaxed out of her cave by distraction and is said to pause her crying for a moment of laughter initiated by the efforts of the gods to save humanity by reinstating the role of Demeter as goddess of the harvest, and here too, the laughter of Grandmother Sun reveals the mythic revelation that death is cyclical. Her daughter dies, but life must continue, as represented by the new young dancers. Her threats to stunt life through her incessant presence giving off constant heat, or her withdrawal emanating bitter cold, pauses the cycles always evident in nature, so the myth recounts the necessity of Grandmother Sun realizing the role she plays in the natural world, therefore, revealing the role human beings must also play as part of this cycle.

In India the worship of the phallus, or lingam, "is a central part of the cult of Shiva but dates from the time of the Indus Valley civilization" (Phillips, Kerrigan, & Gould 44). Shiva is considered to be the destroyer, part of triple divine representation with Brahma, the creator, and Vishnu, the preserver; this role is necessary to the cosmic cycle of birth, destruction, and rebirth. This regenerative cycle follows the cycles of nature, as death secures the lives of the next generation. Also Shiva bringing destruction in most of his myths shows mythic audiences that life and nature are often necessarily indeterminate, harsh, and unpredictable. His connection to fertility is also an essential part of his portrayal, as shown in a myth about him and a group of ascetic sages striving for enlightenment.[8] Shiva in the avatar Nataraja comes to a mountain community where a group of sages live in state of self-deprivation; "some ate nothing but green moss gathered from the dank and dripping caves, while others stretched out in icy mountain pools and wandered the landscape beneath great banks of clouds, refusing all shelter; they either sat meditating in the usual cross-legged yogic position, or stood, as if suspended, on the tip of a single toe" (Phillips, Kerrigan, & Gould 42). Seemingly to negate this form of asceticism, Shiva as Nataraja, enters their community. He poses as a stranger, completely naked, with his hair streaked with chalk and his penis painted red and white; "his wild appearance was matched by his unpredictable behavior—he sang with a wide smile, then danced intensely in a frenzy of sexual energy; at other times he cackled with laughter and screamed wildly" (Phillips, Kerrigan, & Gould 43–4). The wives of the ascetic monks were enticed by his sexually suggestive dance, and they unabashedly watched him. The sages, attempting to remove themselves from all bodily connections, grew enraged at their wives looking this way at another man, so they approached Shiva demeaning him and his dance; they yelled that he should cut off his penis rather than parade it for everyone to see as he was now doing. Shiva announced that no force in the world would ever be able to cut his penis off of him, but that if he chose to do it, he could easily accomplish the task. The sages were delighted to hear that soon this menace and his apparent sexual prowess would be emasculated. Shiva took his member is his hand and smiling cut it off in front of the crowd; he then disappeared before their very eyes. Dumbfounded, the crowd wasn't sure of the immensity of what they had just witnessed.

The weeks that followed proved disastrous; "Shiva's action had terrible consequences. When he cast aside the *lingam,* order collapsed in the universe. The sun's power failed and sacrificial rituals lost their effectiveness. The seasons fell out of their appointed order.... The sages' own vitality faded, and though they held fast to their familiar religious practices they even began to lose their sure faith in the rightness of *dharma,* the universal order" (Phillips, Kerrigan, & Gould 44–5). This connection of Shiva's self-dismemberment to the collapse of the natural world is significant. It suggests that fertility must be fully embraced as an essential aspect of the natural cycle. If one fully shuns a vibrant bodily existence while alive, including a healthy sexual appetite, then it suggests that the seasonal cycles, as evident in nature, are not being fully actualized. The myth proposes that the sages, in removing all physical pleasure from their lives, a common practice in the goal of attaining enlightenment, are not fully embracing nature as it is.

The sages go to the divine Brahma and prostrate themselves before him begging for an answer as to why the natural order has collapsed, and Brahma immediately understands this to be the work of Shiva. Brahma tells the sages that they must embrace the lingam and worship it instead of shun it. The sages then go back home to worship the phallus, and "the seasons moved once again into their rightful path and the sages' own virility returned. For a full year they worshipped Shiva, using images of the *lingam*" (Phillips, Kerrigan, & Gould 45). After the year has passed, the sages were once more greeted by the presence of Shiva, but this time he revealed himself to them in his full splendor. The god Shiva "poked gently to them, saying that they would be cleansed by the ashes of sacrificial fires because they contained his own seed.... With great joy the sages took their images of the *lingam* and washed them in fragrant waters mixed with flowers. Then they washed the great one himself, singing gently" (Phillips, Kerrigan, & Gould 45). The myth's attention to the mildness of Shiva towards the sages and their gentle washing of him suggests that the natural order was restored because nature was embraced as it actually is—full of virility. Sexual life and fertility at the end of the myth are not shunned as obscene, but valued as an essential part of the natural order.

Also in Indian mythology, the maiden Parvati is depicted as being the other half of the god Shiva. Parvati is portrayed as a beautiful maiden who is assured, despite heavy opposition, that she wants to marry Shiva. Shiva, who is said to reside alone in natural areas of the wild, is not at first interested in Parvati. But undeterred, Parvati sends Kama, the god of love, to try and lure Shiva into falling in love with her. Kama tries to engage Shiva with "sounds and scents of spring,"[9] but Shiva only immersed at present in his destructive role, burns Kama to ashes. This connection of attempting to introduce the season of spring to Shiva foreshadows the role that Parvati will play in the life of the destructive god. In his solitary role of the bringer of death, he is only partially actualized; even though he is portrayed with Brahma and Vishnu as a three-fold representation of the cycles of nature, he still must have a personal counterpart that represents life and regeneration in order for the myths surrounding him to fully connect him to the cycles of life.

Parvati is not deterred by the death of Kama; she embraces her role as mythic maiden when she insists on pursuing Shiva, even though he is the harbinger of death and destruction. Parvati's persistence alone is said to be what causes Shiva, and the Hindu divinities to actualize her desire:

> She performs all the traditional mortifications, such as sitting in the midst of four fires in the middle of summer, remaining exposed to the elements during the rainy season and during the winter, living on leaves or air only, standing on one leg for years, and so on. Eventually she accumulates so much heat that the gods are made uncomfortable and persuade Shiva to grant Parvati's wish, so that she will cease her efforts [Kumar].

Parvati's renunciation of her life as filled with human limitations allows her to enter a broader cycle that again is clearly tied to the progression of nature; her mythic choice to endure the elements with superhuman determinism suggests her tie as mythic maiden to the earth. Her refusal to back down from connecting with Shiva displays their collective role; the uniting of Shiva with Parvati actualizes the natural occurrence of life, death, and rebirth.

Shiva and Parvati eventually marry, and at their wedding, Parvati's mother is outraged that her daughter is marrying one so hideously terrifying. This aspect of the myth reveals its overall meaning. In Parvati's bravery at connecting herself forever to the god associated with destruction and death, she is showing that maidenhood is irrevocably connected to death. Her mother, possibly in the role of preserver of life, resists this connection, but Parvati, as mythic maiden, demands that it be fulfilled.

After the wedding ceremony, the marriage is consummated, and the myth indicates that the passion between Parvati and Shiva is so intense that it shakes the cosmos and lasts so long that the gods again become afraid and try to intervene. This fear of even the gods suggests the futility of trying to escape the natural cycle they embody. In addition, when Shiva and Parvati embrace, Parvati's sweat mixes with the ashes of the body of Kama, and he is resurrected (Kumar). Kama's resurrection again shows the actualization of the cycles of nature and life.

Shiva and Parvati ultimately have children, though fitting to his role, Shiva is initially resistant, but also suitable to Parvati's role, she insists on making Shiva more than just a singular tenet of the life cycle. She convinces him to concede and accept the regenerating aspect of life; when they do finally have children, it solidifies the myth's message. Parvati, as mythic maiden, knows that she must lose her maidenhood and become a mother, so that together with Shiva, they fully represent the cycle of life, death, and renewal; "without its female half, or female nature, the godhead of Shiva is incomplete and is unable to proceed with creation" (Kumar). Shiva initially resisted Parvati and her role as mythic maiden, as the bringer of life, but upon their union, they together symbolize the cyclical aspect of life.

The Indian myth of Kali presents another incarnation of Shiva's wife Parvati, but this myth perhaps most distinctly connects the maiden as a representation of death in nature's life cycle. Kali's myth[10] shows her as existing as a beautiful goddess in full maidenhood. She is portrayed as so exquisitely pure, "the lotus flower of perfection" (Leonard & McClure 159) that all of the gods desire her, but Kali deflects their attention, which enrages them. The gods take revenge upon this symbol of innocence and murder her by beheading her with a bolt of lightning; they then throw her head into the underworld, which causes monstrous beasts to emerge out of the depths of the earth. The gods, now fearful of what they have done, go to seek out Kali's head in repentance. They eventually find Kali's head, but they cannot find her body, so they attach her head to the body of a beheaded prostitute they find. This unforgivable act done to the pure Kali transforms her forever into a figure of insatiable hunger.

Kali now longs to consume men, as she is portrayed as becoming sexually voracious. She has sex with every mortal man she can find; she approaches men stricken with poverty, illness, old age, etc., and meets their every carnal desire. She is portrayed as roaming the streets like a prostitute, killing the men after she pleases them, trying, but being unable to, satiate her desire. She is described as callous towards the living. As she walks through the streets, a young child comes up to her and begs for food, but Kali just keeps walking without warning the child that a snake is about to bite him. Kali had been overcome by a hatred of all living things, and at the same time by a desire … to annihilate all creatures as she fed on them. She could be seen crouching at the edge of graveyards; her jaws cracked bones like the maw of a lioness. She killed like the female insect devouring the male; she crushed the beings she brought to life like a wild sow turning on her young. Those she killed, she finished off by dancing on their bodies. Her lips stained with blood exuded a dull smell of butcher shops, but her embrace consoled her victims, and the warmth of her breast made them forget all ills [Leonard & McClure 160].

Finally, Kali becomes tired. She finds an old wise man sitting in the woods. The man's presence moves Kali. She speaks to him about her own murder and subsequent behavior; "I desire and do not desire, I suffer and yet I enjoy, I loathe living and yet I am afraid to die" (Leonard & McClure 160). The man simply tells Kali that all beings suffer; they always have, and they always will. She refutes that she was once a goddess, but was degraded more than anyone she knows, and to this the old man states: "'and yet you were not freer from the chain of things, not your diamond body safer from misfortune than your body of flesh and filth. Perhaps, unhappy woman, dishonored traveler of every road, you are about to attain that which has no shape'" (Leonard & McClure 160).

This myth shows that Kali, once a divine maiden, had to grapple with the reality of death in a mythic representation that is elevated. She quite literally gorges herself on the death of others; she is a contrasting view of the maiden often seen in world myth, where instead of innocence and verdant thriving, she depicts destruction. Still, the representation of Kali is still aligned with her other mythic maiden counterparts, as she is portrayed as living in a state of abundance, only the profusion of her life is death. She, like her consort Shiva, represents the necessary stages of the natural cycle. Kali and Shiva are presented as overtly horrific, as they dance on the evidence of their destruction, but one must be mindful of the fact that the representation of both Kali and Shiva is not a portrayal of evil; it is instead a portrayal of nature as it is. Kali finally becomes tired of her role within this myth, which suggests that the seasonal promise of nature is about to be renewed in her. Kali will always become Parvati, and Parvati will always go back to becoming Kali, just as winter will always move into spring, and spring back to winter.

The mythic maiden is an essential part of world mythology. As evidenced, her myths do not usually keep her locked within her youthful vigor, but instead they show that like the cycles of nature, she must embrace death. Mythically she repeatedly does this to show audiences that the process of life and death is not fatalistic; instead, she reminds one of the promises of renewal and regeneration in nature. Like spring moving into summer, audiences of myth connect their own youth and lives within their prime to a realization that their symbolic autumns will soon approach, and that inevitably winter must come, but in remembering the mythic maiden, one is assured that spring will blossom again and again.

Myths of a Necessary Destruction—Winter

Just as fire is a natural process of regrowth in forest environments, causing fallen trees and decayed matter to be cleared away to assure new growth for smaller plant life to thrive, as well as enabling the fertilization of soil with essential nutrients, so too do human beings imagine similar myths of destruction to explain the natural cycles of death and destruction assuring the generation of new life. As Campbell states, "The world lives on death: that is the insight rendered dramatically"; in addition, "reproduction without death would be a calamity, as would death without reproduction" (*Primitive Mythology*, 177). Myths that portray death and destruction are tied to the myths of the maiden, mother, crone life cycle in that they portray the same cyclical message of the triple goddess. Implicit in the myths of the triad deities is the sense that each goddess represented, Persephone, Demeter, Hecate for example, is a crucial part of the cycle, but that the cycle itself is dominant; no one deity can exist without her counterparts. Myths of death and destruction follow this same pattern. Mythic destruction, even on a grandiose scale, like the annihilation of the earth, is merely one stage of the natural life cycle—winter. Though winter is harsh, it will always concede to the rebirth of spring.

As stated, myths of destruction appear around the world; sometimes they are portrayed in daily terms, such as the consistent cycle of day into night. The Egyptians believed that the end of the world was an event that must be avoided each day:

> Each night the sun god Re ... had to defeat Apophis, the serpent god associated with darkness, evil and trickery.... Ever since humanity had first walked the banks of the River Nile, Re had won the necessary victory, but if one day he were to lose, or even if Apophis were to be killed, the universe would come to an end. Then all would be returned to primeval chaos, to the waters of Nun. The gods themselves would be no more, save the One—called Atumin Heliopolis—who was existent before all things. Creation would have come full circle [Allan & Phillips, *World*, 38].

Sometimes, mythic destruction was portrayed as establishing a new order, so that a new pantheon could prosper, such as the myth where the Babylonian Marduk must kill the giant primordial Tiamet in order to gain his rightful seat as head of the pantheon. The Greeks also established a mythic creation cycle where the primary father Uranus was defeated by his son Cronus through castration, so that Cronus could rule with his siblings, until he too succumbed to the same fate as his father and was defeated by his son Zeus. Myths of mythic characters overtaking other superior deities serve again as representations of the cycles of nature. It is natural for the younger generation to supersede the older generation. Though, the Babylonian and Greek versions of relational take over appear harsh, they are meant to represent the natural cycle of life that ceaselessly demands the death of one generation to continue the next.

The Bantu people of Africa recount a myth of Dikithi[11] who takes his wife and children and leaves the village; they are pursued by the mother of his wife, who has been refused to accompany them by Dikithi himself. The old woman, though, is determined to follow, and she begins to threaten the virility of Dikithi, by stating that she will castrate him. Dikithi and his wife climb a tree to escape her; he then sends locusts and lions to push her away, but she perseveres and continues to threaten him, whereupon he sets her on fire, burning her to death. Dikithi then calls forth his own father and kills him by convincing him to be allowed to be pulled up the tree by a rope around his neck; "when the old man was near the top of the tree, Dikithi took out his knife and cut the rope" (Leeming & Page, *God*, 47). The deaths of both the wife's mother and Dikithi's father is symbolic of one generation bringing about the destruction of the previous generation. It again seems like a harsh myth, but there are many other creation myths that follow this similar structure, such as the defeat of the original Greek pantheon by Zeus and the Olympians.

The sacrifice of the older generation by the younger generation merely shows the necessity of the life cycles of nature. The older generation must concede to the younger one, so that the cycle is fulfilled. These myths, through their violence, represents the struggle of the required harsh acknowledgement of all mortals that their life, according to the natural cycle, is limited. When Dikithi and his wife climb down the tree, which also suggests a tie with vegetation, he states that his father's stomach is full of food, so he calls all the animals and people together, and they feast to secure their own survival. Again this task, which is celebrated by all the animals alongside the people, indicates the interconnectedness of the natural cycle to all living beings.

Many ancient civilizations also believed that the end of the world was inevitable. The Persian Zoroastrians believed that the destruction of the earth would come with first a period of iron, where warriors would ruthlessly attack the living, then after a thousand years a massive dragon would cause more deaths, and finally, again one thousand years later, a great flood would rid the world of all its inhabitants. Once the destruction ended, though, the earth would "be re-created" (Bierlein 241). Many adherents of Christianity and Islam also believe in this inevitable end of the world.

The Pawnee American Indians believed that Tirawa Atius, the creator, set a mythic buffalo in the sky, and made certain that the buffalo would lose one hair a year; after all of his fur was gone, the Pawnee believed that the world would end (Bierlein 248). The Cherokee American Indians believed that the earth floats on a primordial sea, only held up "by rawhide at the four points of the compass" (Bierlein 249). Over millions of years, the rawhide will continue to wear away, until one day it is certain to break, and when it does the earth will plunge into the same waters from which all life emerged; "then, as happened the last time, the Creator will pull the earth back out of the water and re-create the world" (Bierlein 249).

There are many world cultures that account for the destruction of the earth's inhabitants in the form of a great flood. The Hebrew story of Noah accounts for the flood that wiped out all humanity, except for Noah, his family, and a pair of each animal species, as being the result of a divine punishment for the immoral behavior of humans. Similarly, the Mesopotamians recounted a tale where the god Enlil caused a great deluge because humankind was too noisy, which annoyed the god, but king Atra-hasis survived with his family and many animals, so that the earth's inhabitants were replenished. And again in the Assyrian and Babylonian tale of Utnapishtim, he survived a great flood, but also saved his family and many animals so as to repopulate the newly cleansed world after the deluge. The Maya and Incas additionally accounted for a creator who destroyed the first race of people who proved insufficient by a massive flood. The Greek Zeus also mythically caused a massive flood to punish humanity, but Prometheus warned his son Deucalion and his wife Pyrrha to take refuge in a large boat. Quite often, as with these examples, the great flood was caused by the power of a single divinity who was angered or disturbed by the ways of mankind, but in the Hindu version of the flood myth, the deluge merely resulted because the world is always periodically called to end with destruction at the end of each day for Brahma (Allan & Phillips, *Chinese,* 34).

What is central to these tales of a great flood is the concept of renewal after inevitable destruction, so that again, the portrayal of utter destruction in myth simply represents a mythic version of a seasonal state of winter. The newly refreshed world, after the state of mythic death, is the intended message of these myths, as this concept of death for the world is quite similar, again to the notion of the seasonal death and rebirth of nature. The Aboriginal

Worora of Australia, for instance, discuss a great flood that occurred in Dreamtime, so as to make space for the people and animals that would inhabit the "new" earth (Allan & Phillips, *World*, 35).

What is central to myths where the world is destroyed is the concept that new life will emerge from the destruction of the earth's resources and its inhabitants, and again this is a repetition of the basic concept of cyclical nature explored in many mythological tales thus far—all living matter exists for a time, then must die, but from death new life emerges. The mythic end of the world, either through flood, or a more apocalyptic explanation, simply reiterates the natural observation that like plants, animals, and humans, all life is subject to the same seasonal laws. Many cultures, then, accounted for their myths of destruction with acceptance rather than fear, as these cultures "regarded life as an intricate cycle in which the end of one age marked the birth of another, often better, epoch" (Allan & Phillips, *World*, 36). For example, many Tibetan Buddhists believe that the world will end in a "violent cataclysm at the end of the current age that will be followed by a golden age: a 1,000-year era of world peace and enlightenment when the ways of Buddhism will find favour [sic] in all countries" (Allan & Phillips, *World*, 37).

The Norse conception of the end of the world, Ragnarok, exemplifies the necessity of destruction. The myth of Baldur portrays the necessity of death in a way that again ties a representation of a divine death with the portrayal of death in nature. Rosenberg contends that "the fertility myth of Baldur is an integral part of the creation myth. Like other Norse myths, it has been lifted from its earlier, agricultural culture and has been transplanted into the more aggressive Viking Age, with an increased emphasis on death" (219). Baldur's mythic death shows audiences that nature requires death; it shows death in the nuances of the natural world, in the divine, in man, and subsequently in the universe.

The Norse creation myth, as has been discussed in chapter 1, begins with death. Ymir must be sacrificed for the earth to be created from his very body, and Odin, with Vili and Ve, are central to causing his death. It is therefore proper that Odin too will one day have to die so that the natural process of the universe is met. The myth of the death of Baldur recounts this vision. Loki, often defined as a mythic trickster, is sometimes defined as evil in Norse myth, but this portrayal of Loki is misguided when his mythic role is viewed in natural terms, as discussed in chapter 4 of this book. Loki is essential, especially in the myth of Baldur, to continuing the natural order of the universe. Loki is a designated and integral part of the Norse pantheon of the Aesir. Though he often gets into trouble, disrupting the intentions of the other members of the Aesir, they cannot fully get rid of Loki, and this mythic understanding reveals the Norse view that Loki represents aspects of life that will forever be indeterminate and inevitable. Loki's offspring also portrays a mythic understanding of the harsher aspects of life; as also stated in chapter 4, Loki is father to the wolf Fenrir, the underworld goddess Hel, and the Midgard serpent. All of his offspring are essential components in the destruction of the universe.

The Norse gods know that the world will eventually destruct, and the depiction of this devastation is again put into natural terms. First the wolf, Hati, that perpetually chases the sun will finally catch and swallow it, as will the wolf, Skoll, finally catch and swallow the moon. The heavens will be torn apart by a giant named Surt, which will cause massive earthquakes that will destroy the earth's surface and resources and cause Loki, the wolf, Fenrir, and the World Serpent, Jörmungandr, to become unleashed. Odin will battle Fenrir; Thor will attack Jörmungandr, and Freyr will take on Surt, but all three divine beings, Odin, Thor, and Freyr, will be killed by their adversaries. The Norse depiction of Ragnarok shows that everything that maintains order in the known universe must eventually capitulate. The world, according to the myth, systematically created components, such as Loki, Fenrir, the Midgard Serpent, etc., that assured an inevitable destruction. It is also vital to note that Odin foresees his own inescapable destruction; this component makes him an interesting divinity because he is portrayed not as dominant to natural forces, but as equally controlled by them as all mankind. His understanding of his own powerlessness in this respect prepares mythic audiences for their own singular deaths. The myth of Ragnarok shows that death is necessary for all beings, as well as for the earth itself, but the myth also, like nature, provides a representation of rebirth out of death and destruction. After Ragnarok, "the earth will rise out of the sea once again, fresh and green. The eagle will again fly down from mountain crags to capture fish. The daughter of the sun will travel old paths of her mother and will brighten heaven and earth with her light. Fields will produce grain where seeds were never sown" (Rosenberg 226).

Odin's grandsons will become the new pantheon, who along with Baldur will resurrect and join the new divine order. The portrayal of a resurrected existence after Ragnarok shows this devastating event, not as tragic, but as simplistic because it again mimics the natural patterns of nature; the offspring of the eagle will maintain the same patterns its parents biologically passed down, as will the divine representation of the sun, and the fields will produce grain after fire has seared them in preparation. Therefore, according to the myth, even the horrific destruction of Ragnarok is portrayed as only natural and essential for assuring survival; this portrayal reminds audiences that in each death, be it a plant, animal, or human, all living beings are repeating the same seasonal cycles found in the environment.

The myth of Baldur's death follows the predictable patterns of fertility myths, that of life, death, and rebirth, as discussed in chapter 2, "The Earth Goddess, the Male Consort and the Harvest," but it focuses more on the aspect of death than some of its counterparts. Rosenberg states:

> The emphasis upon the finality of death may reflect a later age of people and a shift in their interests. During the fifth century, Norse society became less interested in sedentary, agricultural pursuits, which depend upon the cyclical aspects of nature. Instead, the Norse were beginning to turn their attention to more aggressive and acquisitive pursuits, in which wealth was provided by the sword instead of by the earth.... Baldur is a relic of a bygone religious age.... He is a fertility god in name only.... That Baldur is resurrected at all testifies to the power of the original fertility myth and the great appeal of the idea of rebirth and regeneration [231].

Baldur is portrayed within his myth as the son of Odin and Frigg. He is kind, beautiful, and cherished by almost everyone, but the myth serves to show that he is not the beloved of all. Loki resents Baldur, and because of this, he is to blame for Baldur's death.

The myth states that Baldur dreams of his own destruction, and then reveals his fear that he will soon die to his mother Frigg. Frigg, who is said to hold the ability to see into the future, knows that his dream should be heeded, so she initiates a process to ensure that no creature intends harm upon Baldur. The elements that she inquires of their loyalty to Baldur: "every plant," "animal," "bird," "serpent," "metal," "stone," "illness," "poison," "water," "speck of earth," and "spark of fire" (Rosenberg 232) point to a conception of the interconnectivity of the earth's resources. All elements easily swear to never harm Baldur because they love him, but moreover, because allowing Baldur to forgo death ensures that they too will all be able to escape their own deaths in the impending Ragnarok. This mythic portrayal of nature's elements conspiring against the inevitability of death points to the myth's message—that despite all efforts, death for every resource is part of nature's order.

Frigg returns to Asgard having gained the promise from almost all of nature's resources that they will never harm her son Baldur, so she initiates a celebration where the Aesir hurl items at Baldur knowing that he will never be harmed by them. Loki, ever present in his mythic role of antagonist, resents the attention that Baldur is receiving, but also resents the assurance of the Aesir to assume that they can control nature. Loki tricks Frigg into revealing that she failed to make sure the smallest item, a sprig of mistletoe, would not harm Baldur, thinking that such a small thing would be incapable of bringing destruction upon one so beloved. Yet, the myth reveals that exactly a thing as small as mistletoe can cause all things to unravel, as Loki finds the mistletoe, gives it to the blind god, Hodur, to throw at Baldur, which instantly kills him. Again, myths often portray a small element as possessing the ability to overtake even the most powerful forces; flies, mosquitoes, mice, etc., often are portrayed as overpowering bigger adversaries to show that all of the earth's resources are necessary for the maintenance of the entire ecosystem. Also it should be noted that mistletoe is a plant that seems contradictory to many other plants, as it bears its fruit in the winter; because of this, mistletoe was "often regarded as a symbol of rebirth" (Wilkinson 63). That mistletoe within this myth is depicted as causing death suggests again the continuality of nature's cycles.

Distraught at Baldur's death, the Aesir search for a means to escape this tragic event, so that they may evade their own deaths, as again Baldur's death will lead to the catastrophe of Ragnarok. The symbolism in connecting the death of one to the death of all is important; if the Aesir can succeed in having Baldur escape death, then they are represented as capable of controlling natural forces that demand death and destruction. Of course, though, they cannot succeed at such domination.

The gods send, Hermod, the son of Odin, to the underworld to ask the goddess Hel if she will release Baldur; she answers that she will if the Aesir can get every creature on earth to weep for Baldur. Again, the myth portrays the same pattern of making sure all of the earth's resources interact cohesively, showing again, that this hope is illusory, as an integral part of natural law is an incorporation of contradictory elements. The Aesir find out that a giantess living in a remote cave, Loki in disguise, refuses to weep for Baldur, and with this, they are doomed to accept Baldur's death, which in turn forces them to accept their own deaths.

The Aesir pursue Loki, who transforms himself into a salmon and hides in a stream in the deep wilderness. Alone, he obsesses about how the Aesir might eventually find and capture him, and interestingly the myth points out that Loki's own obsession causes him to create the one item capable of allowing the Aesir to capture him—a net. Seeing that he created this item that inevitably will cause his destruction, he throws it into the fire, but eventually the Aesir find Loki's cave, see the remnants of the net in the fire, understand that he is disguised as a salmon, and now also know the means of which to catch him. This mythic element showcases again Loki's role as a representation of the inevitability of nature; even Loki must succumb to what his own role represents. Again, Loki is not evil; he is simply nature; he is trickery, spontaneity, and he is illness, destruction, and death; these elements are not bad, but inevitable. He, in unwittingly fashioning the means that will enable his own destruction, is fully serving his mythic role; Loki always reminds audiences that a perfectly planned existence is not natural.

The Aesir catch Loki, bound him to a rock, hang a poisonous snake over his head whose venom pours upon his face, causing the earth to shake, and it is this shaking that eventually causes such enormous earthquakes that Loki will become free, will go into the underworld to release his offspring, and will then cause the final battle of Ragnarok to begin.

In Indonesia, the myth of the maiden Hainuwele and the night man Ameta[12] describes the necessity of accepting the cyclical laws of nature. Ameta finds a pig and follows it to a pond where it drowns; he retrieves the carcass and is surprised to find a coconut pierced through its tusk. Knowing that he found something completely new to the ecosystem, he treasures the coconut, wraps it in a blanket "like a baby, and plants it" (Leeming & Page, *Goddess,* 74). In a few days it sprouts forth from the earth as a coconut palm; Ameta accidently cuts himself and his blood falls onto the leaves and seeps into the ground, and in a few days the maiden Hainuwele mystically emerges directly from the natural materials. Hainuwele is described with "unceasing generosity" (Leeming & Page, *Goddess,* 74), but the people upon seeing her begin to dance the Maro Dance. They move in and out around Hainuwele, pushing closer, until finally she falls into a pit in the earth. The people continue to dance and drown out her cries for help. Their dancing tramps the earth down firmly, burying Hainuwele; "it was only after this beautiful and generous maiden had been murdered in this fashion that the people could die and be born again" (Leeming & Page, *Goddess,* 74). According to Indonesian belief, from this myth, after people die, they must return to the earth and visit Hainuwele in the underworld in order to be reborn; "To dance the dance of life, they had first to dance the dance of death" (Leeming & Page, *Goddess,* 74).

This myth carries with it again the message that, like the season of winter, death is essential to life. In first showing Ameta, the hunter, chasing the young pig into the water and causing it to drown, immediately shows the harsh side of existence, but upon raising the dead pig from the water, Ameta's discovery of the coconut sets in motion the pattern of the story—from the death of the pig, nature provides a renewed resource. In Ameta nurturing and planting the coconut shows another crucial stage of the life cycle. Ameta treats this new found object as a child, wrapping it in a swaddling cloth and planting it within the earth to assure its continued life. His action educates future generations on how to assure the propagation of future palms. When the generous Hainuwele, through the ceremonial ritual of dance, is pushed back into the earth, it points to the necessity of death in the natural cycle. The maiden is clearly identified botanically; this connection ties firmly together the notion that humanity and plants are inherently connected. The necessity of sacrificing the beloved Hainuwele shows the importance of this food staple to the Indonesians. Furthermore, the myth concludes with the culmination of the lesson—the ritual dance forever reminds the people of the cost of the assurance of their food staple, but it also reveals to them that indeed their own lives must follow the same natural pattern dramatically shown with Hainuwele's life and death; this is why the people die and return to her before they too can be reborn. The myth directly relates to audiences the fact of death and destruction as a means to assure the continued natural process of regeneration.

As discussed in Hinduism, it is believed that the earth has been created, destroyed, and recreated countless times. This crucial aspect of Hindu belief also can be seen to reflect the seasonal order found in nature. In Hinduism, "the destruction of the earth is inevitable" (Bierlein 237), just as death for all earthly inhabitants is required. Hinduism portrays divine representations to reflect this natural cycle: Brahma creates the world, Vishnu preserves it, and Shiva perpetually destroys it. According to this belief, "a cycle, or 'Day of Brahma,' lasts ... 4,320,000 human years. At the beginning of each such 'Day,' when the Eternal One wakes up, the world is re-created. Every cycle is divided into fourteen *manvantaras*.... Each *manvantara* is followed by a great flood that destroys all living things, except those saved to repopulate the earth" (Bierlein 237). It is said that Shiva, in the form of Rudra, creates a drought that lasts one hundred years, causing the death of most earthly inhabitants; then he enters the sun and causes all the earth's water to evaporate. Then the dry earth is set on fire, purifying it. Finally Rudra breathes out storm clouds from the moisture he obtained from the earth, causing a catastrophic flood. It is Brahma who again out of the watery chaos once more begins to create.

One Indian myth recounts the birth of Shiva by stating that Brahma and Vishnu were arguing about who had the right to ordain himself as supreme deity, when suddenly a pillar of fire in the form of a giant phallus emerged between them.[13] Brahma transformed himself into a goose and flew through the cosmos to see if he could find the source of the phallic fire, and Vishnu transformed himself into a boar and descended into the underworld to find the source. Both gods returned from their quests dumbfounded, and conceded then and there that Shiva, the source of the phallic fire, representing both life and death, must be the equal ruler to the powers of both Brahma and Vishnu. As stated Shiva represents the natural and necessary stage of death within the cycle of life. In myth, destruction, like the season of winter, is often embraced as necessary to enable new creation. The Indian concept of the god Shiva and his consort Kali is that the world, and those who reside on it, must be destroyed, so that new life can emerge. This cycle, of destruction and resurrection, again mimics the order of the natural world. Shiva is not evil, and the destruction he creates is not viewed as negative; his role is simply recognized as essential and endless. This acceptance of the seasonal nature of life often encourages Hindus to arrive at an essential spiritual understanding—that life and identity is an illusion; the goal of samsara is to let go of the world and its illusions to embrace spirituality.

The Indian myth of Prajapati[14] discusses Prajapati's act of creation as self-motivated. He descends to the earth to create offspring, and from his own mouth comes Agni; "Agni's mouth gaped for food and Prajapati grew scared. Here is the food-eater I have created from myself, and there is no food for him but me" (Leeming & Page, God, 153). The myth continues to show the destructive cost of living. The natural cycle can be a vicious one; in order for Prajapati to have offspring, he sets the natural cycles in motion. Agni as portrayed as a constant, unrelenting hunger is in fact portrayed as death itself. Prajapati offers himself to Agni, and out of this offering, the world is created, and the myth states that it is this understanding of the natural cycles of life that allows Prajapati to exist forever in all things; "if you know this, you can save yourself from Death. When you die and are put in the fire, you will be reborn from the fire just as you once were born of your mother and father. For the fire consumes only your body after all" (Leeming & Page, God, 154).

The Kirtimukha from Hindu mythology captures the essential quality of death and destruction within nature, and thus within the lives of human beings. Campbell discusses the myth of the Kirtimukha[15] in relation to the god Shiva and his wife Parvati; he states that a demon had just overtaken the existing pantheon and comes before them demanding that Shiva give Parvati to him. Unimpressed by this demon, Shiva, who is quite comfortable with times of destruction in his roll of destroyer, simply opens his third eye towards the demon, which produces another demon; "even larger than the first. He was a great lean thing with a lion-like head, hair waving to the quarters of the world, and his nature was sheer hunger. He had been brought into being to eat up the first, and was clearly fit to do so. The first thought: 'So what do I do now?' and with a very fortunate decision threw himself upon Shiva's mercy" (Campbell, Myths, 272). Shiva agrees to protect the first demon from the second, but then the second demon finds that he is voracious without something to eat, so he asks Shiva:

"Whom, then, do I eat?" to which the god replied, "...why not eat yourself?" And with that ... commencing with his feet, teeth chopping away, that grim phenomenon came right on up the line, through his own belly, on up through his chest and neck, until all that remained was a face. And the god ... was enchanted. For here at last was a perfect image of the monstrous thing that is life, which lives on itself. And to that sun-like mask, which was now all that was left of that lion-like vision of hunger, Shiva said, exulting, "I shall call you Face of Glory, 'Kirtimukha,' and you shall shine above the doors of all my temples. No one who refuses to honor and worship you will come ever to knowledge of me" [Campbell, *Myths*, 272].

The Kirtimukha mask that hangs above many Hindu temples, as dis-cussed in this myth, reminds worshippers of the nature of life itself. The Kir-timukha is titled the "Face of Glory" by Shiva because it is a microcosm of the earth and its natural, vital processes. The demon consumes itself, putting an end to its own horror, which was created by Shiva to eradicate the first demon. In the demon eating his own body, Shiva understands and confirms his own role within Hindu mythology; as destroyer of the universe, Shiva serves as a representation of nature's cycles. All things, even horrific things, like the Kirtimukha, will come to an end, but implicit in the Kirtimukha's face, is that the process is cyclical. Death and destruction are a necessary part of nature's cycle, just like the season of winter, and Shiva and the Kirtimukha provide mythic audiences with

> the realization that this is just how it is and that it cannot and will not be changed. Those who think ... that they know how the universe could have been better than it is ... without pain, without sorrow, without time, without life, are unfit for illumination. All societies are evil, sorrowful, inequitable, and so they will always be. So if you really want to help this world, what you will have to teach is how to live in it. And that, no one can do who has not himself learned how to live in it in the joyful sorrow and sorrowful joy of the knowledge of life as it is [Campbell, *Myths*, 272].

The face of the Kirtimukha then is not evil, just as Shiva is not evil; it is only one face of nature's constant cycle—the face of winter.

Similarly, the Greek concept of the Phoenix reveals life in the same cycli-cal representation of the Hindu tale of the Kirtimukha. The Phoenix must live for a time, be consumed by fire into a pile of ashes, so that it may rise again into full glory. The Egyptian and Greek Ouroboros also consistently serves as a representation of the cycles of life within nature, as its giant serpent shape is portrayed in the form of a circle showing it as always consuming its own tail. This representation of the serpent shows again the seasons of life in all living beings because it lives and it dies at the same time; there is no beginning and no end. Plato, speaking as Socrates in his *Timaeus*, discusses

the creation of the universe in terms of the Ouroboros, a giant serpent form
that consumes its own tail:

> he made the world in the form of a globe ... making the surface smooth all
> around for many reasons; in the first place, because the living being had no
> need of eyes when there was nothing remaining outside him to be seen.... Of
> design he was created thus, his own waste providing his own food, and all that
> he did or suffered taking place in and by himself.... The movement suited to
> his spherical form was assigned to him ... within his own limits revolving in a
> circle [Plato].

Plato's description of the universe in terms of an Ouroboros significantly portrays the cycle of life for all beings existing on the earth. Here the Ouroboros
is portrayed much like the Hindu conception of the creator Brahman. The
Ouroboros is alone and self-sufficient; it has no need for eyes, ears, hands,
or legs because it is a symbol of the earth itself. The Ouroboros, like Brahman,
shows that all of nature is interconnected, so that all that is perceived as good
or evil really comes from the same source. This conception of life then shows
beginnings, like the season of spring or the birth of a human being, and end-
ings, like winter or death, as irrevocably intertwined with one another because
the Ouroboros represents the broad system of nature itself that has no defin-
itive beginning and no end.

Conclusion

"Crawl to your Mother Earth. She will save you from the void."
—*Rig Veda,* XVIII, 10

Actively identifying nature as the central component of our most beloved world myths allows the myths to provide deep meaning in own our lives. Most world religions require faith to provide certainty of an identity-driven afterlife, but only in nature can one witness with certainty a promise of everlasting renewal.

Allan and Phillips discuss the historical eradication of the belief that many myths provided sacred knowledge to a people; "The fate of myths depended on the attitude adopted by the faith that took their place. Buddhism … was generally tolerant towards the old stories…. Indian Hinduism and Japanese Shintoism went even further, being in large part based on the nations' ancestral beliefs…. Christianity and Islam, however, were both deeply antagonistic to the old, pagan gods" (*World,* 130). Yet, many scholars contend[1] that although major religious movements, like Christianity and Islam, did their best to eradicate existing nature-oriented beliefs, practices still survived that suggest that the mythological and spiritual beliefs of many people were harder to erase than church officials imagined. As stated by Allan and Phillips, often faiths merged together to form an amalgamation of an older and a newer belief system, as evidenced with some Celtic and Slavic practices within Christian rituals. Many traditions, customs, and festivals still practiced today suggest the preservation of ancient beliefs, like celebrating Halloween, bringing a tree indoors at Christmas, dying Easter eggs, dancing around a maypole, etc.

Also, folktales emerged to replace the once sacred myths of a people, as nature spirits, elves, fairies, leprechauns, etc., began to replace the once powerful roles of mythic spiritual representatives. For instance, the Celtic immortals of the Tuatha de Danaan became replaced by folklore accounts of miniature fairies that haunt the woods of Ireland. In many cultures mythic characters became diminished in importance, as was seen in the myths that portrayed male heroes overpowering an older version of a divine matriarch. Many of once divine mythological characters were portrayed as physically diminished in size, becoming small fairies and leprechauns instead of powerful forces. This was a way of declaring the superiority of the new emergent faiths in an attempt to eradicate the older earth-based belief systems. Fairytales also emerged to cast ancient divine beings in sinister or evil portrayals to strip them of their former powerful and sacred roles.

Yet, finding a persistent theme of reverence for all aspects of nature, harsh as well as benevolent, from the mythology of myriad cultures around the world, speaks of nature's vital importance to the lives of human beings, and is something that should not be forgotten or cast aside as remnants of outdated belief systems.

It does not take long when visiting an environmental site that perhaps inspired a myth or when analyzing an ancient text to find clear connections of the influence that nature played to the creators of the myths. And arguably, as this book has conveyed, representations of nature and its cycles within a myth often can be interpreted as the myth itself. The Grand Canyon and Mount Everest inspired myths of divinity, inevitably showing that the divine characters were in actuality the landscape. This can also be applied to epic heroes; the Greek landscape in which the mythical Heracles roamed to commit his labors is full of vast and rugged mountains, and as one looks at them, one wonders if the beginnings of the concept of this hero who wears a lion skin and carries a Paleolithic club came directly from living amongst the rugged terrain of these mountains.

Without giving nature its due praise within our most beloved myths, we fail to see the significance of the myth. Nature is what we humans are; it birthed us, and to it, we will one day return. As the Roman Ovid speaking of the Greek Pythagoras reminds us:

> Nothing retains the form that seems its own, and Nature, the renewer of all things, continually changes every form into some other shape. Believe my word, in all this universe of vast extent, not one thing ever perished. All have changed appearance. Men say a certain thing is born, if it takes a different form from what it had; and yet they say, that certain thing has died, if it no longer keeps the self-same shape. Though distant things move near, and near things far, always the sum of all things is unchanged [362].

Many myths were as sacred to the people who created them as any religious text used in contemporary times is to its devotees, but the natural messages the myths convey, that can provide substantial spiritual meaning in one's life, may be threatened in contemporary times. Without mythic archetypes as representations of natural laws and cycles, we as a people have come to a state of environmental jeopardy. If we forget to praise nature and lose sight of the importance of the environment and our proper place within it, then we inevitably lose ourselves.

Without acknowledging the hundreds of myths that showcase human beings as inextricably linked to the environment, such as the first humans coming directly from the soil, divine beings who serve as direct representations of natural elements, or mythical characters who transform into animals or botanical agents, then we forfeit the insight these myths afford us on the meaning of life and death. As discussed, myths from nature-dependent cultures recount tales that repeatedly present an acceptance of demise on the part of mythic characters, but these same myths also often provide a promise of renewed life after death. Whether mythic rebirth be identified as the creation of a staple crop coming from a deceased loved one, a symbolic reincarnation by means of metamorphosis, or a mythic divine being who dies and resurrects, all of these myths are following the most basic patterns of nature witnessed by people for millennia—that life in the season of spring always emerges from the death of winter, showing mythically that the lives of humans and animals also follow botanical patterns. The myths of nature-dependent communities remind us that we come from the land, and because of this we are equally connected to all of the earth's beings and will also one day return to the land to allow the next generation its time in the sun. This knowledge that all living beings follow the seasons of nature provides a means for audiences of myth to live a life where one embraces the laws of nature in order to thrive vibrantly while alive.

Chapter Notes

Chapter 1

1. Margaret Astrov, *American Indian Prose and Poetry* (New York: Capricorn Books, 1946), 96–7.

2. J. L. Bierlein, *Parallel Myths* (New York: Random House, 1994), 68.

3. Philip Wilkinson, *Myths and Legends* (New York: Metro Books, 2009), 192–3.

4. Tony Allan, Charles Phillips, and Michael Kerrigan, *Artic Myths: Spirits of the Snow* (London: Duncan Baird, 1999).

5. Donna Rosenberg, "The Creation of the Universe and Ife," in *World Mythology*, 3rd ed. (Lincolnwood, IL: NTC Publishing Group, 1999), 510–14.

6. Donna Rosenberg, "The Creation of the Universe and Human Beings," in *World Mythology*, 3rd ed. (Lincolnwood, IL: NTC Publishing Group, 1999), 324–5.

7. J. F. Bierlein, *Parallel Myths* (New York: Random House, 1994), 57–8.

8. Alexander Porteous, *The Forest in Folklore and Mythology* (New York: Dover, 2002), 213.

9. Karen Armstrong, *A Short History of Myth* (Edinburgh: Canongate, 2005), 32.

10. David Leeming and Jake Page, "Okanaga Earth Woman," in *Goddess: Myths of the Feminine Divine* (New York: Oxford University Press, 1994), 12.

11. David Leeming and Jake Page, "Romi Kumu," in *Goddess: Myths of the Female Divine* (New York: Oxford University Press, 1994), 33–4.

12. Anishinaabeg tells of muskrat finally clasping the needed soil from the depths of the primordial sea before the dispossessed beings can find land.

13. J. F. Bierlein, *Parallel Myths* (New York: Random House, 1994).

14. David Lemming and Jake Page, *The Mythology of Native North America* (Norman: University of Oklahoma Press, 1998).

15. Ibid.

16. Ibid.

17. Ibid.

18. Alexander Porteous, *The Forest in Folklore and Mythology* (New York: Dover, 2002), 159.

19. Ibid.

20. Tony Allan, Clifford Bishop, and Charles Phillips, *South American Myth: Lost Realms of Gold* (London: Duncan Baird, 1998), 31.

21. David Leeming and Jake Page, "Faro," in *God: Myths of the Male Divine God* (New York: Oxford University Press, 1996), 64–7.

22. David Leeming and Jake Page, "Wonjina," in *God: Myths of the Male Divine God* (New York: Oxford University Press, 1996), 69–71.

23. Ronald M. Berndt and Catherine H. Berndt, *The Speaking Land: Myth and Story in Aboriginal Australia* (Rochester, VT: Inner Traditions International, 1994), 16–7.

24. Ibid.

25. Tony Allan, Charles Phillips, and Michael Kerrigan, *Artic Myths: Spirits of the Snow* (London: Duncan Baird, 1999), 32–3.

26. Ibid.

27. Snorri Sturluson, *The Prose Edda: Norse Mythology*, trans. Jesse L. Byock (New York: Penguin, 2005), 13–15.

28. J. F. Bierlein, *Parallel Myths* (New York: Random House, 1994), 54–6.

29. Joseph Campbell, *Myths of Light* (Novato, CA: New World Library, 2003), 121.

30. Stephen Belcher, *African Myths of Origin* (New York: Penguin, 2005), 19.

31. Philip Wikinson, *Myths and Legends* (New York: Metro Books, 2009), 154–5.

32. Ibid., 161.

33. Donna Rosenberg, *World Mythology*, 3rd ed. (Lincolnwood, IL: NTC Publishing Group, 1999), 515–7.

34. Philip Wilkinson, *Myths and Legends* (New York: Metro Books, 2009), 98–9.

35. Ronald M. Berndt and Catherine H. Berndt, *The Speaking Land: Myths and Story in Aboriginal Australia* (Rochester, VT: Inner Traditions International, 1994), 50–1.

36. Barbara C. Sproul, *Primal Myths* (New York: HarperCollins, 1991), 287–98.

37. Roslyn Poignant, *Oceanic Mythology* (New York: Paul Hamlyn, 1967), 48–50; David Leeming and Jake Page, "Maui," in *Myths of the Male Divine God* (New York: Oxford University Press, 1996), 25–7.

38. Tony Allan, Fergus Fleming, and Charles Phillips, *African Myth: Voices of the Ancestors* (London: Duncan Baird, 1999), 46–7.

39. Tony Allan, Fergus Fleming, and Michael Kerrigan, *Oceanian Myth: Journeys Through Dreamtime* (London: Duncan Baird, 1999), 73.

40. Tony Allan, Clifford Bishop, and Charles Phillips, *South American Myth: Lost Realms of Gold* (London: Duncan Baird, 1998).

Chapter 2

1. Karen Armstrong, *A Short History of Myth* (Edinburgh: Canongate, 2005); Joseph Campbell, *Primitive Mythology: The Masks of God* (New York: Penguin Compass, 1991).

2. Diane Wolkstein and Samuel Noah Kramer, *Inanna, Queen of Heaven and Earth* (New York: Harper & Row, 1983), 29–31.

3. "Descent of the Goddess Ishtar into the Lower World," trans. M. Jastrow, 1915. Sacred Texts. Web.

4. Ibid.

5. Ibid.

6. Michael Kerrigan, Alan Lothian, and Piers Vitebsky, *Middle Eastern Myth: Epics of Early Civilization* (London: Duncan Baird, 1998), 46–7.

7. Barbara C. Sproul, *Primal Myths* (New York: HarperCollins, 1991), 91–113.

8. Courtney Milne, *Sacred Places in North America* (New York: Stewart, Tabori, and Chang, 1994), 34.

9. Robert Graves, *The Greek Myths* (1955) (New York: Penguin, 2012), 1–2.

10. Ibid.

11. Critics Richard G. A Buxton and G. S. Kirk challenge some of Robert Graves' analysis of mythic origins and interpretations.

12. David Leeming and Jake Page, "Indra," in *God: Myths of the Male Divine* (New York: Oxford University Press, 1996), 150–2.

Chapter 3

1. *Hymns of the Atharva Veda*, trans. Ralph T. H. Griffith, 1895. Web.

2. *Hymns of Orpheus*, trans. Thomas Taylor, 1792. Web.

3. Jeannette Faurot, "Archer Hou Yi and Chang-O," in *Asian-Pacific Folktales and Legends* (New York: Simon & Schuster, 1995), 76–8.

4. Gary Ferguson, *The World's Great Nature Myths* (Guilford, CT: Falcon Guides, 1996).

5. Fergus Fleming and Alan Lothian, *Egyptian Myth: The Way to Eternity* (London: Duncan Baird, 1997), 64–5.

6. Joseph Bruchac, *Native American Stories* (Golden, CO: Fulcrum, 1991).

7. Joseph Campbell, *Primitive Mythology* (1959) (New York: Penguin, 1991), 283–6.

8. James A. Swan, *The Sacred Art of Hunting* (Minocqua, WI: Willow Creek Press, 1999), 37–8.

Chapter 4

1. Larry J. Zimmerman, *American Indians, The First Nations: Life, Myth, and Art* (London: Watkins, 2003), 100.

2. Philip Wilkinson, *Myths and Legends* (New York: Metro Book, 2009), 168–9.

3. Stephen Belcher, *African Myths of Origin* (New York: Penguin, 2005), 40–1.

4. Juliette Wood, *The Celts: Life, Myth, and Art* (London: Watkins, 1998), 40.

5. Charles G. Leland, *Algonquin Myths* (1884) (New York: Dover, 1992), 278–80.

6. Gary Ferguson, *The World's Great Nature Myths* (Guilford, CT: Falcon Guides, 1996).

7. Tony Allan, Fergus Fleming, and Charles Phillips, *African Myth: Voices of*

the *Ancestors* (London: Duncan Baird, 1999), 110.

8. Larry J. Zimmerman, *American Indians, The First Nations: Life, Myth, and Art* (London: Watkins, 2003), 90–1.

9. "Coyote Comes to Life Four Times: Jicarilla Apache Coyote Stories," *Coyote Stories and Poems*. Web. Retrieved October 2, 2014.

10. David Leeming and Jake Page, "Krishna (I)," in *Myths of the Male Divine God* (New York: Oxford University Press, 1996), 28–30.

Chapter 5

1. Gary Ferguson, *The World's Great Nature Myths* (Guilford, CT: Falcon Guides, 1996).

2. J. F. Bierlein, *Parallel Myths* (New York: Random House, 1994).

3. Johannes C. Andersen, *Polynesian Legends and Myths* (1928) (New York: Dover, 1995), 297–302.

4. Sharon Paice MacLoed, *Celtic Myth and Religion* (Jefferson, NC: McFarland, 2012), 67.

5. Tony Allan and Charles Phillips, *World Myth: The Great Themes* (London: Duncan Baird, 2000), 118.

6. Tao Yanming, "Peach Blossom Spring," in *Norton Anthology of World Masterpieces*, eds. Mack Maynard and John Bierhorst (New York: Norton, 1997).

7. Fergus Fleming and Shahrukh Husain, *Celtic Myth: Heroes of the Dawn* (London: Duncan Baird, 1996), 71–2.

8. Fergus Fleming and Shahrukh Husain, *Celtic Myth: Heroes of the Dawn* (London: Duncan Baird, 1996), 72–3.

9. Sharon Paice MacLeod, *Celtic Myth and Religion* (Jefferson, NC: McFarland, 2012), 100–1.

10. Ibid.

11. Jeannette Faurot, "Kaguya Himé," in *Asian-Pacific Folktales and Legends* (New York: Simon & Schuster, 1995), 88–95.

12. Alexander Porteous, *The Forest in Folklore and Mythology* (New York: Dover, 2002), 157–8.

13. Ibid.

14. Ibid.

15. Charles P. Mountford, *The Dreamtime: Australian Aboriginal Myths* (Perth: Rigby, 1965), 46.

16. Gary Ferguson, *The World's Great Nature Myths* (Guilford, CT: Falcon Guides, 1996).

Chapter 6

1. Joseph Bruchac, *Native American Stories* (Golden, CO: Fulcrum, 1991), 89–92.

2. Tony Allan and Charles Phillips, *The Great Themes: World Myth* (London: Duncan Barid, 2000), 58.

3. Ibid.

4. "Blue Corn Maiden and the Coming of Winter," *Native American Legends*. Accessed March 13, 2014, http://www.firstpeople.us/FP-Html-Legends/Blue_Corn_Maiden_And_The_Coming_Of_Winter-Hopi.html.

5. Homer, *Homeric Hymns*, trans. Sarah Ruden (Indianapolis: Hackett, 2005), 75.

6. *The Mabinogion*, trans. Sioned Davies (New York: Oxford University Press, 2007).

7. David Lemming and Jake Page, *The Mythology of Native North America* (Norman: University of Oklahoma Press, 1998), 24–6.

8. Charles Phillips, Michael Kerrigan, and David Gould, *Indian Myth: The Eternal Cycle* (London: Duncan Baird, 1998), 42–4.

9. Nitin Kumar, "Parvati: Goddess of Love and Devotion," *Exotic India* (July 2001). Accessed March 3, 2014, http://www.exotic indiaart/article/parvati.

10. Scott Leonard and Michael McClure, *Myth and Knowing* (New York: McGraw Hill, 2004), 158–161.

11. David Leeming and Jake Page, "Dikithi," in *God: Myths of the Male Divine God* (New York: Oxford University Press, 1996), 46–7.

12. David Leeming and Jake Page, "Hainuwele," in *Goddess: Myths of the Female Divine* (New York: Oxford University Press, 1994), 74.

13. Philip Wilkinson, *Myths and Legends* (New York: Metro Book, 2009), 120.

14. David Leeming and Jake Page, *God: Myths of the Male Divine* (New York: Oxford University Press, 1996), 153–4.

15. Joseph Campbell, *Myths to Live By* (1972) (New York: Penguin, 1993).

Conclusion

1. Tony Allan and Charles Phillips, *The Great Themes: World Myth* (London: Duncan Baird, 2000), 130–1.

Bibliography

Allan, Tony, Clifford Bishop, and Charles Phillips. *South American Myth: Lost Realms of Gold.* London: Duncan Baird, 1998.

Allan, Tony, Fergus Fleming, and Michael Kerrigan. *Oceanian Myth: Journeys Through Dreamtime.* London: Duncan Baird, 1999.

Allan, Tony, Fergus Fleming, and Charles Phillips. *African Myth: Voices of the Ancestors.* London: Duncan Baird, 1999.

Allan, Tony, and Michael Kerrigan. *Japanese Myth: Realm of the Sun.* London: Duncan Baird, 2000.

Allan, Tony, and Tom Lowenstein. *Aztec and Maya Myth: Gods of Sun and Sacrifice.* London: Duncan Baird, 1997.

Allan, Tony, and Sara Maitland. *Greek and Roman Myth: Titans and Olympians.* London: Duncan Baird, 1997.

Allan, Tony, and Charles Phillips. *Chinese Myth: Land of the Dragon.* London: Duncan Baird, 1999.

_____. *The Great Themes: World Myth.* London: Duncan Baird, 2000.

Allan, Tony, Charles Phillips, and Michael Kerrigan. *Artic Myths: Spirits of the Snow.* London: Duncan Baird, 1999.

Allan, Tony, and Piers Vitebsky. *Greek Roman and Myth: Triumph of the Hero.* London: Duncan Baird, 1998.

Andersen, Johannes C. *Myths and Legends of the Polynesians* (1928). New York: Dover, 1995.

Apuleius. *The Golden Ass.* Trans. E. J. Kenney. New York: Penguin, 1998.

Armitage, Simon. *Sir Gawain and the Green Knight: A New Verse Translation.* New York: Norton, 2007.

Armstrong, Karen. *The Great Transformation: The Beginning of Our Religious Traditions.* New York: Anchor Books, 2007.

_____. *A Short History of Myth.* Edinburgh: Canongate, 2005.

Arner, Lynn. "The Ends of Enchantment: Colonialism and *Sir Gawain and the Green Knight.*" *Texas Studies in Language and Literature* 48.2 (2006): 79–101.

Astrov, Margot. *American Indian Prose and Poetry.* New York: Capricorn Books, 1946.

Auerbach, Loren, and Jacqueline Simpson. *Viking and German Myth: Sagas of the Norsemen.* London: Duncan Baird, 1997.

Belcher, Stephen. *African Myths and Legends.* New York: Penguin, 2005.

Berndt, Ronald M., and Catherine H. Berndt. *The Speaking Land: Myth and Story in Aboriginal Australia.* Rochester, VT: Inner Traditions International, 1994.

"Bhagavad-Gita." Trans. William Quan Judge. The Theosophical University Press Online Edition. http://www.theosociety.org.

Bierlein, J. F. *Parallel Myths.* New York: Random House, 1994.

"Blue Corn Maiden and the Coming of Winter." *Native American Legends.* Accessed March 13, 2014. http://www.firstpeople.us.

Bosley, Keith. "Introduction." *Kalevala* by Elias Lönnrot. Trans. Keith Bosley. Oxford: Oxford University Press, 2008.

Bruchac, Joseph. *Native American Stories.* Golden, CO: Fulcrum, 1991.

Burkert, Walter. *Greek Religion* (1977). Boston: Harvard University Press, 1985.

Campbell, Joseph. *Goddesses: Mysteries of the Feminine Divine*. Novato, CA: New World Library, 2013.

_____. *Hero with a Thousand Faces*. Princeton: Princeton University Press, 1949.

_____. "Hinduism." *Hindu Wisdom*. The Joseph Campbell Foundation Website. https://www.jcf.org/.

_____. *Myths of Light: Eastern Metaphors of the Eternal*. New York: New World Library, 2012.

_____. *Myths to Live By* (1972). New York: Penguin, 1993.

_____. *Occidental Mythology: The Masks of God, Vol. 3*. New York: Penguin, 1968.

_____. *Primitive Mythology: The Masks of God*. New York: Penguin Compass, 1991.

"Coyote Comes to Life Four Times: Jicarilla Apache Coyote Stories." *Coyote Stories and Poems*. http://www.indigenouspeople.net.

Davidson, H. R. Ellis. *Gods and Myths of Northern Europe* (1964). New York: Penguin, 1988.

Davies, Sioned. *The Mabinogion*. New York: Oxford University Press, 2007.

"Descent of the Goddess Ishtar into the Lower World." *Civilization of Babylonia and Assyria*. Trans. M. Jastrow, 1915. http://www.sacred-texts.com.

Dobson, Marcia W. "Ritual Death, Patriarchal Violence, and Female Relationships in the Hymns to Demeter and Inanna." *NWSA Journal* 4.1 (Spring 1992): 42–58.

Ellis, Peter Berresford. *Celtic Myths and Legends*. New York: Carroll and Graf, 2002.

Faurot, Jeannette, ed. *Asian-Pacific Folktales and Legends*. New York: Simon & Schuster, 1995.

Ferguson, Gary. *The World's Great Nature Myths*. Guilford, CT: Falcon Guides, 1996.

Fleming, Fergus and Sharukh Husain. *Celtic Myth: Heroes of the Dawn*. London: Duncan Baird, 1996.

Fleming, Fergus, and Alan Lothian. *Egyptian Myth: The Way to Eternity*. London: Duncan Baird, 1997.

Folkard, Richard. *Plant Lore, Legends, and Lyrics* (1892). New York: Forgotten Books, 2012.

Foskett, Mary F. *A Virgin Conceived: Mary and Classical Representations of Virginity*. Bloomington: Indiana University Press, 2002.

Frankl, Viktor. *Man's Search for Meaning* (1959). New York: Buccaneer Books, 1992.

Frazer, James G. *The Golden Bough: The Roots of Religion and Folklore* (1890). New York: Avenel Books, 1981.

Graves, Robert. *The Greek Myths* (1955). New York: Penguin, 2012.

Hamel, Frank. *Werewolves, Bird-Women, Tiger-Men, and Other Human Animals* (1915). New York: Dover, 2007.

Herbert, Marie. "Transmutations of an Irish Goddess," in Miranda Green and Sandra Billington, eds., *The Concept of the Goddess*. New York: Taylor and Francis, 2002.

Hinds, Katherine. *Ancient Celts*. New York: Marshall Cavendish, 2010.

Hollander, Lee M. *The Poetic Edda*. Austin: University of Texas Press, 1962.

Humphrey, Cheryl. *The Haunted Garden: Death and Transfiguration in the Folklore of Plants*. New York: Cheryl Humphrey, 2012.

Hymns of Atharva Veda. Trans. Ralph T. H. Griffith. 1895. http://www.sacred-texts.com.

Hymns of Orpheus. Trans. Thomas Taylor. 1792. http://www.sacred-texts.com.

Kerrigan, Michael, Clifford Bishop, and James Chambers. *Tibetan and Mongolian Myth: The Diamond Path*. London: Duncan Baird, 1998.

Kerrigan, Michael, Alan Lothian, and Piers Vitebsky. *Middle Eastern Myth: Epics of Early Civilization*. London: Duncan Baird, 1998, 46–7.

Krogh, David. *Biology: A Guide to the Natural World*. San Francisco: Pearson, 2009.

Lehner Ernst, and Johanna Lehner. *Folklore and Symbolism of Flowers, Pants and Trees*. New York: Dover, 2003.

Leland, Charles G. *Algonquin Legends* (1884). New York: Dover, 1992.

Lönnrot, Elias. *Kalevala*. Trans. Keith Bosley. Oxford: Oxford University Press, 2008.

Kumar, Nitin. "Parvati: Goddess of Love and Devotion" *Exotic India* (July 2001).

Accessed March 3, 2014, http://www.exoticindiaart/article/parvati.

Leeming, David Adams. *Mythology: The Voyage of the Hero.* New York: Oxford University Press, 1998.

Leeming, David Adams, and Jake Page. *God: Myths of the Male Divine.* New York: Oxford University Press, 1996.

_____. *Goddess: Myths of the Female Divine.* New York: Oxford University Press, 1994.

_____. *The Mythology of Native North America.* Norman: Oklahoma University Press, 1998.

Lowenstein, Tom, and Piers Vitebsky. *Native American Myth: Mother Earth, Father Sky.* London: Duncan Baird, 1997.

MacLeod, Sharon Paice. *Celtic Myth and Religion.* Jefferson, NC: McFarland, 2012.

Milne, Courtney. *Sacred Places in North America.* New York: Stewart, Tabori, and Chang, 1994.

Mountford, Charles P. *The Dreamtime: Australian Aboriginal Myths.* Perth: Rigby, 1965.

Ovid. *Metamorphosis.* Trans. David Raeburn. New York: Penguin, 2004.

Phillips, Charles, and Michael Kerrigan. *Slavic Myth: Forests of the Vampire.* London: Duncan Baird, 1999.

Phillips, Charles, Michael Kerrigan, and David Gould. *Indian Myth: The Eternal Cycle.* London: Duncan Baird, 1998.

Plato. *Timaeus* (c. 360 BCE). Trans. Benjamin Jowett. Retrieved October 7, 2014. http://classics.mit.edu/Plato/timaeus.html.

Poignant, Roslyn. *Oceanic Mythology.* New York: Paul Hamlyn, 1967.

Porteous, Alexander. *The Forest in Folklore and Mythology.* New York: Dover, 2002.

Puhvel, Jaan. *Comparative Mythology.* Baltimore: Johns Hopkins University Press, 1987.

Rosenberg, Donna. *World Mythology: An Anthology of the Great Myths and Epics.* Lincolnwood, IL: NTC Publishing Group, 1999.

Schomp, Virginia. *Myths of the World: The Norsemen.* New York: Marshall Cavendish, 2008.

Scott, James M. *Adoption as Sons of God.* Tübingen: Mohr, 1992.

Sproul, Barbara C. *Primal Myths: Creation Myths around the World* (1971). New York: HarperCollins, 1991.

Stange, Mary Zeiss. *Woman the Hunter.* Boston: Beacon Press, 1997.

Sturluson, Snorri. *The Prose Edda: Norse Mythology.* Trans. Jesse L. Byock. New York: Penguin, 2005.

Stone, Merlin. *When God Was a Woman.* New York: Harvest/Harcourt Brace, 1976.

"The Story of Tuan Mac Cairill." Retrieved November 11, 2014. http://www.sacred-texts.com.

Swan, James A. *The Sacred Art of Hunting: Myths, Legends, and the Modern Mythos.* Minocqua, WI: Willow Creek Press, 1999.

Torrance, Robert M. *Encompassing Nature: A Sourcebook—Nature and Culture from Ancient Times to the Modern World.* Washington, D.C.: Counterpoint, 1999.

Tzu, Lao. *Tao Te Ching.* "Wisdom of Lao Tzu." Retrieved November 6, 2014. http://www.taoistic.com/taoteching-laotzu-book.htm.

Warner, Elizabeth. *Russian Myths.* Austin: University of Texas Press and the British Museum Press, 2002.

Wilkins, W. J. *Hindu Mythology, Vedic and Puranic* (1900). Retrieved June 30, 2014. http://www.sacred-texts.com.

Wilkinson, Philip. *Myths and Legends: An Illustrated Guide to Their Origins and Meanings.* New York: Metro Books, 2009.

Wolkstein, Diane, and Samuel Noah Kramer. *Inanna, Queen of Heaven and Earth: Her Stories and Hymns from Sumer.* New York: Harper and Row, 1983.

Wood, Juliette. *The Celts: Life, Myth, and Art.* London: Watkins, 1998.

Yanming, Tao. "Peach Blossom Spring." *Norton Anthology of World Masterpieces,* eds. Mack Maynard and John Bierhorst. New York: Norton, 1997.

Zimmerman, Larry J. *American Indians, The First Nations: Life, Myth, and Art.* London: Watkins, 2003.

Index